Character Sketches

From the Pages Of Scripture

> God's biographies reveal the secrets of warning and instruction for our daily lives. "Now all these things happened unto them for ensamples (types): and they are written for our admonition . . ."   *I Corinthians 10:11*

Illustrated In the World Of Nature

> "But ask now the beasts, and they shall teach thee; and the fowls of the air, and they shall tell thee: Or speak to the earth, and it shall teach thee: and the fishes of the sea shall declare unto thee."   *Job 12:7-8*

Character Sketches

From the Pages Of Scripture
Illustrated In the World Of Nature

INSTITUTE IN
BASIC YOUTH CONFLICTS, INC.

Printed by Rand McNally and Company
1981

Printed in the United States of America.

**Library of Congress
Catalog Card Number: 76-3050**

ISBN 0-916888-01-0

Dedicated to the vision
of God raising up a vast host of men
who are committed to His standards and their responsibility
to build character and to meet the basic needs of each one in their families

Table of Contents

PART ONE · LOYALTY

ADJUSTING MY SCHEDULE TO MEET THE NEEDS OF THOSE I AM SERVING

STANDING WITH THOSE I AM SERVING IN THEIR TIME OF NEED

BEING A RELIABLE MESSENGER TO THOSE I AM SERVING

KNOWING AND FOLLOWING THE WISHES OF THOSE RESPONSIBLE FOR ME

PART TWO · RESPONSIBILITY

USING ALL MY ENERGIES TO FULFILL THE EXPECTATION OF THOSE WHO ARE COUNTING ON ME

COMPLETING A TASK SO THAT IT WILL ENDURE TESTING

REALIZING THE IMPORTANCE OF THE TASK ASSIGNED TO US

TURNING ROUTINE TASKS INTO ENJOYABLE EXPERIENCES

PART THREE · COURAGE

RESPONDING TO DANGER WITHOUT THOUGHT OF RETREAT

APPLYING THE RESOURCES I HAVE IN CREATIVE WAYS WHEN FACED WITH OVERWHELMING ODDS

FOLLOWING DIFFICULT INSTRUCTIONS IN THE FACE OF DANGER

CONFRONTING AN OPPONENT WITH THE CONFIDENCE THAT I WILL ULTIMATELY SUCCEED

PART FOUR · DETERMINATION

REALIZING THAT MY PRESENT STRUGGLES ARE ESSENTIAL FOR FUTURE ACHIEVEMENT

BREAKING DOWN A SEEMINGLY IMPOSSIBLE TASK BY CONCENTRATING ON ACHIEVABLE GOALS

EXPENDING WHATEVER ENERGY IS NECESSARY TO COMPLETE A PROJECT

REJECTING ANY DISTRACTION WHICH WILL HINDER THE COMPLETION OF A TASK

PART FIVE · ORDERLINESS

PART SIX · INITIATIVE

ACTING WITH AN ASSURANCE OF THE OUTCOME

RESPONDING QUICKLY AND WISELY TO SITUATIONS OF DANGER

PART SEVEN · DECISIVENESS

REFUSING TO RECONSIDER A DECISION WHICH I KNOW IS RIGHT

MAKING PRESENT COMMITMENTS TO AVOID FUTURE FAILURES

DEVOTING ALL MY ENERGY TO A COURSE OF ACTION WHICH I KNOW IS RIGHT

EVALUATING COURSES OF ACTION QUICKLY AND ACCURATELY

God gave man a marvelous intellect with one limitation—he is not to use it to learn the details of evil (Romans 16:19).

Today's pseudo intellectuals are vigorously trying to defend their "right" to use their mind to study all the details of evil so that "Ye shall be as gods knowing good and evil." —quote from Satan (Genesis 3:5)

God never intended that we learn evil with our mind or by experience but rather with our spirit. "Try the spirits whether they are of God." (I John 4:1)

JOHN THE BAPTIST
One mighty in spirit

Multitudes of those who were least expected to respond to the Gospel came to be baptized of him and to listen to his practical wisdom for daily living.

Counsel to publicans—Exact no more than that which is appointed you.

Counsel to soldiers—Do violence to no man, neither accuse any falsely and be content with your wages.

He went before Christ, "In the spirit and power of Elias to turn the hearts of the fathers to the children and the disobedient to the wisdom of the just and to make ready a people prepared for the Lord." (Luke 1:17) "Among them that are born of women, there hath not risen a greater than John the Baptist. Notwithstanding, he that is least in the kingdom of heaven is greater than he." (Matthew 11:11)

A "NEW" APPROACH TO LEARNING

—RESTORING GOD'S BASIC OBJECTIVES

LEARNING WHAT IT MEANS TO BE MIGHTY IN SPIRIT

> WHEN ONE IS MIGHTY IN SPIRIT HE HAS THE ABILITY TO COMPREHEND BOTH THE DEEPER THOUGHTS OF GOD AND THE HIDDEN MOTIVES OF MAN.

The great challenge of our day is to grasp the concept of being mighty in spirit and to see how it differs from being directed by intellect. When one is mighty in spirit, he has the ability to comprehend both the deeper thoughts of God and the hidden motives of man. The practical application of this is illustrated in the lives of such men as John the Baptist, who was mighty in spirit, and Stephen, whose spirit of wisdom the entire assembly could not resist. The multitudes and the professionals came to John to learn practical wisdom and counsel for their lives and their work. In our day we have unknowingly accepted a standard of education which hinders and destroys the potential of being mighty in spirit and emphasizes the idea that the highest achievement in education is to be guided by intellect.

CHRIST

He exposed their motives

"All that heard Him were astonished at His understanding and answers." (Luke 2:47) "For He taught them as one having authority and not as the scribes." (Matthew 7:29) Many fought against Him for He exposed the secrets of their hearts. This is the heritage of one mighty in spirit.

> TO BE MIGHTY IN SPIRIT IS TO JUDGE TRUTH BY THE COMBINATION OF GOD'S SPIRIT BEARING WITNESS WITH OUR SPIRIT IN HARMONY WITH SCRIPTURE.

To be mighty in intellect is to judge truth by our mind. To be mighty in spirit is to judge truth by the combination of God's Spirit and our spirit in harmony with Scripture. In the life of every person there must come a time when he decides which will be pre-eminent—his mind or his spirit (God's Spirit

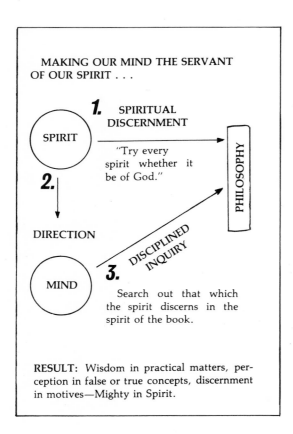

MAKING OUR MIND THE SERVANT
OF OUR SPIRIT . . .

1. SPIRITUAL
DISCERNMENT

SPIRIT

"Try every
spirit whether it
be of God."

2.

DIRECTION

MIND

3. DISCIPLINED INQUIRY

PHILOSOPHY

Search out that which
the spirit discerns in the
spirit of the book.

RESULT: Wisdom in practical matters, perception in false or true concepts, discernment in motives—Mighty in Spirit.

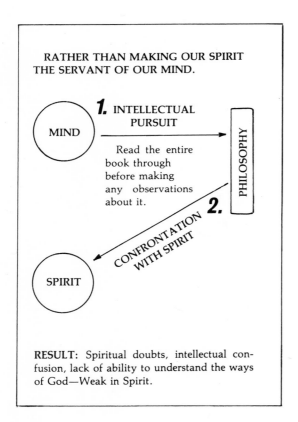

RATHER THAN MAKING OUR SPIRIT
THE SERVANT OF OUR MIND.

1. INTELLECTUAL
PURSUIT

MIND

Read the entire
book through
before making
any observations
about it.

2. CONFRONTATION WITH SPIRIT

PHILOSOPHY

SPIRIT

RESULT: Spiritual doubts, intellectual confusion, lack of ability to understand the ways of God—Weak in Spirit.

with our spirit). One with special mental ability will find it more difficult to submit his mind to his spirit. Thus Paul observes, ". . . not many wise . . . not many mighty . . . are called." (I Corinthians 1:26)

To be mighty in spirit means that we build walls that guard our mind from certain content. This is contrary to the philosophy of those who try to be mighty in intellect. To them all knowledge is God's knowledge. But to the one mighty in spirit, knowledge in the mouth of fools is as destructive as poison in the mouth of man. He heeds the Scripture which commands, "Go from the presence of a foolish man when thou perceivest not in him the lips of knowledge." (Proverbs 14:7)

We are to "Beware, lest any man spoil you through philosophy and vain deceit, after the tradition of men, after the rudiments of the world, and not after Christ." (Colossians 2:8)

> **EVERY PERSON MUST COME TO THE PLACE WHERE HE SUBMITS HIS MIND AS THE SERVANT OF HIS SPIRIT**

If a son or daughter is taught to be mighty is spirit he will learn how to approach any new information by first testing it with his spirit. If his spirit discerns that it is not of God, then he will use his mind as his servant to dig out the facts and concepts which are in error. In this way he fulfills Scripture which commands, "Try the spirits whether they are of God. . ." (I John 4:1), "Keep thy heart with all diligence; for out of it are the issues of life" (Proverbs 4:23), and "Cease, my son, to hear the instruction that causeth to err from the words of knowledge" (Proverbs 19:27).

The dilemma of our day is that we have not defined how to teach young men and young women to be mighty in spirit. We can check them for accuracy of intellect but what is the procedure to check out a man's spirit? If we are to accomplish this higher task we must initiate a program of personal victory in the moral life of each person because the flesh lusteth against the spirit and the spirit against the flesh. For this reason Peter pleads, ". . . I beseech you as strangers and pilgrims, abstain from fleshly lusts, which war against the soul." (I Peter 2:11)

> IT IS NOT NEARLY ENOUGH TO SET UP A CERTAIN LIST OF ACTIVITIES TO REFRAIN FROM BUT RATHER TO GIVE CLEAR DIRECTION ON THE NECESSARY WARFARE TO CONQUER IMPURE THOUGHTS AS WELL AS ACTIONS IN DAILY LIVING

It is not nearly enough to set up a certain list of activities to refrain from but rather to give clear direction on the necessary warfare to conquer impure thoughts as well as actions in daily living. Ultimately we must be concerned with how those under our spiritual care are taking in and digesting Scripture. We must get beneath the surface ideas of Scripture and open up the deeper ways of God so that they will be able to comprehend the larger picture upon which God has built all of life and all of truth. ". . . thou hast hid these things from the wise and prudent, and hast revealed them unto babes." (Matthew 11:25) "But strong meat belongeth to them that are of full age, even those who by reason of use have their senses exercised to discern both good and evil." (Hebrews 5:14) We must integrate the character of Christ into every area of learning since, "In Him dwelleth all the fulness of the Godhead bodily." (Colossians 2:9) And, He is the source of all knowledge.

LEARNING HOW TO BE MIGHTY IN SPIRIT

A person who is mighty in spirit will perceive a wrong motive in a business transaction and spare himself the unnecessary loss of funds. One who is mighty in spirit will discern any impure motives in another and avoid the moral destruction that comes to the simple. One mighty in spirit will be able to appeal to the conscience of the one who is doing wrong rather than arguing with the philosophies of those who would justify their wrong.

DAVID
Wiser than his enemies

The secret of his discernment and wisdom lay in his practice of meditation on God's Word day and night. He "behaved himself wisely" when Saul tried to find fault in him. When Saul's jealousy increased he "behaved himself yet more wisely."

STEPHEN
Wisdom they could not refute

His defense before the council revealed an amazing grasp of Scripture. He had deep insight into God's ways and work among His people. The philosophers of his day "Were not able to resist the wisdom and the spirit by which he spake." (Acts 6:10)

DISCERNING A BASIC
ASPECT OF SPIRITUALITY

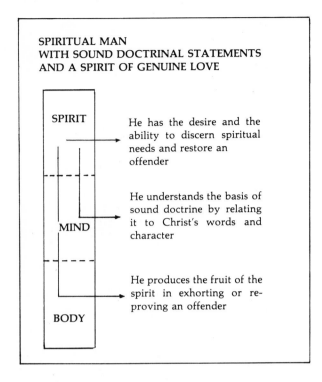

SPIRITUAL MAN
WITH SOUND DOCTRINAL STATEMENTS
AND A SPIRIT OF GENUINE LOVE

SPIRIT — He has the desire and the ability to discern spiritual needs and restore an offender

MIND — He understands the basis of sound doctrine by relating it to Christ's words and character

BODY — He produces the fruit of the spirit in exhorting or reproving an offender

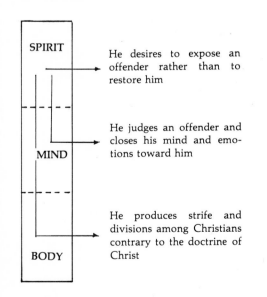

CARNAL MAN
SOUND IN DOCTRINAL STATEMENTS
BUT UNSCRIPTURAL IN HIS SPIRIT AND FRUIT

SPIRIT — He desires to expose an offender rather than to restore him

MIND — He judges an offender and closes his mind and emotions toward him

BODY — He produces strife and divisions among Christians contrary to the doctrine of Christ

"...for whereas there is among you envying, and strife, and divisions, are ye not carnal, and walk as men?"
I Corinthians 3:3

If we teach our generation how to be mighty in spirit a missing dimension in defining sound doctrine will be restored. For centuries we have concentrated primarily on statements of faith. But the tragedy is that a person may be sound in his doctrinal statements but totally unscriptural in his spirit. There are actually three tests of sound doctrine—not just one.

THERE ARE THREE TESTS OF SOUND DOCTRINE—NOT JUST ONE.

First, we are to try every spirit whether it be of God or not. A spirit of contention and division is not of God. Neither is a spirit that seeks to expose other Christians rather than restore them. "Brethren, if a man be overtaken in a fault, ye which are spiritual, restore such an one in the spirit of meekness, considering yourself lest you also be tempted." (Galatians 6:1)

Second, we are to try every statement. "Every spirit that confesseth not. . ." (I John 4:3) These statements must be in harmony with the total message of Scripture. Notice the Scripture says, "every spirit that confesseth" rather than every mind that confesseth. We comprehend the truth of Scripture by our spirit, not our mind. These things are spiritually comprehended. "But the natural man receiveth not the things of the Spirit of God: for they are foolishness unto him: neither can he know them, because they are spiritually discerned." (I Corinthians 2:14)

Third, we are to try the fruit of his life and actions. "By their fruits ye shall know them." (Matthew 7:20) One of the most important aspects of this third test is whether a man follows the steps given by our Lord in Matthew 18 when correcting a brother who has missed the mark. Some would use an offending statement or action as a Scriptural basis for separation, but if the steps of Matthew 18 are not closely followed in a spirit of restoration and long-suffering, a division will be made contrary to the doctrine of Christ, causing bitterness among Christians and unbelief by the world. For this reason Paul warns:

"Now I beseech you, brethren, mark them which cause divisions and offences contrary to the doctrine which ye have learned; and avoid them. For they that are such serve not our Lord Jesus Christ, but their own belly; and by good words and fair speeches deceive the hearts of the simple." (Romans 16:17,18)

LEARNING WHY WE MUST BE MIGHTY IN SPIRIT

There has been and always will be a need to purify the church. This involves strengthening sincere Christians (Romans 15:1) and ridding the church of the impure and the impostors (I Corinthians 5:11-13). Only as Christians are mighty in spirit will they be able to detect those in each category. And only as we follow the steps of Matthew 18 will we demonstrate to a skeptical world the genuineness of our love for each other and the Lord. The mark of a disciple is not how much he disciplines his mind but how much he disciplines his spirit in genuine love. "By this shall all men know that ye are my disciples, if ye have love one to another." (John 13:35) This spirit of oneness is so important in causing the world to believe that it became the burden of our Lord's prayer in John 17:21, "That they all may be one; as thou, Father, art in me, and I in thee, that they also may be one in us: that the world may believe that thou hast sent me."

When we concentrate on being mighty in spirit to the extent that God intends, we will see multitudes of those we would least expect responding to the Gospel in repentance and to the Christian life in a spirit of true wisdom.

THE FIRST STEP TO BECOME MIGHTY IN SPIRIT

With our human spirit we are capable of communicating with the human spirit of each one around us. We sense what is in their spirit by knowing what is in our spirit. "For what man knoweth the things of a man, save the spirit of man which is in him?" (I Corinthians 2:11)

In the same way we can only know what is in the mind of God if we have God's Spirit within us. "Even so the things of God knoweth no man but the Spirit of God." (I Corinthians 2:11) Scripture clarifies that God's Spirit is the source of wisdom and power that we are looking for. "For the Spirit searcheth all things, yea, the deep things of God." (I Corinthians 2:10)

God's Spirit is not something we work for, or wait for, but ask for.

It is very important that the head of each home makes sure that each one in his family knows what steps are essential in receiving this provision which God has given through His Son, the Lord Jesus Christ.

This can be done by personally meeting with each one and explaining the following verses of Scripture and then leading in a prayer to put his faith and trust in Jesus Christ for salvation.

"For all have sinned, and come short of the glory of God."   Romans 3:23

"But God commendeth His love toward us, in that, while we were yet sinners, Christ died for us."   Romans 5:8

"For the wages of sin is death; but the gift of God is eternal life through Jesus Christ our Lord."   Romans 6:23

"If thou shalt confess with thy mouth the Lord Jesus, and shalt believe in thine heart that God hath raised him from the dead, thou shalt be saved."   Romans 10:9

A PRAYER TO BE REBORN IN YOUR SPIRIT . . .

Thank You, God, for loving me and sending Your Son to die for my sin. Right now I repent of my sin and I do receive Jesus Christ as my personal Savior.
Now as Your child I turn my entire life over to you so you can glorify Yourself through me.

Amen

I. THE HOME MUST BE THE LEARNING CENTER

God's educational objectives were designed to be carried out in the home long before anyone ever thought about a school. The school can be an effective extension of the home but can never take its place. Educators realize that the most effective learning is achieved in living experiences rather than classroom theory. The difficulty has come in that parents often do not have the alertness or the ability to turn everyday situations into teaching experiences. Neither do they have in the back of their mind a well thought-out body of content which must be communicated to each child at different levels of maturity.

A further challenge involves the parents' ability to create the interest and maintain the discipline for learning which is required by the son or daughter. It is not difficult to see why parents have so willingly delegated their teaching responsibility to others. If we are to make the home the learning center, the following goals must be established:

A. RECOGNIZE HOME SITUATIONS WHICH CAN BE TURNED INTO VITAL LEARNING EXPERIENCES

Most parents would be amazed at the vast and varied amount of learning which is possible by taking hold of opportunities as they come. Reject the concept of having to put up with your child going through phases. There are no phases of parental endurance but rather phases of childhood learning.

B. USE THE SCRIPTURE AS THE BASIC CURRICULUM OF CHARACTER SKILL, CONCEPTS AND INFORMATION WHICH EACH SON AND DAUGHTER SHOULD LEARN

Many parents are unaware that God does not expect them to design curriculum but rather to share with their children what God is teaching them from Scripture and from life. This then becomes the unique heritage that each child has and prepares them to edify and be edified by others outside the home toward spiritual maturity. "Till we all come in the unity of the faith, and of the knowledge of the Son of God, unto a perfect man, unto the measure of the stature of the fulness of Christ." (Ephesians 4:13)

C. DISCOVER AND RECHANNEL THE INTEREST AND MOTIVATION OF EACH CHILD FOR LEARNING

We do this by listening and asking questions which will allow us to see through their eyes and feel through their emotions, defining and reinforcing God's goals for their lives, creating curiosity for vital information (salting the oats) and providing opportunities for each one to record and share what they are learning (Life Notebook).

D. TRANSLATE FAMILY CONFLICTS INTO SPECIAL ASSIGNMENTS OF LEARNING AND SPECIAL OPPORTUNITIES FOR APPLYING BASIC PRINCIPLES OF CLEARING CONSCIENCE, ASKING FORGIVENESS, YIELDING RIGHTS, ETC.

16

E. EVALUATE EVERYTHING IN THE HOME ON THE BASIS OF HOW IT CONTRIBUTES TO LEARNING AND LIVING SCRIPTURE

Every home has its own atmosphere. This atmosphere can be a powerful influence for instilling character learning. Areas of consideration are music, reading material and home furnishings.

Music is a basic form of worship and can create inner ideals as well as express them. Three types of music should be introduced within the home—bright, cheery music as the day begins, soothing music prior to mealtime and devotional music before ending the day.

A bookshelf which contains character-building volumes, especially the biographies of men and women in God's hall of fame, is essential. Books have shaped the future of almost every great leader. For this reason it is important that parents make sure that the concepts of every non-technical book are not in violation with God's principles and that its author has the kind of a life that parents would want their sons or daughters to imitate.

If two or three people recommend a book, it may well be worth reading. If people report that it has changed their lives to be more godly, it is worth buying. By removing books of little or no value, your sons and daughters will find it less confusing to choose the right books. Just as a shepherd goes into a pasture ahead of the sheep and removes all the poisonous plants, so parents must review the reading material to which their children are exposed.

Pictures and beautifully-made wall plaques with key Scripture messages, precise character definitions, the meaning of each person's name, hymns and godly reminders help instill spiritual maturity in a family. In addition to these, there is a wealth of reinforcing teaching material which can and should be visible on the walls of the home. The purpose of each of these items is to create a godly atmosphere in the home which will be different from the world.

F. MAKE THE HOME THE HEADQUARTERS FOR MEANINGFUL SPIRITUAL ACTIVITY

A godly atmosphere in a home provides a powerful setting into which others may come to hear the Gospel and to see the Christian life in action. Special events can be planned by each one in the family for those in his or her "world of influence."

HOW TO USE THIS BOOK

The primary purpose of this book is to place in the hands of fathers basic concepts of Scripture and interesting facts of nature which those in his family have not yet heard. For this purpose it is suggested that this book remain in the father's possession and under his supervision until all the concepts are discussed with all the family.

We suggest that you select one meal each week during which you discuss the Scriptural concept of one chapter. Begin the meal by informally asking the concept question for the chapter you are considering.

Ask each person around the table what he would do in that situation. Don't force anyone to answer and don't allow anyone to ridicule another's answer. Allow the discussion to continue as long as the interest is maintained.

Then, after the meal, read the Scripture story that corresponds to the concept question. See which one can identify the character in the story first.

After reading the story encourage anyone to make further comment on it. Then explain the unique feature of the animal of that chapter which illustrates the character quality in the story.

After this dismiss your family, but if some want to learn more about the nature story or the Scripture story, you can give them the additional material in the chapter which is designed for this purpose.

CONCEPT QUESTIONS

1. If you were responsible for one thousand soldiers and your general told you to pursue the enemy who had equal strength, but you knew that tomorrow you would have twice as many men, what would you do?

page 37

2. If you were living under the rule of a mean and wicked leader and you overheard two of his assistants plotting to kill him, what would you do?

page 49

3. If your grandfather left instructions before he died that you were not to live in a certain city but a mission board wanted to send you there, what would you do?

page 61

II. THE FATHER MUST BE RESPONSIBLE FOR TEACHING

God never intended for a father to lose his role as a "teacher." As a father or grandfather Scripture commands him to "Teach. . .thy sons, and thy son's sons." (Deuteronomy 4:9) If a son or daughter ceases to look to their father as a "teacher" they lose one of the most vital and lasting relationships in their lives. But in order for him to have this position his sons and daughters must want to learn from him. Thus it is his responsibility to win their confidence, think through what he intends to share and create curiosity in their minds. He must expect to earn the privilege of teaching—not demand the right to do so. If a father has "lost his audience" because of division or disharmony in the home, it is all the more important that he work to regain it. The following factors must always be kept in mind:

A. LEARN TO COMMUNICATE TO THE SPIRIT OF YOUR CHILD

Learning stops between two people when the spirit of either one has been wounded. A father must prepare to spend as much time maintaining an open spirit as he does presenting information. A child's spirit may close if he thinks that there is favoritism toward another child, or that his father's work is more important than he is, or that he can never please his father or that he is a burden to the family and the home. The test of an open spirit is whether a son or daughter will trust their father with the secrets of their deepest wishes and emotions.

B. EXPLAIN YOUR RESPONSIBILITY AS THEIR "UMBRELLA OF PROTECTION"

One of the greatest motivations for a father to live a godly life is the awareness that any failure on his part provides an opportunity for Satan to bring destructive temptations to those under his spiritual care. "No man can enter into a strong man's house, and spoil his goods, except he will first bind the strong man; and then he will spoil his house." (Mark 3:27)

This truth explains to sons and daughters the importance of being under the father's authority and maintaining close communication with him. One of the most powerful relationships a father can have with his sons and daughters is the agreement that they will use temptations as a signal to pray for the other and will contact each other and simply ask for prayer when under special temptation.

C. TEACH YOUR CHILDREN TO BE COLLECTORS OF WISDOM

A son or daughter wants to know what pleases his father. His statement to them should be, "You would make me a very happy father if you would be wise sons and daughters as you grow up." "A wise son maketh a glad father. . . " (Proverbs 10:1) He could then suggest that they begin a Life Notebook in order to record insights, experiences and projects in Scripture. This notebook will become a practical basis for working together, clarifying ideas, organizing information and developing a life message. For example, one such project would be to reorganize the book of Proverbs under categories such as the fool, pride, the slothful man, a strange woman. Gathering pictures to visualize each concept and memorizing key verses would develop exceptional ability in discernment and discretion.

D. TEACH YOUR CHILDREN TO MAKE DECISIONS ON THE BASIS OF A ONENESS OF SPIRIT WITH YOU AND THE LORD

Sons and daughters will be under constant pressure to conform to the world's standards, and they will be continually making decisions in the areas of activities, dress standards, friendships, music, vocational goals, etc. The first defense against worldly pressures is to teach them how to stand alone. This ability is the heritage only of those who have discovered God's principles for living as a superior way of life. Therefore, each new decision provides an important opportunity for the father to explain God's principles of life and how the natural inclinations of the world are opposed to them. The father should ask his sons and daughters to discuss with him any decision they are not positively sure he would be in favor of. They should be willing to drop it as long as he has any reservation about it being God's will. It is as important for them to do this for small decisions as it is for major decisions.

III. MEALTIMES MUST INCLUDE DISCUSSION OF LIFE CONCEPTS

When a father explains a basic truth upon which life is built, he is teaching a principle. When he weaves together a combination of truths for a life situation, he is teaching a concept. Today, a flood of false concepts is engulfing the home and school and church, and the mealtime provides one of the most important opportunities for a father to discuss them with his family. The following skills are essential in doing this:

A. LEARN TO THINK IN TERMS OF CONCEPTS

Behind almost every decision that your son or daughter faces are underlying concepts which are either Scriptural or unscriptural. It is essential that you not just give your opinion, but rather that you identify and analyze each concept upon which their decision is based.

This means that you must first search out God's concepts in each area of life from Scripture and from the counsel of wise men. Then you must be aware of the subtle undermining which constantly takes place against God's thinking. The wise father will expose the destructiveness of the world's thinking before his sons and daughters become emotionally attached to a decision to follow it.

Carefully planned questions, illustrations and stories which are casually but appropriately shared by the father during a mealtime discussion will provide the daily exhortation so necessary in each life. "But exhort one another daily. . .lest any of you be hardened through the deceitfulness of sin" (the accepting of **ungodly** concepts). (Hebrews 3:13) One of the most powerful tools against any concept is mocking. Those in the world usually mock God's standards before presenting their alternate views. Either your children will have a godly contempt for the philosophies of the world or they will have an ungodly reaction to the ways of God which you have been seeking to teach.

During dinnertime, the father must be skilled in showing a godly and wise contempt for the logical-sounding but distorted conclusions of the world with a clear reinforcing of Scriptural concepts which the very spirit of their children reaffirm. God illustrates this spirit in I Corinthians 1 and 2, Colossians 2, I Timothy 6, II Timothy 3 and Jude. ". . .Hath not God made foolish the wisdom of this world?" (I Corinthians 1:20)

CONCEPT QUESTIONS - continued

4. If you followed your parents' instructions to date a certain person who really wasn't your choice but whom you learned to enjoy being with, what would you do if they asked you to break up?

page 73

5. If you were the pastor of a church that was in desperate need of funds, and a wealthy man offered your church a large sum of money if you attended the dedication of his business venture which you knew violated Scriptural principles, what would you do?

page 87

6. If a friend whom you wanted to see become a Christian agreed to attend your church if you would first attend an activity with him which you knew would displease your parents, what would you do?

page 99

7. If a friend gave you a box of record albums to throw away which were causing him to stumble spiritually, and you found a few Christian-type songs among them which could be used in the music library at church, what would you do?

page 111

8. If your boss put you in charge of one hundred employees and your father showed you how it would be much more efficient to divide this responsibility with others, what would you do?

page 123

9. If you were very grieved because your father was being cheated in a business deal by his brother but wouldn't do anything about it, what would you do?

page 137

10. If you were telling your friends how important it was to be courageous when some big, mean men came around the corner to beat you up, what would you do?

page 149

11. If you asked your father how you could be better liked, and he told you to befriend that nice group from church which you knew was rejected by most others outside of church, what would you do?

page 161

B. CONQUER PRIDE BY SHARING WHAT GOD IS TEACHING YOU

Most fathers fail at this point. They have important information to teach, but they cannot understand why their children lose interest in what they are saying or are easily distracted by competing thoughts. There are usually two reasons. Either he has not created sufficient curiosity for what he wants to say, or they are resisting a spirit of pride within him of which he may not even be aware.

God resists the proud and so does a man's family. Just as it is important for the father to maintain an open spirit with each child, so it is important to communicate to that spirit. But this is only possible if he has an attitude of humility. The concepts he teaches must grow out of the painful lessons that God has taken him through. In this way he is on their level, humbling himself by telling them how God has been dealing with him rather than speaking on an authoritative level and telling them what he thinks they should know.

It is so easy for a father to expect his children to pay attention, but he must give up this right. He must use their inattention as God's gauge to him of whether he has adequately prepared both himself and them for what he is trying to share. Most men feel inadequate in effective conversation with their children, but this is certainly a cause for claiming the promise of James 1:5, "If any of you lack wisdom, let him ask of God, that giveth to all men liberally, and upbraideth not; and it shall be given him."

If a father is to be successful he must ask his family to look at him as a learner and expect many times of failure in clearly explaining himself. If he allows these failures to drive him back into the Word, God will give him the grace of new desire and power which will be that much of a greater heritage for his children.

C. CREATE CURIOSITY BEFORE COMMUNICATING CONTENT

It is a common fallacy among fathers to think that their children are not interested in spiritual matters. But fathers have the ability to create great anticipation and response to these truths. This is done by using the interests and concerns of his sons and daughters to create curiosity for information which he knows will meet deep needs in their lives. The phrase—you can lead a horse to water but you can't make it drink—is not entirely accurate. You can salt the oats. In the same manner you must learn to sprinkle "salting statements" in your conversation which will direct the natural curiosity of your children to consider the concepts of Scripture. Christians are to be the salt of the earth. This means that we must learn the skill of

creating thirst in the hearts and minds of all those around us for the refreshing truth of God's Word. Our Lord was a master at creating curiosity by asking questions and giving parables which forced his listeners to ask further questions. Expect your children to have at least one question in their mind whenever you start talking to them. "Is this really important for me to hear?"

A wise father will design a preliminary question, statement, story or situation which will answer this question before he even tries to present the concepts of Scripture. This is a practical application of breaking up the fallow ground before the seeds of truth are planted in it.

NOTE TO FATHER:

Before the meal, study for yourself the background information and character sketch of the Scripture story so that you can share additional points of interest about its people and events. The mother and the Christian school are then able to reinforce and amplify what you as the father teach your children.

HOW WELL DO YOU KNOW THE WAYS OF ANIMALS?

The significant precedent for learning the ways of animals is given in God's dealing with Adam. Adam's first task was to name each animal as God brought them to him. He would never have been able to give them precise names if he had not thoroughly understood their ways.

MATCH THE FOLLOWING STATEMENTS WITH THE PROPER SPECIES ON THIS PAGE.

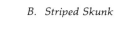

A. River Otter

B. Striped Skunk

C. Black-Headed Gull

D. Yellow-Shafted Flicker

E. Great Horned Owl

F. Eastern Hognose Snake

1. **WHAT ANIMAL MAKES ITS DAILY CHORES FUN?**

   Answer: page 116

2. **WHAT SPECIES AVOIDS DANGER BY PLAY-ACTING?**

   Answer: page 142

3. **WHAT ANIMAL HAS SUCH AN EFFECTIVE WEAPON THAT IT HAS FEW ENEMIES?**

   Answer: page 166

4. **WHAT BIRD NESTS IN THE WINTER TO PROVIDE FOR ITS YOUNG IN THE SPRING?**

   Answer: page 30

5. **WHAT BIRD GETS A MEAL BY USING ITS TONGUE TO IMITATE A WORM?**

   Answer: page 304

6. **WHAT BIRD AVOIDS DANGER BY KEEPING ITS NEST CLEAN?**

   Answer: page 254

MATCH THE FOLLOWING STATEMENTS WITH THE PROPER SPECIES ON THIS PAGE.

7. WHAT ANIMAL CAN DIG ITSELF OUT OF SIGHT IN NINETY SECONDS?

Answer: page 354

A. *Raccoon*

8. WHAT ANIMAL IS SO INQUISITIVE THAT IT GETS INTO TROUBLE?

Answer: page 280

B. *Wolverine*

9. WHAT SPECIES THRIVES AS A RESULT OF GOING THROUGH MAJOR STRUGGLES?

Answer: page 180

C. *Badger*

10. WHAT ANIMAL RELENTLESSLY TRACKS DOWN ITS PREY?

Answer: page 216

D. *Common Crow*

11. WHAT ANIMAL HAS A BUILT-IN COMB TO GROOM ITS FUR?

Answer: page 242

E. *Red Fox*

12. WHAT ANIMAL IS SPANKED WHEN IT DOESN'T FOLLOW THE WISHES OF ITS PARENT?

Answer: Page 66

F. *Cecropia Moth*

13. WHAT ANIMAL RELIES ON ITS WIT RATHER THAN ITS STRENGTH?

Answer: page 366

G. *Beaver*

14. WHAT BIRD STATIONS "LOOK OUTS" WHILE IT FEEDS?

H. *Grizzly Bear*

Answer: page 104

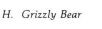

The wisdom which God gave to Solomon included a thorough understanding of the world of nature. ". . . He spake also of beasts, and of fowl, and of creeping things, and of fishes. And there came of all people to hear the wisdom of Solomon, from all kings of the earth, which had heard of his wisdom." (I Kings 4:33-34)

MATCH THE FOLLOWING STATEMENTS WITH THE PROPER SPECIES ON THIS PAGE.

A. Wood Duck

B. Whistling Swan

C. Canada Goose

D. Eastern Chipmunk

E. Woodcock

F. Short-Tailed Shrew

G. King Salmon

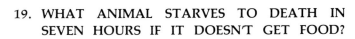

15. WHAT BIRD CAN FLY UP TO ONE HUNDRED MILES AN HOUR BECAUSE IT HAS A LEADER?

Answer: page 292

16. WHAT BIRD WILL RISK ITS LIFE TO PROTECT ITS MATE?

Answer: page 42

17. WHAT SPECIES NEVER SEES ITS YOUNG HATCH?

Answer: page 204

18. WHAT BIRD CAN IMITATE THE SOUND OF RAIN?

Answer: page 80

19. WHAT ANIMAL STARVES TO DEATH IN SEVEN HOURS IF IT DOESN'T GET FOOD?

Answer: page 330

20. WHAT ANIMAL BUILDS SPECIFIC ROOMS IN ITS HOME FOR DIFFERENT PURPOSES?

Answer: page 266

21. WHAT BIRD BEGINS TRAINING ITS YOUNG BEFORE THEY ARE HATCHED?

Answer: page 154

> In Scripture God assumes that we know the ways of animals. For example, if we do not know the response of a bear we will neither appreciate nor understand the warning, "Let a bear robbed of her whelps meet a man, rather than a fool in his folly." (Proverbs 17:12)

MATCH THE FOLLOWING STATEMENTS WITH THE PROPER SPECIES ON THIS PAGE.

22. WHAT SPECIES MAINTAINS A HIGHLY EFFECTIVE COMMUNICATION SYSTEM THROUGH ITS TASTE?

Answer: page 54

A. *Short-Tailed Weasel*

23. WHAT BIRD CAN SEE A FISH FROM TWO HUNDRED FEET IN THE AIR AND CATCH IT?

Answer: page 342

B. *Pied-Bill Grebe*

24. WHAT BIRD FLIES AROUND THE WORLD EVERY YEAR?

Answer: page 192

C. *Spotted Sandpiper*

25. WHAT ANIMAL HAS EARNED THE REPUTATION OF NEVER RETREATING?

Answer: page 130

D. *Osprey*

26. WHAT ANIMAL HAS THE EQUIVALENT OF AN IN-HOUSE SANITATION SYSTEM?

Answer: page 230

E. *Honeybee*

27. WHAT BIRD USUALLY RESPONDS UNWISELY WHEN DANGER APPROACHES?

Answer: page 316

F. *Woodchuck*

28. WHAT BIRD MAKES ITS NEST ON THE WATER?

Answer: page 92

G. *Arctic Tern*

Loyalty

CHARACTER · CURRICULUM

PART ONE

ADJUSTING MY SCHEDULE TO MEET THE NEEDS OF THOSE I AM SERVING

STANDING WITH THOSE I AM SERVING IN THEIR TIME OF NEED

BEING A RELIABLE MESSENGER TO THOSE I AM SERVING

KNOWING AND FOLLOWING THE WISHES OF THOSE RESPONSIBLE FOR ME

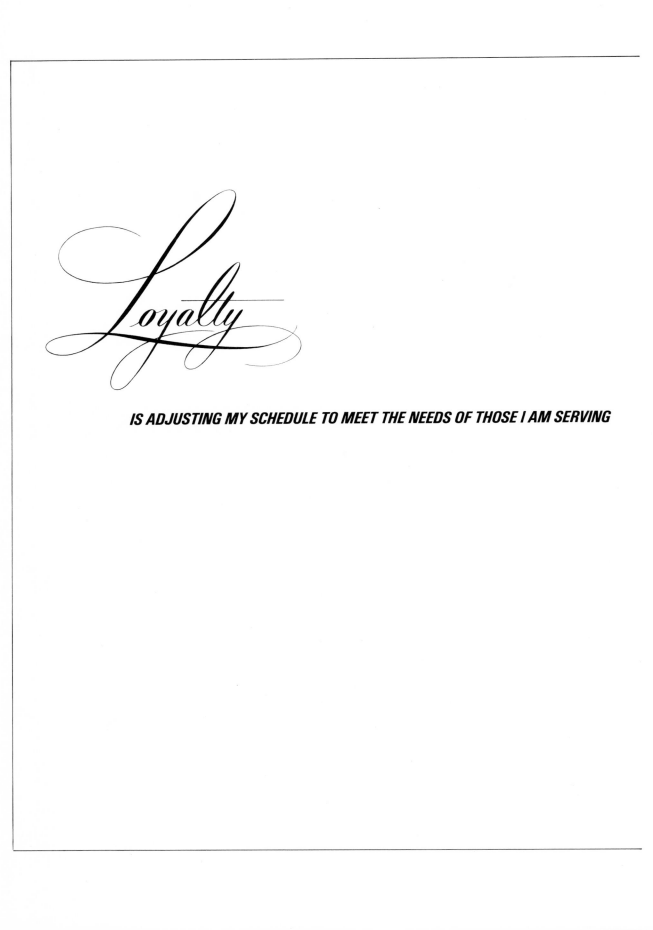

Loyalty

IS ADJUSTING MY SCHEDULE TO MEET THE NEEDS OF THOSE I AM SERVING

LIVING LESSONS ON LOYALTY . . .

FROM THE PAGES OF SCRIPTURE

At the turning point of his career, a general was given the opportunity to become commander-in-chief of his nation's army. He did not understand the true meaning and implications of loyalty and could not even obey his superior's first order. He paid a bitter price for his unwillingness to adjust his schedule to meet the needs of those he served.

ILLUSTRATED IN THE WORLD OF NATURE

THE GREAT HORNED OWL   *Bubo virginianus*

A deep-woods inhabitant, the horned owl ranges in size from eighteen to twenty-five inches. The female is slightly larger than the male. This bird, also known as the hoot owl and the "tiger of the air," is considered the most powerful of the North American owls.

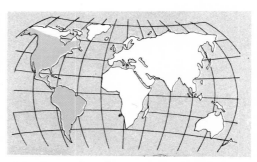

The range and habitat of the great horned owl

LOYALTY

HOW DOES THE GREAT HORNED OWL ILLUSTRATE LOYALTY IN ADJUSTING ITS SCHEDULE?

A faint crunch sounded deep in the frozen Northwoods as a great horned owl fractured the glazed snow surface on a large oak limb. The chilling February wind played with the tufts of feathers on this crouched figure as she surveyed the nearby trees. She gave little attention to the snow or the wind. Her keen eyes were in search of something more important.

Suddenly, she spotted what she was looking for. Her large, powerful wings spread and lifted her to another tree for a closer investigation.

The reward of her search was an abandoned crow's nest. It passed her inspection. She began pecking away its frozen crust of snow and added a few branches and breast feathers. With the adaptation complete, it became her home and within a few days it contained three white eggs.

Now began the months of dedicated sacrifice which are carefully given by the horned owl in a remarkable way.

This early nesting was an unusual sight in the frozen forest. It was a full two months before other birds would do the same—and for good reason. The cold days and colder nights made the owl a prisoner of her nest. If she left the nest to find food for herself, she would run the risk of her eggs freezing. So she went without much food during the crucial incubation period.

But a new hardship revealed another disadvantage of early nesting. One afternoon the sky darkened, and heavy thick snow pelted the mother owl. It clung to her feathers as well as the protruding edges of the nest. The owl fought to shake off the deepening snow but never left her eggs.

After four weeks of keeping the eggs warm, three cream-colored, downy owlets hatched. Now the reason for the early nesting became apparent. The owlets opened their pleading mouths and the parents began their race to keep them filled. Their appetites were enormous. The task of feeding would be impossible were it not for the mother's early nesting. This gave her the advantage of being able to spot a passing meal on the floor of the forest. Leaves had not yet grown on the trees, and the lingering snow provided a sharp contrast to the rodents for which the parents searched.

In three months the owlets would grow from three inches to over two feet. Their tremendous and rapid growth makes it necessary for the parents to secure enormous quantities of food. And it is for this reason that the parent bird adjusts its schedule and remains stationary during the cold months of winter, depriving itself of food so that it can better meet the needs of its rapidly-growing young.

The strong, bony structure of the horned owl's beak allows it to crush bones and tear through thick skin and tough muscles.

CHARACTERISTICS AND PHYSICAL FEATURES OF THE GREAT HORNED OWL

The horned owl demonstrates loyalty by building its schedule around the needs of its young. One indication of loyalty occurs when the owl builds its nest. Rather than choosing the warmer spring months, it nests during the cold months of late winter. Small prey are not afforded their usual ground cover during this time because of lack of foliage. This enables the parent owls to meet the tremendous food requirements of their young.

HOW CAN AN OWL GET A LARGE RODENT THROUGH ITS SMALL MOUTH?

The mouth structure of the horned owl actually extends from ear to ear. It is much larger than just the beak. Its sharp, hooked bill is used to tear a larger catch in two, but usually it will stuff the entire catch into its mouth at once.

The horned owl may use its beak *to tear its catch, but normally a small animal such as this house mouse is eaten whole.*

Extent of mouth opening

33

The owl either expands or contracts its iris to adjust to available light.

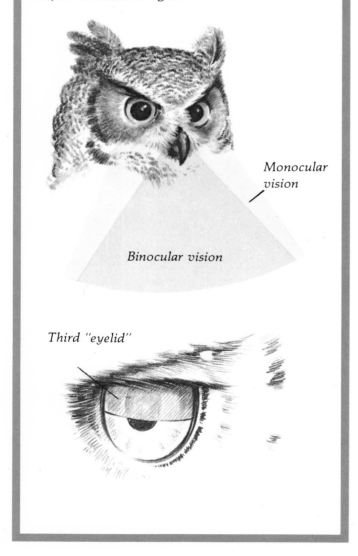

Monocular vision

Binocular vision

Third "eyelid"

DOES AN OWL DIGEST BONES AND HAIR?

Hair, bones and feathers are indigestible and are regurgitated in two to four-inch long "castings." Unlike a mammal, the owl does not have teeth with which to grind its food. It must use its beak for tearing large pieces of meat into manageable sizes and then rely on a muscular motion to shake the food into the gullet. There the powerful gastric juices of the owl's digestive system reduce the meat to liquid.

WHY IS IT IMPORTANT FOR AN OWL TO SEE BOTH DAY AND NIGHT?

It is vital for the owl to see at night as well as during the day. The daylight hours are short during the time of the year when it needs to gather the greatest amount of food for its young, and much of what it hunts is more active during the night.

HOW CAN AN OWL SEE AT NIGHT?

An owl has more rod cells in its retina than most other birds do. These gather whatever light is available and allow it to "see in the dark." Binocular vision—an overlapping of each eye's field of vision—gives it a greater ability to judge distances.

WHY DOES THE OWL HAVE THREE EYELIDS?

The third eyelid regularly cleanses and moistens the eyes of the owl. It is like a built-in wiper system which prevents the owl's eye from becoming dry. This feature is necessary to preserve the keen vision and accuracy of the eye for hunting.

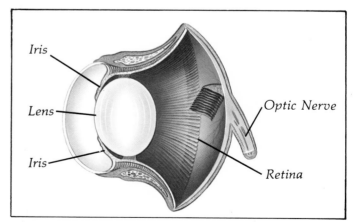

Iris

Lens

Iris

Optic Nerve

Retina

Interior view of the eye of an owl

WHERE ARE THE REAL EARS OF AN OWL?

The feathery tufts we see on the owl have nothing to do with hearing. The real ears are precisely positioned in different locations on either side of the owl's head. This results in a sound reaching each ear at a different instant. The time interval between the same sound reaching each ear gives the owl the ability to accurately pinpoint the exact source of sound.

WOULD AN OWL LOSE ITS CATCH WHILE FLYING BACK TO THE NEST?

The owl has four pairs of extremely sharp and powerful claws—two sets on each foot. They are arranged in such a way that they come down on the prey like sets of crossed ice hooks. The claws or talons are so sharp that they can quickly sink into even thick skin and flesh. This grip ensures a safe return of its catch to the nest.

IN WHAT WAY ARE AN OWL'S FEET LIKE TENNIS SHOES?

The owl's foot is equipped with non-skid pads. These pads work the way tennis shoes do on a gymnasium floor and aid in retaining its grip on prey.

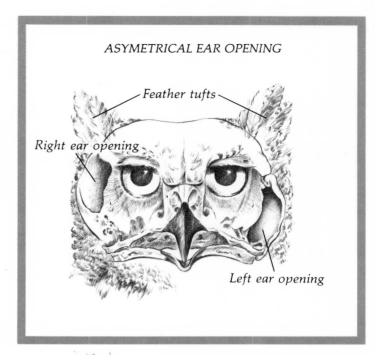

ASYMETRICAL EAR OPENING

Feather tufts

Right ear opening

Left ear opening

Claws or talons

Pads

WHAT ENABLES AN OWL TO FLY SILENTLY?

The intricate feather structure of the leading edge of the wings enables the owl to fly noiselessly. As air passes over the feathers, it is broken up and the sound level of the flapping is reduced to almost nothing.

WHY DOES THE OWL NEED SILENT WINGS?

For its full-time job of satisfying the enormous appetites of its young, the great horned owl must use every possible advantage in hunting. The feather structure of these "silent wings" gives an added advantage as it enables the owl to approach and surprise its prey without a sound.

WHY DOES THE OWL'S DIET CHANGE DURING THE NESTING PERIOD?

The parent horned owls eat far less than usual during the time that their young are growing. They are tireless in their search for food and usually eat only what the owlets cannot digest in order to make sure that they are adequately fed.

Extended wing showing frayed edge of feathers which enable it to fly silently

Leading edge of owl's wing feather

HOW DOES SCRIPTURE ILLUSTRATE THE IMPORTANCE OF ADJUSTING MY SCHEDULE?

Twice an ambitious general marched out to battle, and twice he was defeated. The cause of each defeat was his failure to learn a lesson in timing. Twenty thousand men were killed in the first battle, but the second confrontation was fatal to only one.

Three days before the second battle, the king called his newly-appointed general and gave him urgent instructions. "Assemble the fighting men of the nation within three days and report here with them."

The general left to assemble the army. The events of that moment were strikingly similar to those of the earlier battle. Prior to that first battle, two advisors had debated which was the better plan—to pursue the enemy immediately with a smaller army or to take a few extra days and mobilize a larger army. The latter course had been chosen and it proved to be disastrous. Little did the general realize how vital it was for him to learn from that experience.

Anxiously the king waited. Each hour that passed gave his enemy a further advantage. Finally the appointed hour arrived on the third day. The king went out expecting to see the troops, but to his amazement, no troops were in sight—nor was the general.

In desperation the king called a trusted warrior. He explained the growing danger to their kingdom and commanded him to pursue the enemy with the remaining troops that were stationed in the city. An air of panic swept over the city. Orders were shouted out by commanding officers. Soldiers grabbed their weapons as they rushed into formation and marched out to pursue the enemy.

News of what was happening reached the general. He immediately abandoned his efforts to mobilize the army and hurried to join the king's troops. Little did he realize that he was rushing to his own death. Among the king's troops was a demoted rival who despised and hated him.

As the troops reached a huge rock by the road, the latecomer aggressively assumed his appointed position of leadership, but his enemy saw his chance. The troops watched intently to see what would happen.

As the displaced rival walked up to greet the general, his sword slipped out of its sheath. With studied casualness, he grasped it with his left hand. In an effort to distract attention, he asked with interest, "Are you in good health, my brother?" As though he intended to give a kiss of greeting, he gently touched the man's beard in a gesture of respect. Then he quickly grasped the beard with his right hand and viciously stabbed him through with the unnoticed sword.

The stunned victim staggered back. A moment later he collapsed in his own blood in the middle of the highway. The troops stood in astonishment as they watched their leader die.

Had he followed the schedule given to him his murderer would have remained in the capital city, and the new general could have continued and gained an easy victory. Amasa's failure to adjust his schedule to meet the needs of the king was one more example of the disloyalty which had characterized his life and ultimately caused his death.

From II Samuel 20:1-13

The type of weapon *Joab used to kill Absalom is not known. It is likely that it was merely a hard piece of wood sharpened at one end. By holding three of them together they would have formed a deadly weapon.*

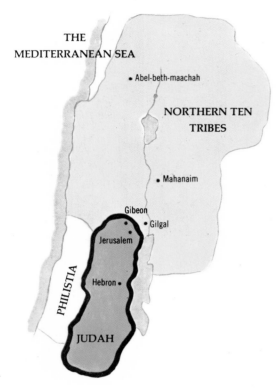

THE MEDITERRANEAN SEA

• Abel-beth-maachah

NORTHERN TEN TRIBES

• Mahanaim

Gibeon
• Gilgal
Jerusalem

PHILISTIA

Hebron •

JUDAH

When Amasa failed *to appear in Jerusalem, David sent his army northward under the direction of Abishai. Joab took over the leadership at Gibeon after murdering Amasa and pursued Sheba as far as Abel-beth-maachah.*

The sword *which was worn by wealthier or higher ranking soldiers was a bronze dagger 7 to 10 inches in length and was ideal for hand-to-hand combat.*

THE HISTORY OF DISLOYALTY THAT PRECEDED AMASA'S FAILURE TO ADJUST TO HIS LEADER'S SCHEDULE

The complex background of Amasa's role in Israeli history involves several ambitious men and a bloody struggle for leadership. Family loyalties and jealousies exerted their influence as the delicate balance of power changed wildly back and forth.

THE KING'S SON SECRETLY TURNS THE NATION AGAINST HIS FATHER

Absalom, third son of King David, had a very attractive sister who was wickedly mistreated by their half-brother, the crown prince. Absalom designed a plot to kill this half-brother who had disgraced his sister and, in so doing, eliminated the chief contender for his father's throne. Next Absalom planted seeds of disloyalty among all those who were discontent in his father's kingdom. Soon he convinced the majority of the nation that he would make a better king than his father. On a given day, he gathered his troops and marched toward his father's capital city, Jerusalem.

David, an experienced military strategist, realized that an immediate attack upon him in Jerusalem would be disastrous. He needed time to organize his defenses so he fled toward the Jordan River with all who remained loyal to him.

THE KING'S WISEST COUNSELOR SEEKS REVENGE FOR AN OFFENSE HE NEVER FORGAVE

When Absalom entered Jerusalem with his forces, Ahithophel was there to join him. Ahithophel had served wisely as David's counselor, but he was the grandfather of Bathsheba, the beautiful wife of Uriah against whom David committed his great sin. It seems that Ahithophel never forgave David for killing his granddaughter's husband.

So at this crucial time, Ahithophel sided with Absalom and shrewdly advised him to attack David immediately with the troops he had already assembled. But another counselor who was a secret spy for David gave contrary advice. He suggested that the entire nation be conscripted to go after David, even though it would require more time. When Ahithophel's wiser counsel was rejected, he realized that Absalom's defeat was imminent so he went home, put his house in order, and hanged himself.

THE REBEL'S COUSIN IS CHOSEN TO LEAD THE ARMY

Absalom had a cousin named Amasa. He was chosen to assemble all the men of Israel to war against David. While he organized his troops, two other cousins of Absalom, Joab and Abishai, were putting together an army of loyal, experienced and well-trained soldiers for King David. In the battle that followed, David's men were greatly outnumbered, but David anticipated that his seasoned soldiers under his general's skillful leadership would still have an advantage over a largely non-professional army fighting in unfamiliar territory.

When his men went out to battle, David gave strict orders not to intentionally harm his son Absalom; however, when Joab found Absalom dangling from an oak tree in which he was entangled by his long hair, he disobeyed David's orders and thrust three darts through his heart. Now that their leader was killed, Amasa and his defeated troops fled to their homes, fearful and apprehensive of their future.

THE KING REPLACES HIS OWN GENERAL WITH THE ENEMY'S LEADER

When David learned that Joab had killed Absalom against his orders, he decided to remove this senior general from leadership. At the same time, reports reached David that the entire nation which had rebelled against him wanted to reinstate him as king—all except the men of Judah who had sided with Absalom in initiating the revolt. David decided that the best way to remove their resistance was to offer their commanding general the position that Joab presently held. Amasa's defeat was thereby reversed and he was made commander-in-chief of the nation's army.

Elated by such an offer, Amasa became overly ambitious in bringing back the king. In so doing, he and the men of Judah failed to give proper recognition to the other ten tribes of Israel. A vicious argument resulted between the men of Judah and the northern ten tribes.

A NEW REBEL LEADER EMERGES AND THREATENS TO DIVIDE THE KINGDOM

At the height of the argument between the tribes of Israel, Sheba, a rebellious and self-appointed leader, saw his opportunity and rallied the northern ten tribes around himself. David knew that in order to avoid a civil war or, even worse, the permanent division of the kingdom, he must act quickly before Sheba had a chance to organize an army.

He commanded Amasa, his new senior general, to mobilize the fighting men of Judah within three days in order to subdue the rebellion. When Amasa failed to appear at the appointed time, David reluctantly weakened his defenses at Jerusalem by sending his personal army to pursue Sheba.

Amasa finally joined David's men in Gibeon and was met by Joab, the general he had just replaced. Joab used this opportunity to eliminate his despised rival. In a gesture of greeting, he treacherously thrust his sword through Amasa's ribs, killing him in front of the troops Amasa had expected to lead to victory.

AMASA CHARACTER SKETCH

WHAT CAUSED AMASA TO BE DISLOYAL TO HIS UNCLE, KING DAVID?

It is possible that Amasa's cousins, Joab and Abishai, as well as other members of David's family treated him with contempt. Amasa was the son of Abigail and Jether the Ishmaelite (I Chronicles 2:17). Abigail was King David's sister and was also the sister of Zeruiah, the mother of Joab and Abishai (I Chronicles 2:16). II Samuel 17:25 indicates that Amasa was an illegitimate child. This stigma and the fact that his father was an Ishmaelite may have resulted in extra pressure or even ridicule as a boy.

By failing to respond properly to this pressure, he may have become resentful and disloyal to the God who created him as well as to the family in which he was placed. This is an explanation for his actions in siding with Absalom, another family outcast, and in becoming the rival of his cousins Joab and Abishai.

WHY DIDN'T AMASA LEARN HIS LESSON THE FIRST TIME?

When given the chance by David to be his commander, he failed at his very first task because he knew no more about being loyal to the one he was serving than he knew years before. By choosing to follow Absalom instead of David, Amasa associated with disloyal men in a rebellious cause. His rebellious friends regarded loyalty as a weakness rather than an important strength (cf. Psalm 1:1).

WHY DID AMASA FAIL TO KEEP HIS APPOINTMENT WITH DAVID?

According to the Hebrew method of inclusive reckoning, "within three days" (II Samuel 20:4) meant that Amasa had only one full day to accomplish his task of mobilizing the army. David's command was not at all unreasonable, for many years later the scribe Ezra issued almost the exact same command and it was obeyed without difficulty (Ezra 10:7-9).

It is likely, however, that the men of Judah were not as quick to follow Amasa as they had once been. His recent history as a general was poor, and he may have experienced considerable resistance. Instead of meeting David promptly on the third day with the soldiers he already had, he evidently decided to disregard David's order and take more time to recruit more men. It is ironic that Amasa was using the same strategy that Ahithophel had warned Absalom against.

Because he had not learned from another's mistake, he sacrificed the advantage of speed and surprise for the advantage of numbers. Amasa was doing things his way and in his time, never realizing that his act of disloyalty would cost him his life.

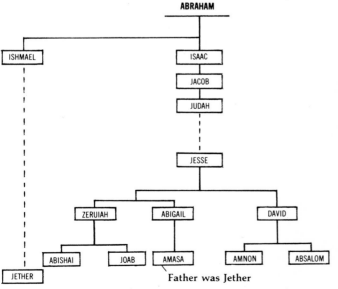

Although Amasa's father Jether *was a distant relative of the tribe of Judah, there was no family loyalty between the two lines. The Ishmaelites made Arabia their home and became known as Arabians (Genesis 25:18). Rivalry in the form of Israeli-Arab conflicts between the lines of Isaac and Ishmael has persisted throughout the centuries (cf. Genesis 16:12).*

GENERAL AMASA

Loyalty

IS STANDING WITH THOSE I AM SERVING IN THEIR TIME OF NEED

LIVING LESSONS ON LOYALTY . . .

FROM THE PAGES OF SCRIPTURE

A court official learned of a plot to kill his king. Because of his willingness to stand by the one he was serving even in his time of need, a dramatic series of events resulted. His people were saved from the fate of a cruel decision as a result of his loyalty.

ILLUSTRATED IN THE WORLD OF NATURE

THE CANADA GOOSE   *Branta Canadensis*

The Canada goose is the most familiar member of its family. It can attain a wingspread of up to seventy-six inches and is commonly seen in the spring and fall, flying in V-formation to and from its breeding grounds. This species is the only goose with a white chin strap.

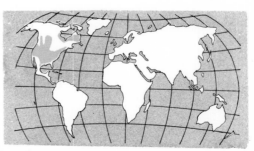

The range and habitat of the Canada goose

LOYALTY

HOW DOES THE CANADA GOOSE ILLUSTRATE LOYALTY IN RESPONDING TO ADVERSITY?

The long migration flight finally terminated for the Canada geese. The nesting colony, flying in a large wedge, returned at last to the breeding grounds where they had been reared.

The colony rested with sentinels standing guard while others fed on grain and tender shoots of plants. Within a few weeks the serious task of nesting began. The paired geese searched for a suitable location for their nests.

One goose and gander, just three years old, chose an abandoned shoreline beaver lodge for their nesting site. The beaver lodge met the necessary requirements of proximity to the water and afforded protection from enemies. All considerations for safety had been taken into account—except one.

A nearby wooded area housed a raccoon family. Raccoons are a treacherous threat to all waterfowl. They raid nests indiscriminately for eggs and for newly-hatched chicks. But the geese had no way of knowing that any were so near. Oblivious to their danger, the pair heaped grass and sticks on top of the lodge as the nest took form.

After the five eggs had been laid, the female began incubating them. But four weeks later, a deadly assailant skirted the abandoned lodge area during the early hours of a spring night. A mother raccoon, searching for food for her growing young, spotted the nest and approached it confidently.

The female was guarding the nest alone, but she quickly signalled her mate when she faced the murderous attacker. A vicious struggle began, and the male flew immediately to her aid. As a result of their united defense, the female suffered severe bleeding and a broken wing, but they succeeded in driving the attacker away.

Undaunted by its initial failure, the persistent raccoon repeated its attack the next night. Again the geese valiantly defended their nest, and this time the female's remaining useful wing was broken.

On the third night their vigil was threatened by the determined raccoon as she again tried to make her way past the parent geese. In her display of loyalty the female lost her life, but because of her sacrifice she was able to preserve her nest. That morning, in the care of the remaining male, five downy goslings hatched and within hours they were enjoying the protection of the water.

CHARACTERISTICS AND PHYSICAL FEATURES OF THE CANADA GOOSE

The allegiance of the female goose saved her nest from destruction because she was willing to defend it at all costs. Early in life, she carefully chose the one to whom a lifelong commitment would be made.

WHAT HAPPENS WHEN TWO GANDERS WANT THE SAME MATE?

When a male Canada goose is attracted to a partner, he must be prepared to battle for her. If he makes his intentions known and another goose does the same, they will engage in a contest of strength.

WHICH PARTNER HAS THE FINAL WORD IN MATING?

If two males battle over a mate, the winner is not assured of success with the watching female. Even though he has defeated the competitor, the victor must still win her acceptance of him. He attempts this by showing special attention to her until she either accepts or rejects him as a mate.

Success in a battle *between ganders does not guarantee that the victorious male will be accepted by the female.*

HOW WILL A "PAIRED" FEMALE GOOSE RESPOND TO AN INTRUDING MALE?

If a rival approaches, both geese will probably drive it away. Once the female has accepted a partner, they establish a relationship which is likely to last for a lifetime. This lifetime partnership is one explanation for the strong bond of loyalty which the Canada geese display.

WHAT IS AN INCUBATION PATCH?

When each egg arrives, the female plucks out down feathers from her breast and places them around the egg. As she continues to remove these feathers, a bare spot eventually appears which is referred to as the "incubation patch." The body heat of the female is transferred to the egg as it is in direct contact with her skin. These eggs are periodically turned to maintain consistent heat.

HOW DO FEATHERS HELP HATCH EGGS?

The eggs must maintain a temperature of 100.4° F. to 101.3° F. Down feathers were highly valued by the pioneers as excellent insulators of warmth. Their ability to lock in heat enables the parents to leave the nest for brief periods of time and attend to their own personal needs. With the down feathers under and around the eggs and the warm incubation patch gently pressed against the top of them, the high temperature which the eggs require is ensured.

HOW LONG WILL A GOOSE SIT ON INFERTILE EGGS?

The female has been known to continue sitting on a nest of infertile eggs up to five months past the time in

Incubation patch

Down filled nest

The female *periodically turns her eggs. The exact reason for her doing this is not certain, but one explanation is that this movement maintains an evenly distributed temperature.*

which they were to be hatched. When eggs are destroyed early in the nesting season a new clutch may be laid.

WHAT WOULD BE A LIKELY NESTING SITE?

Nests are usually built in secluded places such as islands or the top of beaver or muskrat dwellings. By choosing inaccessible places the parents are better equipped to protect their young from predators.

HOW DO THE PARENT GEESE CLEAR THE WATER OF DANGER?

The day after the goslings hatch, they will enter the water for the first time. They will swim in potentially dangerous water—vulnerable to the attack of snapping turtles, bullfrogs or large fish such as pike or muskie. The female signals her mate and he beats the water wildly with his wings and makes loud squawking noises. This technique frightens enemies away and protects the young goslings from danger.

HOW DOES A GOOSE DEMONSTRATE LOYALTY TO A WOUNDED MATE?

If a goose is shot down by a hunter during the fall migration flight, its mate has been known to circle back, risking death itself, in order to help its partner. If one is wounded, the other will remain with it until it is healed. If the partner cannot be found the other will often stay behind to look for it, enduring the hardships of winter in that area in order to continue its search.

Just as geese fly in formation, *so they also swim in formation. A family will form a line with the gander taking the lead. The female brings up the rear to guide goslings that might lag behind.*

Gander clearing water of danger for goslings

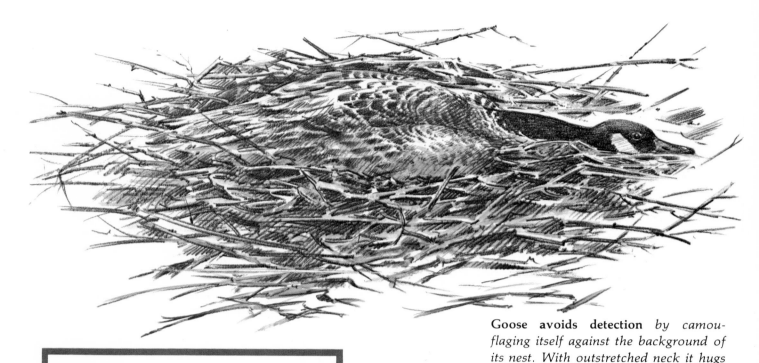

Goose avoids detection *by camou-flaging itself against the background of its nest. With outstretched neck it hugs the ground and remains motionless.*

NATURAL ENEMIES OF THE GOOSE

WHAT ANIMALS ARE A THREAT TO THE GOOSE?

Although mature geese have few natural enemies, they are very alert to predators which endanger their goslings. Those they fear the most are the raccoon and fox. Large fish or snapping turtles can attack from the water as the young goslings are learning to swim. The possibility of the destruction of the eggs from winged enemies such as the crow or raven requires constant vigilance.

HOW DEEP WOULD THE SNOW HAVE TO BE BEFORE A GOOSE WOULD LEAVE ITS NEST?

Several years ago in Alaska, an unseasonable late spring snowstorm came to a breeding ground of the Canada goose. The snow continued falling to a depth of three feet. Days later as the snow melted away, an amazing picture of protection was revealed. Scores of dead geese were still on their nests. They had chosen to suffocate rather than leave the eggs they were protecting.

The period of greatest vulnerability *for the goose begins at incubation and continues until the gosling is a few weeks old. The protective parents have many dangers to face: the raven which feasts on unhatched eggs, the fox which preys on the awkward goslings, severe weather conditions which could snuff out life.*

HOW DOES SCRIPTURE ILLUSTRATE LOYALTY IN RESPONDING TO ADVERSITY?

As the king entered his magnificent palace, two guards stood at attention. Their stern faces concealed the hatred they harbored toward the king they were guarding. Often they had talked to each other about how they would like to kill him.

One day they conceived their plan. It would be easy for them to kill their king since they guarded the door of his bedchamber. They were sure that others would sympathize with them. The king was difficult to get along with. Even his former queen despised him.

As they whispered the details of their plan to each other an alert listener sat nearby. They paid little attention to him, never realizing that a lower court official would be loyal to such a despised king, especially since his family had been brought there as exiles from another land. They were sure that he hated the king, too. But they were wrong. This man had learned the lesson of loyalty. He had purposed to stand by the one he served, even in a time of need.

Overhearing their plot, he realized quickly that the king was in great danger. When the guards walked away, he left that part of the palace and immediately sent a message to the king. When the king heard the message, he was amazed. Could the report be true? He called in a trusted servant and ordered him to investigate the facts.

The report was true, and swift action was taken. The two guards were quickly apprehended, confronted with the evidence and immediately impaled. The king's life had been spared through the faithful official's report. The events were carefully recorded in a book.

But the story doesn't end there. Two great and unexpected rewards resulted from this brave man's loyalty. The first reward came months later when the king was unable to sleep. He thought that if one of his servants read aloud, he might be able to fall asleep. The servant read from the book of records the account of how the king's life had been saved. The king remembered that he had never rewarded the man who protected him, and he decided to raise this loyal subject to a new level of honor.

The second and greater reward came because the one whom Mordecai had raised as a daughter learned from his example. The same loyalty which he displayed toward the king was instilled in her life.

In the face of grave danger, she remained loyal to her own people and saved them from cruel destruction. This event is still remembered and celebrated by millions of descendants of those who were saved by her courageous and loyal actions.

From Esther 2:21-23

THE LEGENDARY LOYALTY OF MORDECAI—
STANDING BY THE ONE HE SERVED IN HIS TIME OF NEED

This account takes place during the reign of Ahasuerus (486-465 B.C.), known through Greek and Roman historians as an extravagant, immoral and cruel tyrant of the Persian Empire. Through no effort of his own he inherited the wealthiest and most powerful position in the world, developed by the brilliant administrative energies of his father. He inherited the empire but not the ability to govern it. His Grecian campaign is an infamous example to military scientists of blatant miscalculation and overconfidence.

A KING'S AIDE THWARTS ASSASSINATION ATTEMPT

After the campaign, when the mood of the empire toward their king was at a low ebb, two of his court attendants—Bigthan and Teresh—began plotting the king's assassination. The conspirators were unaware that their plan to eliminate the despised king was discovered by Mordecai. Even if they had known, they would have expected the support of a displaced Jew living in a foreign land with unsympathetic customs. They did not realize that Queen Esther was Mordecai's cousin, trained and raised in his home as his own daughter. Mordecai saved the king's life by informing him of the plot through Queen Esther. After an investigation, Bigthan and Teresh were executed as a public example.

THE KING SHIFTS STAFF APPOINTMENTS TO PROTECT HIMSELF, UNKNOWINGLY ELEVATING A MURDEROUS MAN

Shortly after this incident King Ahasuerus reorganized his leadership and appointed Haman, a man whom he thought was loyal and had his interests at heart, second in command over his kingdom. His responsibilities included guarding the kingdom against any threat to the king's security, and in an effort to quickly establish Haman's authority and prestige the king commanded all of the court officials to bow down before him. Mordecai claimed exemption from the new law as a Jew and refused to bow.

Haman was insulted by Mordecai's refusal to bow to him and determined to avenge this lack of reverence. With dual motives of personal vanity and a desire to increase his wealth and the wealth of the kingdom, he devised a plan to destroy the entire race. Because of Haman's position, the king routinely signed into irrevocable law a proclamation allowing the complete destruction of all people of Jewish origin throughout the 127 provinces of the Persian Empire.

THE PLAN THAT MEANT LIFE OR DEATH FOR THE QUEEN

But God used Mordecai's past loyalty to the king and Esther's loyalty to Mordecai to save His people. Mordecai informed Esther of the grave situation caused by Haman's cruel decree and instructed her to appeal to the king. Esther, fearing for her life, requested Mordecai and all the Jews in the capital to fast for three days before she brought such a bold request before her husband. After successfully gaining an audience, she invited the king and Haman to a small banquet she had prepared. Esther knew that if she arranged for two meetings, one to prepare the king for her request and the other to actually present her case before him, she might have a more sympathetic ear. Both Haman and the king were present at the first meeting, and the king agreed to attend the second banquet.

Elated by the queen's invitation, Haman became overconfident. Assured that the king would endorse any request which he might make, he boldly constructed a gallows on which to hang Mordecai.

A SLEEPLESS NIGHT SAVES THE NATION

But that very same night the king was reminded that Mordecai had never been rewarded for saving his life from the would-be assassins. The next morning, before Haman had a chance to secure what he thought would be quick approval, King Ahasuerus instructed him to publicly honor Mordecai by leading him through the streets.

Later that day Haman, humiliated by this turn of events, attended the second banquet where Esther revealed her Jewish identity and exposed the background of Haman's decree to destroy her people. The shocked king, recognizing that the law he had signed was not intended to benefit himself but represented a personal ambition of Haman instead, realized that he could no longer trust Haman and eliminated him. Haman was hanged on the same gallows he had prepared for Mordecai.

Mordecai, the only person who had proved his loyalty beyond doubt, became Haman's natural replacement. He quickly used his position and his expertise in law to compose a new decree which allowed the Jews to defend themselves. On the appointed day, God gave the Jews a great victory over their enemies and preserved the race from genocide.

Today the loyalty and courage of Mordecai and Esther and the deliverance which God worked through them is reviewed each year by Jews throughout the world during the celebration of the feast called Purim.

Ahasuerus ruled in Babylon *for twelve years under his father Darius before he became the sole ruler of the Persian Empire after Darius' death in 486 B.C. He was later assassinated by Artabanus, the head of the palace guard, in 465 B.C.*

Legal documents *such as the chronicles which were read aloud to King Ahasuerus, were often enclosed in clay envelopes on which a duplicate or summary of the contents was inscribed before being baked. The envelope was impressed with the seal of the writer or an official.*

50

MORDECAI CHARACTER SKETCH

WHY DIDN'T MORDECAI WANT TO SEE A GODLESS KING KILLED?

Mordecai was a wise man who had learned from the mistakes of his forefathers. He knew from the words of the prophet Jeremiah that rebellion against God-ordained authority had been responsible for the captivity of his family and nation for over a century (Esther 2:5,6). Jeremiah had predicted a curse for any nation that rebelled against the king of Babylon and a measure of blessing for any nation that remained submissive (Jeremiah 27:6-11). Mordecai was also familiar with the prophecy of Isaiah which transferred that principle to Cyrus, the first king of the Persian Empire (Isaiah 45:1-3). Conscious of God's hatred of rebellion against authority and aware of God's creativity in working through even the cruelest of kings to accomplish His purposes, Mordecai's loyalty to the king remained steadfast (Esther 2:22).

WASN'T MORDECAI DISPLAYING CONTEMPT FOR AUTHORITY WHEN HE REFUSED TO OBEY THE KING'S COMMAND TO BOW BEFORE HAMAN?

Bowing down before a Persian monarch was interpreted as an act of worship rather than an act of respect. Haman commanded worship as a god, a demand beyond his sphere of jurisdiction which Mordecai refused. His decision was based on higher loyalty to a specific law of God (Exodus 20:3-5). It is very likely that Mordecai believed that as a Jew he was exempt from obeying this command and that the command itself was illegal according to the laws of the Medes and Persians which could not be repealed (Esther 1:19; 3:4). There is strong indication that the Jews enjoyed special privilege from certain Persian laws, namely, any law which would force them to disobey a specific law of God. This privilege was due in part to Daniel's strong influence during the reign of Cyrus the Persian (cf. Daniel 3:28-30; Ezra 1:1-3). The fact that Haman was hesitant to challenge Mordecai's claim and his contempt for the Jews' privileged laws seem to confirm this view (Esther 3:6,8).

WHY WAS IT SO DIFFICULT FOR MORDECAI TO ASK ESTHER TO INTERCEDE BEFORE THE KING?

Esther had not been called into the king's presence for thirty days. Unless given a special dispensation, the automatic penalty for one entering the king's inner court without permission was execution. The Greek historian, Herodotus, mentions an incident which had recently occurred which gives an insight into Ahasuerus' character and temperament.

While passing through Lydia, a rich man named Pythius generously entertained Ahasuerus' troops and contributed an enormous sum of money toward the Grecian campaign. He then requested that the king exempt the eldest of his five sons from the army to be of comfort to him in his declining years. The request was reasonable enough, but the enraged Ahasuerus ordered the son to be sliced in half and commanded the army to march between the two halves as an example of what he considered to be a lack of dedication. It is no wonder that Esther asked Mordecai and all the Jews in the city to fast for three days preceding her bold entrance to the king.

"Then took Haman the apparel and the horse, *and arrayed Mordecai, and brought him on horseback through the street of the city, and proclaimed before him, Thus shall it be done for the man whom the king delighteth to honor."*

MORDECAI

IS BEING A RELIABLE MESSENGER TO THOSE I AM SERVING

LIVING LESSONS ON LOYALTY ...

FROM THE PAGES OF SCRIPTURE

The sons and daughters of a great man were given unusual instructions by him before he died. Their response to those instructions became the basis for an urgent message to an entire nation.

ILLUSTRATED IN THE WORLD OF NATURE

THE HONEYBEE *Apis mellifera*

The honeybee usually measures .5 inches and has a life expectancy of thirty-eight days. Its hive may be constructed in a sheltered tree hollow, on a limb, or under eaves of houses. The secret of the phenomenal cooperation and productivity of the hive is found in the bees' ability to communicate accurately to each other.

The range and habitat of the honeybee

LOYALTY

HOW DOES THE HONEYBEE ILLUSTRATE LOYALTY IN GIVING RELIABLE MESSAGES?

The beehive presents an amazing picture of efficiency. To ensure productivity among thousands of bees, a delicate chemical balance must be maintained. The queen bee must lay two to three thousand eggs each day. The heavy-bodied, large-eyed drone bees must be on the lookout for future queen bees. And the worker bees must mature, passing in sequence through six distinct stages of development and responsibility.

Each worker bee functions in the roles of cleaner, nurse, storer, repairer, guard and finally scout during its brief lifetime of cooperative effort.

But what happens when a hive is damaged and vital functions are impaired, including the queen bee's reproductivity? In a remarkable way, the body functions and abilities of the other bees change in order to assume new responsibilities for the emergency state. How does each bee know what duties to assume? What keeps the hive from becoming totally chaotic and unable to function?

The secret is contained in the message of the honey the bees pass among themselves. Each bee contributes a distinct glandular secretion to the honey according to the function it performs. When all secretions are present in sufficient supply the hive is balanced, functioning normally. When one secretion is inadequate or missing, such as that which comes from a queen, a moaning sound travels throughout the hive. All the bees throb as though they were afflicted with fever. This is their signal to quickly adapt themselves—even change roles—in an effort to make up the loss and re-establish the balance of the hive.

Without precise communication, a crucial imbalance could go unnoticed in the beehive and it would inevitably collapse. The bees demonstrate loyalty for their common goals and to each other through their amazingly accurate system of intercommunication.

CHARACTERISTICS AND PHYSICAL FEATURES OF THE HONEYBEE

During their brief lifetime honeybees demonstrate unusual skill in communication. They are precise, reliable messengers to the members of their hive. But the reliable communication of a scout bee is its last responsibility in life. Five different tasks have preceded the final one and each successive stage represents an interdependent role in the cooperative world of the bee colony.

DOES A BEE BEGIN WORKING AS SOON AS IT IS BORN?

The bee cannot begin its first task immediately after birth because its wings are still damp after emerging from the waxy cell. Within a few hours, the bee loses its disheveled appearance. Its wings dry and harden. Then it applies itself to its initial responsibility—cleaning the cells of the hive. The cell from which it emerged can be used to raise another bee.

An average colony *of sixty thousand bees contains one mature queen and approximately one hundred drones. The majority of the population—worker bees—bear the burden of maintaining the hive, caring for the larvae, and gathering and preparing the nectar.*

A damp honeybee *emerges from its waxy cell after three weeks of development.*

Drone

Worker bee

Queen bee

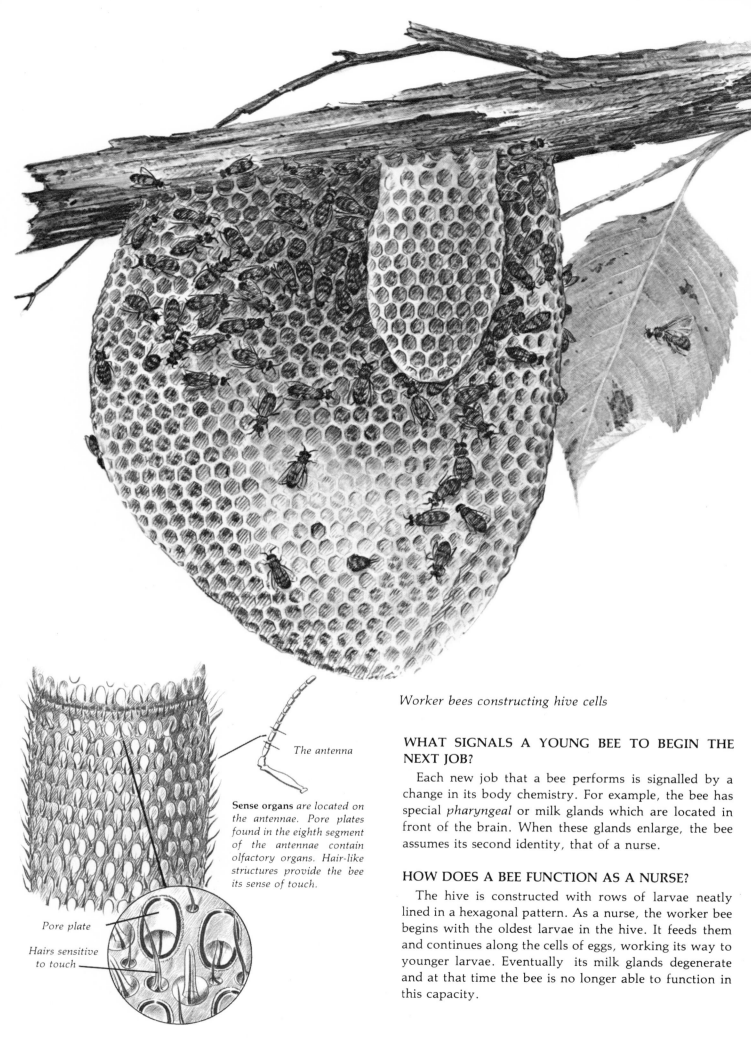

Worker bees constructing hive cells

The antenna

Sense organs *are located on the antennae. Pore plates found in the eighth segment of the antennae contain olfactory organs. Hair-like structures provide the bee its sense of touch.*

Pore plate

Hairs sensitive to touch

WHAT SIGNALS A YOUNG BEE TO BEGIN THE NEXT JOB?

Each new job that a bee performs is signalled by a change in its body chemistry. For example, the bee has special *pharyngeal* or milk glands which are located in front of the brain. When these glands enlarge, the bee assumes its second identity, that of a nurse.

HOW DOES A BEE FUNCTION AS A NURSE?

The hive is constructed with rows of larvae neatly lined in a hexagonal pattern. As a nurse, the worker bee begins with the oldest larvae in the hive. It feeds them and continues along the cells of eggs, working its way to younger larvae. Eventually its milk glands degenerate and at that time the bee is no longer able to function in this capacity.

BACK LEG *By scraping the back legs together, pollen is removed and placed on the pollen basket.*

MIDDLE LEG *This leg is equipped with tiny hairs which sweep pollen from the body and front legs. It also has a spike-like protrusion which removes wax from the wax gland on the abdomen.*

FRONT LEG *Special hairs on this leg are designed to collect pollen. At the joint is a brush that the bee pulls its antenna through in order to clean it. Also at the joint is a tool for cleaning the eyes.*

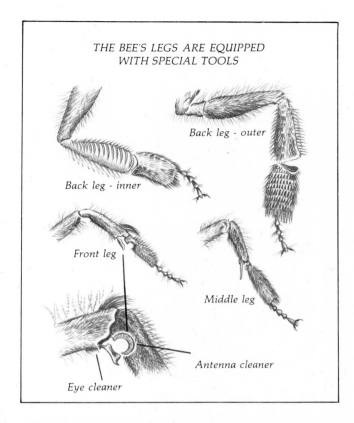

THE BEE'S LEGS ARE EQUIPPED WITH SPECIAL TOOLS

Back leg - outer

Back leg - inner

Front leg

Middle leg

Antenna cleaner

Eye cleaner

DO BEES PROCESS THEIR OWN NECTAR WHEN THEY RETURN FROM THE FIELD?

No. The nectar is transferred to a worker bee who is in its third stage of development. During this stage, the worker receives nectar from returning forager bees and stores it in special cells prepared for this purpose. Honey sacs in its belly have enlarged, increasing the bee's ability to store and transfer nectar.

DOES A BEEHIVE EVER BECOME OVER-POPULATED?

A bee colony is able to accommodate all its new members through systematic enlarging of the hive. In the fourth stage of development, a worker bee uses special wax-making glands. New cells are constructed with wax in order to house all the eggs laid by the queen bee.

WITH SO MANY BEES, HOW CAN AN INTRUDER BE DETECTED?

An elaborate guard system is established to make certain that no intruding bee enters. It would seem impossible for a guarding bee to be able to pick out a stranger among the thousands which belong to its hive; however, quick identification is accomplished through 1,200 scent organs which are on the antennae of the guard. An intruder which could disrupt the balance of the bee colony, steal nectar, or eat eggs, is destroyed immediately.

Forager communicating the precise location of the source of pollen

59

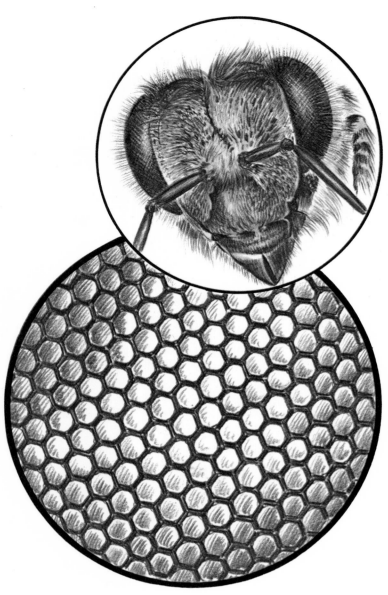

HOW DOES A BEE DESCRIBE THE TASTE OF A FLOWER?

The scout or forager bee brings back a sample for each of the other bees to taste.

HOW DOES A BEE COMMUNICATE DISTANCE?

When a bee returns to the hive, it relates the distance of the nectar source by its body motion. A circular motion tells foragers that the food is within 100 yards. A figure eight ceremony indicates that the nectar is over 100 yards away. The rate of a "tail wagging" motion is in direct proportion to the distance of the nectar.

HOW DOES THE POSITION OF THE SUN AFFECT THE FORAGER BEE'S MESSAGE?

The bee uses the sun as a reference point to signal the direction of the nectar source from the hive. If the bee points its body vertically on the comb of the hive, it signals that the flowers are located away from the hive in the same direction as the sun. A downward position indicates, conversely, that the flowers are in the opposite direction. Or a message given at a 40° angle on the comb directs the watching foragers to leave the hive at a 40° angle from the sun.

WHAT IF A BEE GIVES INACCURATE DIRECTIONS?

Directional information must be precise since the foragers take only enough honey with them to reach their destination. Honey works as their fuel. If they carry too much, they will not have room for more nectar. If they carry too little, they will fall to the ground and die before reaching their destination unless they can locate another source of glucose.

ABOVE *The compound eye with its 8,500 facets gives the bee nearly 360° vision.*

BELOW *A forager bee returns to the hive with precise instructions which it relays by body motions. Both of the motions pictured below relate to the distance of the nectar source from the hive. A circular motion is used when the nectar source is less than one hundred yards away. If the source is greater than one hundred yards away, a figure eight is employed with a "tail wagging" motion. The closer the source, the more intense the body movement.*

Figure eight

Circle movement

HOW DOES SCRIPTURE ILLUSTRATE LOYALTY IN GIVING RELIABLE MESSAGES?

The prophet was deeply grieved. On every side, the nation had turned its back on God's way of life. Confusion, lawlessness and destruction from the Chaldean army were some of the immediate consequences. But the prophet knew that a far greater judgment was being prepared against those who remained in the land. How could he warn the people and turn them back to the ways of God?

One day God told the prophet to go to a certain family and invite them to one of the rooms in the Temple and offer them wine. When the family came into the room and sat down at the table, the prophet set out jugs full of wine and cups in front of each person. Then he said, ". . . drink the wine."

Those at the table awkwardly glanced at one another. They were caught in a dilemma. On the one hand, God's own prophet was telling them to drink wine. On the other hand, their ancestor had given his entire family strict instructions before he died that neither they nor their children should ever drink any wine.

He had also given them other instructions which were strange to the people around them. They were not to build houses nor to own fields of crops or vineyards, but they were to live in tents throughout their lives. This was so opposite to the way of life of all the people around them who were building beautiful houses and getting bigger farms and vineyards. It was so different, in fact, that it welded this family together, and they became a single unit following the instructions of their father. But now they were being asked by the prophet to violate one of their father's instructions. What should they do?

The tense silence was broken by a united response. "We will not drink this wine, for our father commanded us and our children not to drink wine, and we have all obeyed his voice in all that he has commanded us to do."

At that moment the Word of the Lord came to the prophet. He was instructed to use this family's example of obedience in a special message to the rest of the nation. If the people would obey the commands of the Lord in the same way this family had obeyed their father's strict instructions, they would receive the same rewards.

What were the rewards? Those in this family were friends of a former king and should have been killed or carried away captive by the Chaldeans. Had they owned houses and land, this would have happened. Not only were they allowed to live and stay in their own country, but they enjoyed the unusual harmony and love of a closely-knit family. In addition to this, God added one more great reward. He promised that from this Rechabite family there would always be godly descendants.

From Jeremiah 35

61

THE MESSAGE OF THE RECHABITES
THAT PIERCED THE CONSCIENCE OF A NATION

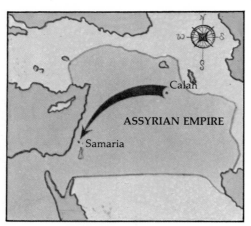

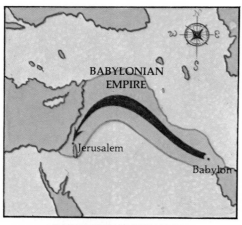

Like their ancestor Abraham, the Rechabites lived in portable tents probably made of black goat's hair. A goat's hair curtain divided the tent into two sections, one for men and one for women. Weapons and clothing were hung from hooks overhead.

ASSYRIAN INVASION

BABYLONIAN INVASION

Masters of psychological warfare, *the Assyrians' reputation for brutality and torture preceded them as they prepared an attack from Calah. Because of their mobility, the Rechabites were spared from their brutal assault in 722 B.C. by fleeing southward. Later, when the Babylonians swept into Judah in 586 B.C., the nomadic Rechabites again escaped captivity.*

God had repeatedly warned the nation against disobedience by reminding them of His commands through His prophets. Punishment had been delayed for many years. But the nation had become increasingly proud and stubborn, and it was now time for severe discipline—the invasion of an enemy.

PUNISHMENT BECOMES INEVITABLE AS TIME RUNS OUT FOR THE NATION

Jeremiah, the prophet, knew that the Babylonian army under the direction of Nebuchadnezzar would soon conquer the land and take the people into captivity. Now the prophet's job was to prepare the people for the penalty which their disobedience had caused. The nation needed to understand why they were being punished in order to learn the lesson God intended.

A MESSAGE THAT TOOK OVER 200 YEARS TO DEVELOP

It must have been an encouragement to Jeremiah when he discovered that God had prepared a message in a family called the Rechabites for him to use at this specific time.

Over two hundred years earlier a man named Jonadab, the head of his family, gave his children three precise commands. One, they were to abstain totally from drinking wine, thus avoiding the temptation toward excess and drunkenness. Two, they were not to build homes. And three, they were not to grow fruit or to buy land which would have required them to live in one fixed position throughout the year.

Not only did Jonadab stipulate these three requirements for his own sons, but he commanded them to tell their children and their children's children as well, thus perpetuating the simple style of living. The Rechabites had faithfully obeyed Jonadab's command for all the intervening years, and now God instructed Jeremiah to test the strength of their family loyalty.

CONTRADICTING COMMANDS FROM AUTHORITIES

At that time Jeremiah was the prophet through whom God spoke. He summoned the Rechabite family members and ushered them to one of the rooms in Solomon's temple. Then Jeremiah set the forbidden wine in front of them and said, "Drink wine." (Jeremiah 35:5)

This invitation presented a conflicting directive from a man of God. They faced one of the most difficult decisions: to whom should they remain loyal —a deceased forefather whose enigmatic restrictions had been voiced two centuries earlier, or a godly prophet through whom God was speaking in their day? The choice for many might have been difficult, but these men discerned that Jeremiah's directive was not a command from God but rather an invitation from the prophet. So committed were they to obedience that an immediate, united response was voiced by the men, "We will drink no wine; for Jonadab, the son of Rechab, our father commanded us, saying, Ye shall drink no wine, neither ye, nor your sons forever" (Jeremiah 35:6).

A FAMILY'S OBEDIENCE BECOMES A NATIONAL EXAMPLE

By remaining loyal to their ancestor's command, the Rechabites provided Jeremiah with the clear illustration that he needed to appeal to the conscience of the rebellious nation of Judah. This family faithfully obeyed Jonadab's three laws given only once centuries before. The nation of Judah had been given the very Law of God and were constantly reminded of it by the prophets, yet they refused to obey. A greater contrast could not have been found, and Jeremiah was able to use this illustration to communicate God's message to the people. If the Rechabites had failed to remain obedient, they would have destroyed a message which had taken over two hundred years to develop.

THE RECHABITES CHARACTER SKETCH

DID GOD PREPARE THE RECHABITES FOR THE MESSAGE THEY WOULD ILLUSTRATE?

God is not a hard taskmaster nor is His will unreasonable (Matthew 11:28-30; Romans 12:2). Although Jonadab's three commands might have been difficult for most families to follow, such was not the case for the Rechabites. I Chronicles 2:55 states that the Rechabites were descendants of the Kenites through Moses' father-in-law (cf. Judges 1:16) whom we know from Exodus 3:1 was a keeper of flocks, a dweller in the wilderness. We also know that the Kenites had no fixed residence, wandering from place to place (cf. Judges 1:16; 4:11 and I Samuel 15:6). Jonadab was only strengthening a tradition which had held the family together for years.

WHY WAS JONADAB CONCERNED THAT HIS FAMILY MAINTAIN A DISCIPLINED LIFE?

Jonadab was aware of the subtle attraction that Baal worship held on the people of Israel. The idolatrous feasts were often nothing more than an excuse for drunkenness and immorality. Having witnessed the destructive results of Baalism during the reign of Ahab and his wicked wife Jezebel, Jonadab participated in King Jehu's zealous eradication of Baal from Israel (II Kings 10). He witnessed Jehu's loss of zeal for the Lord once he exchanged the discipline of army life for the luxuries of the palace (cf. II Kings 10:31). To protect his children from the temptations of idolatry, Jonadab kept them away from wine, out of the cities and free from this world's goods (cf. Amos 6:4-7).

WAS IT DIFFICULT FOR THE RECHABITES TO REFUSE JEREMIAH'S REQUEST?

The Rechabites had been summoned to the temple by a great prophet. Seated before this noted religious leader, the men were instructed by him to violate their forefather's strict command (Jeremiah 35:5). Two hundred years had passed since the command had first been issued. One might think that their adherence to the tradition would have weakened and diminished over this long period of time. One might also think that the Rechabites, awed by the presence of this great man of God, would be swayed to violate or at least consider violating their convictions. At the very least they would be reluctant to offend Jeremiah or cause any embarrassment.

But the Rechabites did not, even for a moment, consider the possibility of compromise. With boldness and spontaneity they unanimously proclaimed the message which years of obedience had instilled in their lives. In a non-apologetic manner the men refused the invitation to drink. Because of their message of unwavering obedience, an even greater message was communicated to the nation through Jeremiah (Jeremiah 35:13-17).

DID GOD REWARD THE RECHABITES FOR THEIR OBEDIENCE?

Because the Rechabites had no possessions and were free to move about, they were spared from both the Assyrian and Babylonian captivities. Unless Jonadab had forbidden his children to build homes, it is likely that they would have settled in Israel rather than Judah because of Jonadab's friendship with King Jehu. Instead, their flexibility enabled them to move south into Judah before the collapse of the Northern Kingdom in 722 B.C. Since they had no possessions, they were later spared from the Babylonian captivity in 586 B.C. (II Kings 24:14). The Rechabites had honored their father's commands and while their fellow countrymen were living in slave camps in foreign countries, they lived in freedom and peace in the land of their birth.

"Neither shall ye build house, *nor sow seed, nor plant vineyard, nor have any, but all your days ye shall dwell in tents, that ye may live many days in the land where ye be strangers.*"

THE RECHABITES

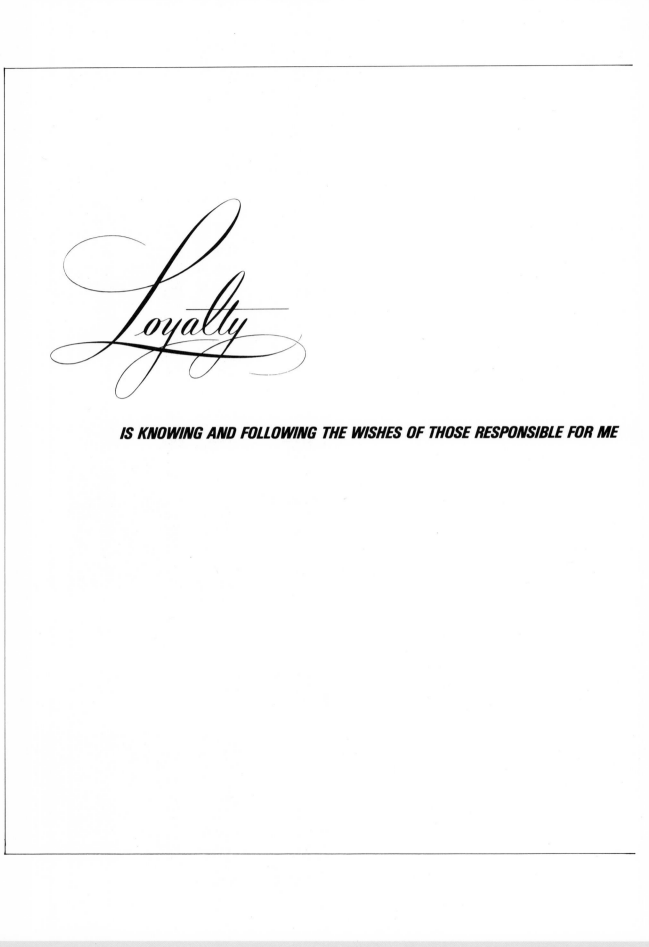

Loyalty

IS KNOWING AND FOLLOWING THE WISHES OF THOSE RESPONSIBLE FOR ME

LIVING LESSONS ON LOYALTY . . .

FROM THE PAGES OF SCRIPTURE

Although a young man wanted to assist a great and mighty prophet, he did not yet understand what it meant to know and follow the wishes of the one he was serving. Until he learned this aspect of loyalty, the task for which he was chosen would never be his.

ILLUSTRATED IN THE WORLD OF NATURE

THE GRIZZLY BEAR   *Ursus horribilis*

The powerful grizzly bear is well-known for its protectiveness and great strength. It lives about twenty-five years, achieving a length of seven to eight feet and a weight from 500-800 pounds. The only bear with a hump on its shoulders, the grizzly wanders widely within its habitat of timber range and mountains.

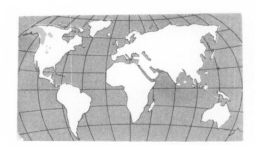

The range and habitat of the grizzly bear

LOYALTY

HOW DOES THE GRIZZLY BEAR ILLUSTRATE LOYALTY IN FOLLOWING UNSPOKEN WISHES?

In a western timber range three grizzly yearlings playfully explored the woods near their den. Their aimless wandering took definite direction when one cub caught the scent of food. The three began to follow the smell of a dead carcass and were lured farther and farther away from the protection of their mother.

Wolves had buried their game near the entrance of their den, and the cubs' curiosity drew them closer and closer to danger. One of the cubs sniffed its way to within thirty feet of the wolf den and found the body of a caribou, half hidden by dirt and brush.

Four wolves crouched nearby, ready to spring. They had circled behind the entrance when they spotted the cubs approaching and without warning began their deadly attack.

As sharp cries from the cubs pierced the air, the mother bear came roaring to their defense. The wolves then included her in their attack and fought savagely, trying to separate her from her young. The battle intensified until the bears managed to fight their way to a nearby hill for safety.

At this crucial moment, the third and weakest of the cubs ignored the protective wishes of its mother. Leaving the safety of the knoll, it naively sniffed out the cache and was surrounded in seconds by the savage pack.

Now the mother was forced to expose herself and the other cubs to a second death struggle. The leader of the wolf pack returned from hunting and quickly joined the battle, distracting the raging mother while the other four wolves concentrated on the weakest cub.

Recognizing the desperate plight of her cub, the mother bear broke away from the lead wolf and roared furiously toward the others. She wildly swung her powerful paws in defense. Then, with the same fury and power, she drove all three cubs through a thick patch of brush and into a glacial stream.

The smallest cub cringed on the shore, frightened and dripping with blood. The mother continued pushing it out into the water until the wolves no longer followed, ending the near-fatal attack.

The wounds which the young cub suffered were a lasting reminder of the consequences of not following the instruction of the one responsible for it.

CHARACTERISTICS AND PHYSICAL FEATURES OF THE GRIZZLY BEAR

The female grizzly takes great care in protecting and training her young. She is fiercely loyal to her cubs throughout their extensive training, and in return she expects them to pay attention to the instruction she gives. Her protective dedication is so noteworthy that even Scripture refers to it. "Let a bear robbed of her whelps meet a man, rather than a fool in his folly." (Proverbs 17:12)

WOULD A CUB SURVIVE IF IT LOST ITS MOTHER?

Its chances for survival would be significantly reduced. The cub would have to learn from its own experience rather than learning by building on the experience of its mother. Some of the things the cub will learn from her are to fear its natural enemies, to avoid man and to prepare for its long winter rest.

WILL AN UNTEACHABLE CUB STARVE TO DEATH?

Cubs must be trained in proper eating habits. Under the guidance of their mother, cubs learn which foods are available at what times, where to find and how to eat them. The bear's life depends upon its ability to eat the right kinds and the right amounts of food during each season of the year. If a bear has not learned to prepare itself for hibernation, it will be forced to wander in search of food during months when there is none available. Malnutrition would be a serious threat if the cub counted on eating during that time.

IN WHAT SIMPLE TASK IS A BEAR SMARTER THAN A MAN?

Man's method of lifting a stone is usually to pull it toward him. When it rolls, he must jump out of the way in order to avoid being hit by it. The bear's method is to lift it on its side and then sweep it away from itself. During the course of the summer, it will turn many stones in pursuit of grub worms which live beneath the forest covering.

Mother bear teaches *young cubs the art of turning stones in search for grubs and insects.*

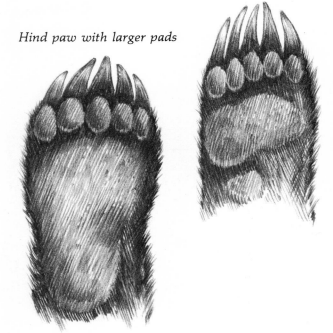

Hind paw with larger pads

Front paw with larger claws

Length of front claw - 5 inches

The grizzly's powerful arm muscles *and long claws equip it for digging rodents out of their dens or tearing decaying logs for grubs and honey.*

Woodchuck looks on *from escape hatch as grizzlies dig fruitlessly.*

WHAT DOES A BEAR CONSIDER A DELICACY?

During the summer the mother bear instructs the young cubs where to find one of the most enjoyable parts of their diet—the sweet berries of the forest. The cubs also learn how they can find and eat wild honey from the comb. Their tough hide makes most of their body impervious to the sting of a bee.

IF THE DIGGING SPEED OF A BEAR AND A GOPHER WERE MATCHED, WHO WOULD WIN?

Gophers, which are known for their digging ability, are no match for the speed of a bear. The bear is an extremely fast digger, using three to five inch claws and arm and shoulder muscles to dig out gophers, ground hogs and other rodents. The bear is omnivorous—its diet encompassing a wide variety of meats and greens.

WHAT FISHING TECHNIQUES DOES THE BEAR EMPLOY?

The bear is aware of the time of year when salmon return to their spawning grounds. These determined fish become the mainstay of the bear's diet during the peak of their migrational run. It had been previously thought that the bear swept fish out of the water with its paws. In reality, the bear wades into the stream, pinning the fish against a surface—either a rock or the bed of the stream—and then carries its catch to shore in its mouth.

WHAT WOULD CAUSE A BEAR TO SPANK HER CUBS?

The grizzly mother is in almost constant communication with her cubs during their training period. Their independent spirit and highly inquisitive nose can lead them into serious trouble unless she exercises resolute protection. For all misdemeanors, the cubs are soundly spanked and sent bawling ahead of the mother. In spite of her watchfulness, they often receive the natural consequences of their premature independence such as the stinging, unpleasant spray of a striped skunk.

COULD CURIOSITY KILL A CUB?

A curious cub could attempt to explore or even try to eat a porcupine without realizing the deadly effect of its quills. Since the quills are constructed with many little barbs similar to those on fishhooks, it is almost impossible for the bear to remove them. Each unsuccessful attempt to pull the quills out only drives them deeper into the flesh. The encounter could be fatal.

WOULD A CUB BEAR RUN FROM AN APPROACHING HUNTER?

The grizzly cub is born without a natural fear of its enemies. The mother must teach it that there are very real dangers to be avoided. One of the lessons involves learning a healthy respect for the father bear. Other enemies which it must learn to avoid are the wolf, the puma, and most of all, man. The mother has the ability to swiftly sense danger, and she takes special care to teach her young what to do when it approaches.

WHAT DOES A BEAR EAT JUST BEFORE ENTERING ITS WINTER DEN?

Nothing. By so doing it begins its extended inactivity with its stomach and intestines clean and empty.

DOES THE GRIZZLY PUT VERY MUCH TIME OR EFFORT INTO ITS DEN?

Unlike the black bear which is content just to find a natural cavity or hollow tree in which to spend the winter, the grizzly bear digs its own den. It removes 200-300 cubic feet of earth in order to dig a tunnel three feet wide, four feet high and six to twelve feet long. The grizzly burrows in on the north slope of a hill. This exposure ensures deep snow insulation during the bitter, cold days of winter. The hillside location also provides drainage, preventing spring rains from flooding the den.

HOW DOES A BEAR MAKE ITS BED?

The bear makes special provision for its comfort and warmth during the long winter months. It takes care to construct a bed by gathering evergreen branches, cushioning the hard surface of the den floor with leaves and needles.

DOES A GRIZZLY BEAR REALLY HIBERNATE?

Technically, no. The grizzly can be aroused from its sleep by an intruder and would be alert to its surroundings within a few minutes. True hibernators such as the woodchuck or ground squirrel would not be aroused from their death-like state. In fact, a grizzly may appear at the entrance of its den in mid winter. The grizzly usually retires just before a heavy snowstorm.

DANGERS THE GRIZZLY CUB MUST LEARN TO AVOID

The cub does not naturally fear man

The quills of a porcupine *are very uncomfortable and sometimes fatal to the inquisitive cub.*

The spray of a striped skunk *leaves a stinging and unpleasant reminder to the cub that this is an animal to leave alone.*

GRIZZLY BEAR DEN

North slope

Sleeping chamber

The female grizzly *will give birth to one to three pound-and-a-half cubs during the winter rest.*

HOW MUCH WEIGHT DOES A BEAR LOSE AFTER FASTING FOR FOUR MONTHS?

Because the bear is inactive during this period, very little energy is expended and, as a result, little if any of its stored fat is lost.

WHAT ARE THE BENEFITS OF THE WINTER REST?

The grizzly bear benefits from the rejuvenation process which takes place during the winter nap. Its front paw claws, worn down to stubs from months of digging, grow back to their normal five-inch length. Its stomach is clean and rested. The cubs which are born during this period are protected early in life in the warm den, and the bear wastes no energy searching for unavailable food in the lean winter months.

HOW DOES SCRIPTURE ILLUSTRATE THE IMPORTANCE OF FOLLOWING UNSPOKEN WISHES?

Two men entered the city and sat down to rest. The old and mighty prophet looked at his younger assistant.

"Why don't you wait here, for the Lord wants me to go on to the next city." The younger man wondered what the prophet meant. God had called him to learn from the older man and assist him. He noticed that the prophet was earnestly watching to see what his response would be. Sensing what the prophet's real wishes were, he answered, "I purpose before God that I will not leave you."

These words seemed to please the old man, but as they walked on to the next city his assistant wondered what kind of test he was being put to and why.

At the next city the same thing happened. The old prophet said, "You stay here. God has called me to go to the river Jordan." This time the younger man answered more quickly, "I promise before God I will not leave you."

When they reached the river, the mighty prophet took his cloak and struck the water. The sight of the cloak reminded the younger assistant of an incident that had happened in the past. Suddenly, he realized why the prophet was testing him.

The cloak hit the water; the river divided, and they walked across on dry ground. When they reached the other side, the old prophet turned to his assistant and asked, "What wish shall I grant you before I am taken away?" "I want a double portion of your spirit," answered the assistant.

"You have asked a hard thing," replied the prophet, "but if you stay with me until I am taken up, your wish will be granted. If you do not stay with me, you will not receive your request."

These words confirmed what the younger man suspected. The prophet wanted to see if he had learned a quality of loyalty that he had not fully demonstrated when he was first called. He remembered in vivid detail the day he was plowing in the field. The mighty prophet came up to him, threw his cloak over his shoulders and kept on walking. That gesture signified the special honor of being chosen as his assistant. He had stood, pondering whether he would forsake all to follow. By the time he made his decision he had to run to catch up to the older man. Had he now learned to follow without any hesitation?

Shortly thereafter, a fiery chariot appeared and the prophet was taken out of sight. Only his cloak was left behind—a reminder to Elisha that loyalty to a leader involves being sensitive to his wishes. And what was the reward of learning this lesson of loyalty? It was a double portion of his spirit.

From I Kings 19:19-21 and II Kings 2:1-14

THE LOYALTY WHICH ELISHA DISPLAYED BY KNOWING AND FOLLOWING THE WISHES OF THE ONE HE SERVED

After a time of severe drought, rain returned to the sun-parched land and signs of life appeared. Elisha was busy preparing his father's fields, expecting the first yield in over three years.

A CHOICE BETWEEN A CLOAK AND A PLOW

He was plowing in the field when he saw the prophet, Elijah, approaching in the distance. Elijah threw his shaggy, animal-skin cloak over Elisha's shoulders. The many implications of the decision he was being asked to make must have raced through his mind. He noticed that Elijah, impatient for a decision, continued on his journey to the wilderness of Damascus.

BURNING HIS PAST TO FREE HIMSELF FOR THE FUTURE

Embarrassed to hesitate any longer, the young farmer decided to change vocations and hurried after his new master. Elijah granted him permission to say good-by to his parents. Elisha used the ox yokes of wood and probably his farmer plow and ox goad as fuel to offer his team of oxen for a farewell feast. This was a public demonstration to all those present that his decision was meant to be final. His life would no longer be the same.

TRANSFORMING A FARMER INTO A SERVANT

The years between Elisha's call and Elijah's translation are not recorded in Scripture. Apart from delivering a message of judgment to King Ahab and another to his son, Ahaziah, we know little of Elijah's activity. Virtually nothing about Elisha is recorded other than that he was known as the one who poured water on the hands of Elijah (II Kings 3:11). It is likely that Elijah spent much of his time preparing Elisha for the job of being God's messenger to a rebellious nation. He had to teach him to stand alone in the midst of persecution without compromising God's message.

One of their joint responsibilities seems to have been the administration of various schools of prophets. They likely taught God's Law and the history of His dealings with the nation of Israel, so that they in turn could instruct the people who had forsaken God for Baal.

A TEST TO MEASURE LOYALTY

Elijah knew that he would soon leave the earth and that it was God's intention for Elisha to be his successor. He felt that it was time for Elisha to be granted freedom from his authority to develop his own ministry. At the same time he provided the perfect test to discover the true motivation of Elisha. Was he restless and discontent with his position as servant, anxiously awaiting the day when he could be his own boss? Or had he learned to be a true servant? Elijah knew that for him to succeed as God's representative, he must have a servant's heart. Three times Elijah gave Elisha the opportunity to remain behind, and three times Elisha swore that he would serve him as long as he remained alive. His motivation was pure and his response immediate. Elijah agreed to grant Elisha a request. His quick response was for a double portion of Elijah's spirit with which to carry on his ministry. The request was not Elijah's to give, but God was pleased to reward this devoted servant with a double portion of Elijah's spirit.

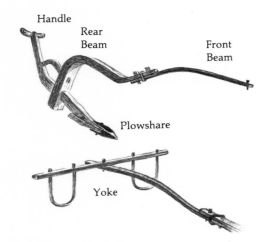

The plow *Elisha used was probably made of two wooden beams. The front beam was hooked to a yoke, and the rear beam was fastened to the crosspiece. The upper part of the crosspiece formed the handle, and the lower part held the plowshare.*

Since eating utensils *were not used, it was important to have plenty of water to wash hands at the close of every meal. This was one of the routine jobs for household servants.*

ELISHA CHARACTER SKETCH

WHY WAS IT DIFFICULT FOR ELISHA TO DECIDE TO FOLLOW ELIJAH?

There were four things which could have discouraged Elisha from accepting this call. First, he came from a prominent family and had the prospect of inheriting considerable material goods. The fact that Shaphat, Elisha's father, owned at least twelve teams of oxen immediately after three and a half years of drought meant that he was able to hire at least eleven men to work the teams and that he had a large amount of land (I Kings 19:19). Elisha was in the position of foreman and was evidently helping to manage the farm. Second, he had a good relationship with his family and it must have been difficult for them to part. Third, he was leaving the position of heir to his father's inheritance and foreman over at least eleven servants to assume a position of servitude. He was known, not as Elijah's co-laborer, but as his humble servant (cf. II Kings 3:11). Fourth, he was leaving a secure and peaceful life for one of danger, disrespect and physical hardship (II Kings 2:23). Elijah was being hunted like an animal by Queen Jezebel for killing the prophets of Baal (I Kings 19:2). King Ahab also hated Elijah and thought of him as his personal enemy (I Kings 21:20).

WAS ELISHA BEING DISOBEDIENT BY REFUSING TO REMAIN BEHIND?

Elisha was Elijah's companion for at least six years (cf. I Kings 20:22,26; 22:1,51). During that time he learned to discern carefully the true wishes and desires behind his master's words. He would have been able to distinguish between a test and a command by the very inflection of his voice. That Elijah was pleased by Elisha's refusal to remain behind is clear. Elisha was no doubt aware of a similar situation which involved Elijah's former servant. After Queen Jezebel ordered an all-out effort to kill him, Elijah fled to Beersheba in the kingdom of Judah. In a similar situation, he requested that his servant remain behind while he went into the wilderness to die. It is significant that, although the servant was not disobedient, it is the last mention of him in Scripture, and he was soon replaced by Elisha (cf. I Kings 19:2,3).

WAS ELISHA GREEDY IN ASKING FOR A DOUBLE PORTION OF ELIJAH'S SPIRIT?

The expression found in II Kings 2:9, ". . . let a double portion of thy spirit be upon me," is a strange one. Literally it reads, ". . . let a mouth or two of thy spirit be upon me." The same Hebrew idiom appears in Deuteronomy 21:17 in the Mosaic Law. It refers to the right of the first-born son to receive twice the inheritance of his younger brothers since it was to be his responsibility to take over as head of the family. Elijah was considered the spiritual father of the "sons of the prophets" he had just visited in Bethel and Jericho (II Kings 2:3,5). Since Elisha was to be his successor and assume the responsibility of maintaining Elijah's ministry, he was merely asking for a share of the spirit that possessed Elijah, twice as large as that of the other followers of Elijah. The request demonstrated faith, dependence and humility—not greed.

The mantle *that Elijah wore was a supplementary garment made of an animal skin. In pleasant weather it was more conveniently worn over the shoulders. Moses commanded that there be tassels on the corners of this garment, together with a blue cord, to remind the people of the heavenly origin of His statutes. Numbers 15:38-40*

ELISHA

Responsibility

PART TWO

IS USING ALL MY ENERGIES TO FULFILL THE EXPECTATION OF THOSE WHO ARE COUNTING ON ME

LIVING LESSONS ON RESPONSIBILITY . . .

FROM THE PAGES OF SCRIPTURE

A tragic and pathetic chapter in Scripture was written when one man failed in a vital responsibility. But there was a reason why he was not able to accomplish it. The reason was hidden at first, but later it became very evident. Because the man failed in this one aspect of responsibility, the courses of two nations and his own family were tragically reversed.

ILLUSTRATED IN THE WORLD OF NATURE

THE AMERICAN WOODCOCK *Philohela minor*

The American woodcock, a migratory bird, inhabits swamps, wet woods and thickets. It is known as a solitary and secretive species, averaging eleven inches in size. Three to four buff-colored eggs hatch in a shallow nest of twigs and leaves. Within two weeks the hatchlings are able to fly.

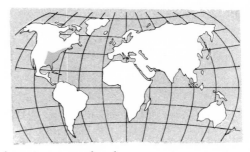

The range and habitat of the American woodcock

RESPONSIBILITY

HOW DOES THE WOODCOCK ILLUSTRATE RESPONSIBILITY IN FULFILLING EXPECTATIONS?

The woodcock carefully led her family in search along the surface of the marshland. The ground was too dry for the probings of her bill to find the food she needed for her young.

Changing direction, she searched under the leaves of a nearby wooded area. This effort yielded some grub worms, but there weren't enough. The woodcock is used to eating its weight in food every twenty-four hours. How could she make the provision for her young?

Several days earlier her four eggs had hatched. The slight depression in the hardwood leaves served as their home for only a few hours. Soon they were on their feet imitating their mother's movements, their fragile bills probing the ground for the earthworms near the surface. Worms are one major source of nourishment, but now the ground was parched. The worms had burrowed deep to find moist soil and were far beneath the surface.

It was time to demonstrate to her young the highly creative technique of getting worms when other means fail. In preparation for this unusual procedure, the woodcock deliberately flattened out on the ground. Next, she spread out her wings. In this position, she beat the ground by rapidly flapping them against the earth. Then she stopped for a moment, listening intently before resuming her unusual effort.

In a short time the woodcock family was enjoying its long-awaited meal. Each young chick was busily finding worms along the parched surface in the very place where their earlier efforts had been fruitless. What made the difference?

Earthworms instinctively know that if they are deep within the ground when a hard rain falls, they will drown unless they can quickly get to the surface for air. Because of this danger, the body of the worm is very sensitive to the vibrations from the surface. When the woodcock rapidly flutters its wings from above, the beating sounds like raindrops to the worms and they burrow upward toward the surface. As the worms come within reach, the woodcock pierces the ground with its bill and pulls them out.

The young woodcocks observed an important aspect of responsibility by the example of their mother using all her energies to fulfill the needs of her young.

CHARACTERISTICS AND PHYSICAL FEATURES OF THE WOODCOCK

The woodcock illustrates the quality of responsibility by using its unique eyes, bill, ears, feet and wings to their full potential. Its energetic use of these unusual features equips the shorebird for survival.

WHAT DO A WOODCOCK AND TIMBER DOODLE HAVE IN COMMON?

A woodcock and a timber doodle are one and the same bird. A woodcock is also known as an owl snipe or a big mud snipe.

WHAT MAKES A WOODCOCK'S VISION DIFFERENT FROM THAT OF OTHER BIRDS?

A woodcock's eyes are set far back on top of its head. This means that as it probes the ground in search of food, it can still be alert to various enemies which might otherwise be able to surprise it from the rear. With the eyes in this position, the range of a woodcock's vision is 360°.

WHAT IS BINOCULAR VISION?

Binocular vision occurs when the field of vision of both eyes overlap. The woodcock has the unique feature of binocular vision both ahead of it and behind it.

WHAT COULD CATCH A WOODCOCK?

The female woodcock trains her young to be alert. With their specially positioned eyes, they can detect the approach of a predator enemy such as a coyote or fox. Because of the woodcock's 360° vision, it is unlikely that many animals could surprise it.

WHICH IS LARGER, THE MALE OR FEMALE WOODCOCK?

As is true in most other species of birds, the female woodcock is slightly larger than the male.

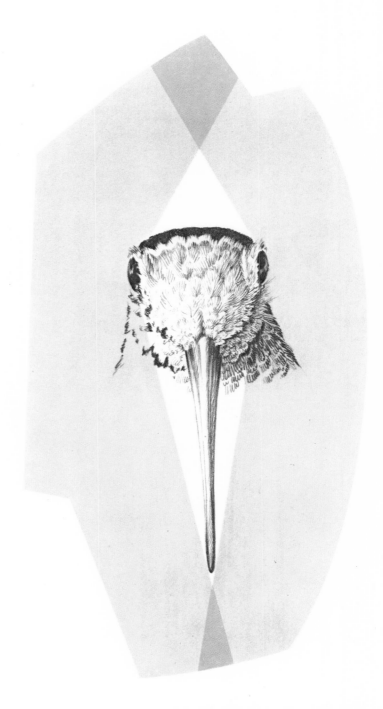

ABOVE *The placement of the woodcock's eyes gives it a visual range of almost 360°. This feature helps to eliminate the danger of surprise attack by preying animals.*

RIGHT *The appearance of the male and female woodcock is virtually identical. Only the larger size of the female distinguishes it from its mate.*

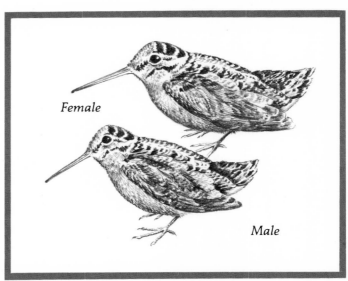

Female

Male

WHAT MOTIVATES A WOODCOCK TO WORK AFTER DARK?

The woodcock's chief source of food is the night crawler, a worm which makes its way up to the ground surface during the cool hours of darkness in the summer months. For this reason the woodcock migrates at night and happens to be one of the first birds to return to its breeding grounds.

HOW LONG DOES IT TAKE BEFORE A WOODCOCK CAN LEARN TO FLY?

Within two weeks of birth the tiny woodcock can fly short distances. In twenty-five days the woodcocks are almost fully grown.

IS THE WOODCOCK A LONG-DISTANCE FLYER?

No. The woodcock's flight tends to be short and erratic. Its agility in maneuvering between trees and brush does enable it to fly through dense underbrush and thickets.

WHERE ARE A WOODCOCK'S EARS?

The ears of the woodcock have an unusual location. Rather than lying at the side of the head as is customary in most birds, they are found between the eyes and the bill.

CAN A WOODCOCK SEE UNDERGROUND?

Because the ears of the woodcock are located close to the bill, they are able to guide it in searching for worms. These ears detect the slightest movement beneath the surface and allow the bird to accurately grasp a worm with its three-inch bill. So highly developed are the ears that they are the equivalent of a woodcock being able to "see" underground.

HOW CAN A WOODCOCK HEAR WITH ITS FEET?

The woodcock can sense with its feet the slight motion caused by a worm propelling itself underground. Because the woodcock's feet are sensitive to vibrations beneath them, they assist in detecting the position of a worm.

ABOVE *The timberdoodle is basically a nocturnal bird, feeding and migrating during the evening hours, resting during the day.*

LEFT *The woodcock's three-inch bill aids the bird in securing its favorite food, the earthworm.*

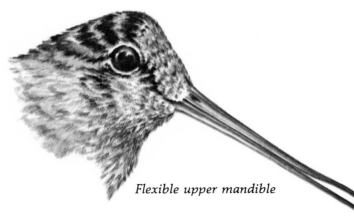

Flexible upper mandible

LEFT *The flexible upper mandible enables the woodcock to grasp worms underneath the surface of the earth. The end of the three-inch bill is equipped with nerves sensitive to touch which relay signals, alerting the bird to the position and proximity of the worm.*

HOW DOES A WOODCOCK GET THE WORM WITHOUT THE MUD?

The woodcock's bill has a feature which is unique to some species. It has a flexible upper mandible which enables only the tip to move in a tweezer fashion. It is able to push its closed bill three inches into the ground and then open only the flexible tip to pick up the worm.

HOW DOES THE WOODCOCK KNOW WHEN IT HAS A WORM IN ITS BILL?

The flexible end of the bill has many delicate nerve endings. These highly developed sense organs feel the worm and signal the woodcock to pull it out of the ground.

WHAT WOULD A WOODCOCK DO IF AN ENEMY APPROACHED?

It probably would remain motionless. When danger threatens most birds flush, but many times the woodcock remains still. You could be within inches of the bird, but it might not break its frozen position. One photographer, after spotting a woodcock, actually moved branches and twigs away from the bird in order to achieve a better picture. The woodcock did not stir.

WOULD IT BE DIFFICULT TO SPOT A WOODCOCK?

The coloration of the woodcock blends perfectly with its surroundings. Unless the bird moved, one would be unable to recognize it against the marshland foliage of its home. The moist countryside in which it lives provides a background against which the bird can easily blend.

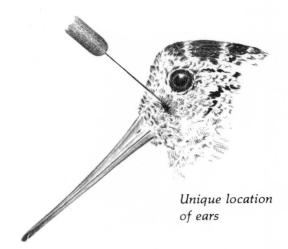

Unique location of ears

Special positioning of ears *allows the woodcock to detect sub-surface movement.*

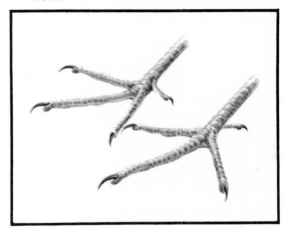

The woodcock's feet *are sensitive to vibration and they, too, assist in locating the position of its food.*

Woodcock frozen in position, relying on protective coloration.

In the early spring *the woodcock performs its courtship ceremonies. Aerial displays may last all night.*

Three outermost primary feathers

HOW DOES A WOODCOCK WHISTLE?

By using its wings. The outermost primaries, three feathers on the end of each wing, enable the bird to make an unexpected whistling sound in flight. When the woodcock senses that it is in danger of being discovered or trampled, it flies quickly away, and the sound from these three feathers startles its enemy as it escapes to safety.

HOW DOES A MALE USE ITS WINGS TO ATTRACT A MATE?

During the mating season the male makes special use of these three feathers. It uses them to create a melodious courtship song. After twilight it will fly high in the air until it is hardly visible. Then, with fixed wings, it will plummet toward the earth. The wind passing through outstretched feathers creates a melodic sound. The male may continue the strange exercise and music throughout the night.

WHAT IS THE WOODCOCK'S MOST DEADLY ENEMY?

The woodcock's most deadly enemy is not a four-footed one. Electric light or telephone wires lying at the flight level of the bird kill more woodcocks than any living predator. Flying at power-line level, the unsuspecting bird many times collides with the thin, out-stretched wire.

The woodcock's outermost primary feathers *provide it with a sharp whistle which catches an observer by surprise. The few seconds it takes for a startled intruder to recover buys the time needed for the woodcock to fly away to safety.*

HOW DOES SCRIPTURE ILLUSTRATE RESPONSIBILITY IN FULFILLING EXPECTATIONS?

The high priest's heart pounded as he grasped the gate post and eased his heavy body onto a seat. His failing eyes stared intently down the winding road. Beyond the horizon a desperate battle was being fought, but he was concerned about something of far greater importance.

He recalled the bitter rebuke that a man of God had given him. He was accused of utterly failing in the discipline of his sons. Others had also warned him concerning this. He had tried to do something about it, but he knew it had been a feeble effort.

But now an even greater danger alarmed him. The men in that battle were in a desperate situation. Their lives and futures depended on victory, and they needed to know that God was on their side.

The priest knew that the nation was looking to him and to his two sons for spiritual leadership, but he was old and he knew that his sons were in no condition to assume such an important responsibility. Because of these crucial circumstances, he had consented to a very dangerous plan. He allowed his sons to take their nation's most sacred treasure, the Ark of the Covenant, into battle. The Ark would reassure the people of God's presence and urge them on to victory.

But the consequences of its loss were grave to consider. If the battle were lost, the treasure would be captured and the nation would grieve over that even more than losing the battle.

In the distance he heard a commotion. A runner had returned from the battle. The old priest leaned forward on his seat and searched his face for an expression. He saw grief and despair in the messenger and listened to the details.

Horrified, he learned that the battle had been lost, 30,000 men had been killed, his two sons were dead and their nation's most sacred treasure had been captured.

At this last news he jerked and trembled. His huge body fell backward. He hit the ground with a heavy thud and lay lifeless. His neck was broken.

The consequences of that day were more far-reaching than he imagined. The nation that conquered them scorned their God, and His own nation decided to have a king rule over them like other nations. Thus, they rejected God's direct leadership.

But why had the priest failed? Why had his sons become gluttonous and immoral? The answer is found in a failure—a lack of discipline in his life. He had a problem of self-control in the area of eating. As his sons grew up, they were very aware of this weakness.

Eli's lack of self-control in this area opened the way for Satan to defeat his sons in related areas of self-control. The discipline and training for leadership which could have saved their lives and the nation's future were never given.

From I Samuel 4:1-18

As high priest, Eli wore the garb of the official mediator between a holy God and His sinful people. The beautiful breastplate with its twelve precious stones represented each of the twelve tribes of Israel.

The brazen altar in the courtyard of the Tabernacle was used for various sacrifices offered to the Lord. Eli's sons used large forks called "flesh hooks" to pull their favorite cuts out of the fire.

GOD'S PRESENCE LEFT A NATION BECAUSE ELI FAILED TO FULFILL THE EXPECTATIONS OF THOSE WHO WERE COUNTING ON HIM

The high priest Eli took office during a period in history which has come to be known as "Israel's Dark Ages." The nation's leaders were disorganized and even the institution of the priesthood seems to have been confused.

AN HONOR IS BESTOWED UPON A MAN WITH THE WRONG ANCESTOR

Eli was a descendant of Aaron's younger son Ithamar and not of the chosen priesthood line of Eleazar. It appears that the line of Eleazar could produce no qualified man for the position of priest. As a result, Eli was chosen as high priest and received the responsibility of judge as well. Because of these circumstances it is safe to assume that at age fifty-eight he was an extremely capable man and no doubt impressed the leaders with his zeal for the Lord.

A BLIND MAN WAS BLIND TO HIS RESPONSIBILITY

It must have been a great honor to have been chosen by the Lord to stand before Him as the representative of the people. But with honor comes responsibility. Eli's chief responsibility would have been to train his sons to succeed him as high priest, a duty that he failed to perform. Years later, the ninety-eight year old Eli, almost totally blind with cataracts in both eyes and unable to perform his duties, could not allow either of his sons, Hophni or Phinehas, to replace him.

LACK OF DISCIPLINE MAKES A MOCKERY OF GOD'S CHARACTER

Eli had failed as a father. He was grieved daily with reports of his sons' irreverent activity as priests. The sacrificial system—designed to teach God's character of righteousness, justice, grace and mercy—was being grossly distorted by Eli's sons. In the Mosaic Law (Leviticus 7:29-34) the Lord had provided for the priest in a practical way. Whenever a man came to sacrifice an animal to the Lord as a peace offering, the right thigh and breast were to nourish the officiating priest. The sons of Eli were not content with what the Lord had provided and refused to limit their tastes to the portion God allowed. They even demanded the fat on the meat which belonged to the Lord and was forbidden for any Israelite to eat (Leviticus 3:16). This gluttony was literally stealing from the Lord Himself. In addition, they introduced to tabernacle worship the shocking "sacred" prostitution common at the surrounding Canaanite shrines.

A FAMILY DISHONORED—A NATION DEFEATED

Since the priests did not correctly teach the Law of God and the history of Israel, the nation was unable to benefit from their past failures. When they lost four thousand men in battle against the Philistines, they should have immediately realized the significance of the defeat. With an understanding of their nation's history they would have interpreted this as God's reproof. Rather than crying out to God in repentance, they increased their wickedness by treating the Ark of the Covenant of the Lord in the manner of a pagan idol and marching it into battle. Their ignorance cost them the very presence of the glory of God and the lives of thirty thousand additional men.

ELI CHARACTER SKETCH

WHY DID ELI LOSE THE RESPECT OF HIS SONS?

Because Eli did not learn to control his weight, he lost the respect of his sons and was unable to teach them self-control. I Samuel 4:18 states that he was old and heavy. As young men, Hophni and Phinehas never learned to control their appetites. They were gluttonous and sensual (I Samuel 2:12-17, 22). The Mosaic Law taught that children of the third and fourth generations would be influenced by the iniquity of their fathers (cf. Exodus 20:5; Numbers 14:18; Deuteronomy 5:9).

WHY DIDN'T ELI DISCIPLINE HIS SONS?

It is likely that Eli's awareness of his own problem caused him to be weak and unwilling to deal with a similar problem in his sons' lives. The Law of God specifically explained the disciplinary action which Eli, as priest and judge, should have known. In Deuteronomy 21:18-21, clear steps of action are given. First, the father is instructed to confront his stubborn and rebellious son with his wrongdoings. After refusing to obey, the son was to be brought before the elders of the city. The Lord's judgment on Aaron's two sons when they rebelled against their father in performing the tabernacle ceremonies was a sobering example from which Eli should have learned (Leviticus 10:1,2).

WHAT WERE THE CONSEQUENCES OF ELI'S NEGLIGENCE?

The immediate consequences of Eli's negligence were the death of his sons, disrespect for the priesthood, and the departure of the glory of the Lord from Israel. There were other long-range consequences. A man of God predicted that none of Eli's descendants would live past their prime and that they would be replaced by a more faithful priest (I Samuel 2:31-32). The prediction was partially fulfilled when Solomon deposed Eli's descendant, Abiathar, from the high priesthood. The complete fulfillment is mentioned in the prophecy of Ezekiel where descendants of Zadok rather than Eli are to be honored in the future kingdom of God (Ezekiel 44:15,16). Because he refused to discipline his own sons, Eli died with a broken and grieved spirit, realizing that he was personally responsible for the spiritual decline of the nation he had judged for forty years.

The Lord allowed the priests *to eat the thigh of the right leg and the breast. Although these were excellent cuts of meat, they did not satisfy Eli's sons, Hophni and Phinehas.*

ELI

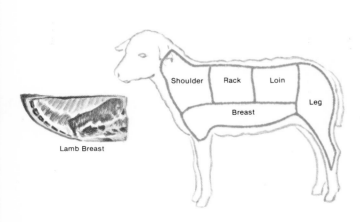

Lamb Breast

Shoulder   Rack   Loin   Leg   Breast

Responsibility

IS COMPLETING A TASK SO THAT IT WILL ENDURE TESTING

LIVING LESSONS ON RESPONSIBILITY . . .

FROM THE PAGES OF SCRIPTURE

A king conceived the idea of an important plan of action, and a construction project was begun which would make it possible for the plan to be carried out. Great crowds of people were on hand to witness the undertaking, but instead they watched in horror as swift tragedy struck. The reason—one precautionary measure had been overlooked.

ILLUSTRATED IN THE WORLD OF NATURE

THE PIED-BILL GREBE *Podilymbus podiceps*

The pied-bill grebe spends most of its life in the water, the element for which it is ideally suited. An inhabitant of both fresh and salt water, this fifteen-inch bird has a wingspread of twenty-three inches. The migratory grebe weighs only one pound.

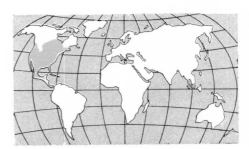

The range and habitat of the pied-bill grebe

RESPONSIBILITY

HOW DOES THE PIED-BILL GREBE ILLUSTRATE RESPONSIBILITY FOR LASTING ACHIEVEMENT?

Warm winds bent cattails over the nesting grebe and her young. An unnatural darkness covered the southern horizon and rapidly filled the entire sky. Several sandpipers and terns returned to their shore nests in sand and clumps of grass on the island as the rain intensified.

In a short time whitecaps formed on the inland lake, and they were pelted with heavy drops of rain. Lightning flashed through the thick clouds and torrents of rain descended. Amid the storm a small bird remained on her nest as it precariously bobbed in the water.

The grebe had arrived early that spring and had made a skillful decision in selecting this particular clump of reeds for her nest. Her area was east of the tributary's entrance in a narrow inlet, away from the open stretches of the lake's expanse. Painstaking care in construction was a hidden accomplishment, betrayed by an apparently haphazard appearance.

As the grebe nestled even closer to her eggs, the sudden spring storm continued to rage. Not since arriving had there been such a torrential downpour. This would certainly put all the grebe had done in building the nest to its most severe test.

As the storm continued, streams that fed the lake swelled well beyond their banks. The waters gushed rampantly into the lake creating even larger whitecaps. Their treacherous crests crashed upon the shore and beat against the nests of frightened shore birds. Helpless, these birds watched as their eggs were washed out of their nests into the turbulent waters.

A different drama was taking place at the nest of the grebe. The nest appeared to be in even greater danger than the others because it was in the water, subject to all the heaving swells of the waves. However, in selecting her nesting area, the grebe had chosen a part of the lake where the waves were lower, broken by the land strip that jutted against the shoreline.

The nest bobbed with each swell and was unaffected by turbulent flooding. The grebe and its eggs rested safely in the carefully-built shelter.

In making the nest, the grebe had employed an amazing engineering feat which served as a precaution for just such a time as this. It had fastened the nest loosely to the reeds, and had designed it to float up and down with the waves. By choosing the location carefully and constructing the nest against the danger of sudden spring storms, the grebe and her young escaped destruction.

Severt Andrewson

CHARACTERISTICS AND PHYSICAL FEATURES OF THE PIED-BILL GREBE

In choosing the site and material for its nest, the grebe takes precautionary measures so that it will remain unnoticed by animals who might prey upon it. The grebe gathers plant material and arranges it among reeds. The material is carefully chosen but haphazardly arranged so that the nest appears simply as a mass of dead vegetation.

HOW DOES THE PIED-BILL GREBE PAINT ITS OWN EGGS?

In an effort to camouflage the eggs, the grebe completely covers them over with vegetation gathered from the nearby waters. She does this whenever she leaves the nest. It isn't long before these materials stain the whitish eggs. This procedure causes them to be even less noticeable to any enemy that would prey upon them.

In the water a grebe closely resembles a small duck. What distinguishes the grebe is that it floats at a higher level than a duck normally would. When danger approaches, the grebe is able to control the level of its buoyancy to the point where only its head is visible above the surface.

When the grebe leaves its home *it only swims away for short periods of time, carefully covering the eggs with vegetation from the nest before leaving. By covering the eggs it achieves two purposes. They are kept warm, and they are hidden from the sight of preying animals.*

Pied-bill grebe's nest, *loosely anchored to reeds, rises and falls with the level of the water.*

IF YOU SAW A GREBE IN THE WATER DURING NESTING SEASON, WOULD ITS NEST BE NEARBY?

Probably not. The grebe takes special precautions to avoid being seen near its nest. When approaching the nest, it will swim underwater to the edge, then quickly slip up on top of it, push away the vegetation and settle down over the eggs.

HOW DOES THE GREBE OUTWIT UNWELCOME VISITORS?

The grebe keeps constant vigil against predators. It is especially watchful for such enemies as the raccoon or the vicious mink. When it hears a suspicious sound or spots an approaching enemy, it engages in a very clever maneuver. First, it quietly pulls vegetation over the eggs. Then it quickly slips off its nest and swims underwater for a considerable distance. When it finally surfaces, the mink or raccoon has no idea from what direction it came.

WHY DOES THE GREBE HAVE AN AWKWARD WADDLE?

The placement of the grebe's feet makes it efficient in the water but very awkward on land. It is a superb swimmer—its feet resembling paddles in their out-stretched position for maximum speed. The lobes of the feet are then folded back to give the least resistance when the bird moves forward.

The grebe's body *is designed for proficiency in water but is cumbersome on land. Because of this limitation, the grebe spends little time out of the water except for flying.*

In an effort to protect the eggs, *the grebe covers its nest with decaying vegetation. Eventually the creamy white eggs become stained, blending with the background of the nest material.*

WHAT ARE THE SECRETS BEHIND THE FLOATING NEST?

The nest of the grebe is a masterpiece of precautionary construction. It is uniquely designed to escape many land predators as well as torrential floods. The grebe begins construction by diving to the bottom of the lake and bringing up plants and mud. These are then piled on a preliminary platform of green stalks which in their fresh condition will easily float.

The platform is small enough to avoid easy detection, yet large enough to bear the weight of the eggs as well as the nesting grebe. The final touch comes as the grebe loosely attaches this floating nest around the stalks of nearby cattails. This both anchors it and allows it to float up and down with the waves.

HOW DO YOUNG GREBES KEEP WARM?

The pied-bill grebe usually lays from five to seven eggs. Grebe chicks will climb up on their mother's back and crawl underneath her feathers to stay warm while waiting for the rest of the brood to hatch.

IS IT TRUE THAT THE GREBE ACTUALLY EATS FEATHERS?

Yes. The grebe eats a considerable amount of feathers. This is not done to provide nourishment, but is another amazing illustration of wise precaution.

The main diet of the grebe is fish, but many bones in fish could pierce the digestive tract of the grebe. To safeguard against this, as much as two-thirds of the stomach consists of feathers. These protect the lining and also hold back the bones until they are soft enough to be digested.

Grebe chicks will climb *up on their parent's back to dry off and keep warm while waiting for the rest of the eggs to hatch. After the brood is hatched, they may continue to use this haven as a refuge from preying fish and turtles.*

The grebe teaches its chicks to eat feathers *to prevent sharp bones from puncturing its intestinal tract.*

TOP: *Lobes are spread apart to achieve maximum force.* LOWER: *Lobes are folded back to reduce resistance as the grebe swims through the water.*

The grebe relies on its lobed feet *for swimming and diving as it searches for fish under water.*

WHAT FINAL PRECAUTION DOES A GREBE PROVIDE FOR ITS CHICKS?

Although the chicks can quickly adapt to the water, they are also weak and tire easily. For this reason the parents demonstrate a care which is uncommon to many birds. Since the chicks are vulnerable to the attack of a turtle, snake, or even a large fish, a parent will swim under a chick and then surface. The chick can then rest on the back of its parent before it is gently set back into the water. The parent may even dive under water with its young on its back if it suspects an attack from the air.

HOW DOES A GREBE STAY DRY EVEN WHEN IN THE WATER?

The feathers of all waterfowl would become waterlogged were it not for a special gland at the base of the tail. This gland secretes an oil which when rubbed over the feathers makes them water repellent. This procedure is called preening.

CAN A GREBE INSTANTLY CONTROL ITS BODY WEIGHT?

It appears to do so by sitting lower and higher in the water. But instead of changing its weight, it is exercising a unique procedure. It is forcing the air out between its feathers, thus making it heavier than the water. By controlling the amount of air, it can adjust to any degree of submerging it chooses.

HOW DOES THE GREBE OUTWIT A HUNTER?

The grebe has learned to disappear so fast under the water that it baffles both predator and hunter. It can dive thirty feet beneath the surface and remain there for eighty seconds. Then it will cautiously approach water level, allowing only its head to break the surface. Because of this skill, it has earned the title, "water witch."

HOW HAVE THE FEATHERS OF THE GREBE ACTUALLY ENDANGERED ITS SURVIVAL?

The feathers possess attractive qualities which prompted man to kill this bird by the tens of thousands in past years. The species was becoming seriously endangered and might have become extinct, but due to protective legislation and its own precautions it is now a flourishing bird.

HOW DOES SCRIPTURE ILLUSTRATE RESPONSIBILITY FOR LASTING ACHIEVEMENT?

Thirty thousand valiant men from the royal army marched with their king on this special mission. They marched to the triumphant sound of trumpets, lyres, harps, tambourines and cymbals. Crowds stood along the road and then followed the huge procession. Many details had been carefully worked out in preparation for this day. But in spite of all preparations, one vital precaution had been overlooked.

Finally they reached their destination. It was the home of a religious leader. His home contained the most sacred and valuable treasure of the entire kingdom—the Ark of the Covenant. God Himself dwelled above this treasure, and wherever it went it brought blessing to those who revered it, but destruction to those who despised it.

Many years earlier this ark had been taken out to battle, and it had been captured by the enemy. But wherever it went, a devastating plague had broken out. After seven months of great anguish, the enemy placed this treasure on a cart and watched as two cows carried it back to its own land. Ever since that time it had been entrusted to the care of this leader, and the treasure had remained in his home.

The troops stood at attention, and all the people eagerly watched as the king and several men went up into that hillside home. The Ark of the Covenant was carefully lifted and placed on a new cart. Two oxen began pulling the cart along

the main road amidst joyous cheering and music from the crowds and troops.

Two of the leader's sons who had cared for this treasure during the previous years were given the honor of walking next to the cart and in front of the procession along with the king. All was going well when sudden tragedy struck. The cart halted abruptly; the music was stilled; those at the head of the procession stopped and kneeled beside the body of one of the sons. The hushed crowd wondered what had happened.

The son had been killed by God. The oxen had stumbled and the cart had almost tipped over. He had thoughtlessly reached out to steady it. But no one was to touch the ark or he would suffer the consequence of death.

Why had this happened? One precaution had been overlooked. When God gave instructions on how to make this sacred ark, He also gave precise direction on how it was to be moved from one place to another. A permanent pole was attached to each side of it. Only these two poles were to be touched by four men who would carry it on their shoulders. They were never to touch the ark.

Had they reviewed these instructions, their work would have endured testing. Neither the imbalance of the cart nor God's swift punishment would have occurred, and the efforts of the king and the family of Abinadab who had housed the ark would have been crowned with success.

From II Samuel 6:1-19

For over seventy years the house of Abinadab enjoyed the special privilege of caring for the most sacred object used in the nation's worship of God—the Ark of the Covenant of the Lord.

THE NATION'S MOST VALUABLE POSSESSION IS STORED IN THE HILLS

The significance of the ark was that God had chosen to reveal Himself through it. The ark was to reside in a room called the Most Holy Place inside the tabernacle. Normally, the only one allowed in the presence of the ark was the High Priest on the Day of Atonement. But conditions were far from normal, and after troubling the nation of Philistia for seven months and causing the death of over fifty thousand Israelites, the ark was being stored for safekeeping in the house of Abinadab. Members of this household were to guard this valuable treasure and protect others from mishandling it.

THIRTY THOUSAND MEN TRANSPORT A SACRED OBJECT

Now the Ark of the Covenant was to resume its central position in ceremonial worship. The nation was enjoying victory over their enemies and the godly King David was anxious to resume the orderly worship of God as prescribed in the Mosaic Law. David gathered thirty thousand representatives who walked the twelve miles from Jerusalem to the house of Abinadab in Keriath-jearim. Eleazar had either died or retired during the seventy years since the ark entered his father's home, but two other members of the house of Abinadab, Uzzah and Ahio, were evidently given the responsibility of caring for it. David allowed Uzzah and Ahio to take part in the ceremony assuming that they would be familiar with the method prescribed in the Law for transporting the ark.

A THOUGHTLESS ACT IS PUNISHED BY DEATH

Holding the ends of the two golden poles which supported the ark, they lifted it onto a new cart driven by a team of oxen. As David and the people celebrated this momentous occasion the oxen suddenly stumbled and nearly upset the cart. Uzzah quickly reasoned that it would be better to disregard the command not to support the ark than to allow it to fall to the ground. He thoughtlessly grabbed it in order to keep it on the cart. The Lord's response terrified King David and the people alike, for He immediately struck dead the well-intentioned but disobedient Uzzah.

A MOVE THAT LASTED OVER 400 YEARS

This sobering death caused David to delay the procession for three months. He searched the Scriptures for the reason for this judgment. Only after following the precise direction given by God did the ark finally enter the capital city of Jerusalem where it was to remain for over four hundred years.

The Ark of the Covenant was so named because it contained the responsibilities of the people in God's covenant with Israel written on two tablets of stone.

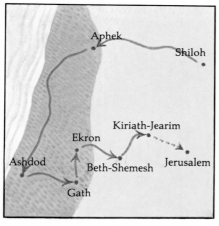

After being captured in battle and remaining for seven months in various cities of Philistia, the ark was sent to Beth-shemesh and then to the house of Abinadab in Keriath-jearim. Later King David brought the ark to Jerusalem.

THE HOUSE OF ABINADAB CHARACTER SKETCH

WAS ABINADAB RESPONSIBLE FOR UZZAH'S PREMATURE DEATH?

Abinadab failed in his responsibility to teach his sons to preserve the integrity of the Law and so was responsible for the later consequences in his family. Although Kiriath-jearim was not one of the designated cities of the Levites, it is almost certain that Abinadab was a Levite. It would have been very strange for his son Eleazar to be consecrated for the responsibility of caring for the ark if such were not the case. The primary responsibility of the Levite tribe was to preserve the Law of God in all of its purity by seeing that its requirements were faithfully and precisely upheld. God required the Levites to set the example for the rest of the nation.

WHAT WAS THE FALLACY OF UZZAH'S REASONING?

When Uzzah noticed the oxen stumble and the cart tip, he had to make a quick decision. He knew that if the sacred ark were to fall it would dampen the joy of the celebration of King David and the thirty thousand men. He quickly took matters into his own hands and chose what he considered to be the lesser of two evils. If Uzzah had reasoned correctly, he would have realized that God was in control of the steps of the oxen. For example, when the Philistines sent the ark back to the nation of Israel, Scripture states that the two cows kept their heads to the ground and turned neither to the right nor the left (I Samuel 6:12), making their way directly to their destination. When the oxen stumbled, Uzzah should have realized that this was God's sign to King David and the people that they were not doing God's work in God's way.

WHY DID THE LORD DEAL SO SEVERELY WITH UZZAH FOR WHAT SEEMED TO BE GOOD INTENTIONS?

When the idolatrous priests of Philistia returned the ark to Israel from their country, they placed it on an unused cart. In Numbers 4:15, the Law clearly stated that any person who touched the pieces of furniture used in the tabernacle would surely die. Two poles were provided for the Levites to carry the ark without touching it. One very important aspect of God's character is the fact that He cannot break any of His promises—whether the promise be a blessing or a curse. To break just one promise would cause His people to lose confidence in His Word. Uzzah's disregard for God's strict command indicated a laxity within the house of Abinadab in their responsibility for caring for the sacred ark. In a public disgrace to the family, Uzzah lost his life because the training which passed down for generations did not withstand the test. God had no other alternative than to deal severely with him as promised.

Only Kohathite Levites *were to transport the ark after the priests had covered it with the inner veil, a skin covering and a blue cloth. They were to touch only the extended poles—never the ark itself.*

UZZAH

IS REALIZING THE IMPORTANCE OF THE TASK ASSIGNED TO US

LIVING LESSONS ON RESPONSIBILITY . . .

FROM THE PAGES OF SCRIPTURE

God looked for a man who would be able to demonstrate responsibility in a task which up to that time He Himself had carried out. A young man was chosen for this purpose, but because he did not realize the importance of the task assigned to him, his right to reign as king was removed from him and from his heirs forever.

ILLUSTRATED IN THE WORLD OF NATURE

THE COMMON CROW *Corvus brachyrhynchos*

Despite the encroachment of civilization upon its natural habitat, the crow not only has survived but has actually increased in number. This omnivorous bird is twenty inches in length. Congregating in large flocks which may reach forty thousand in size, crows inhabit parks, woods and fields, displaying strong group loyalty.

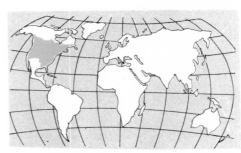

The range and habitat of the common crow

RESPONSIBILITY

HOW DOES THE CROW ILLUSTRATE RESPONSIBILITY IN PERFORMING A TASK?

A distant sound broke the stillness of the afternoon. Indistinct at first, the noise grew in volume until a muffled flapping of wings filled the air. Gleaming, black-feathered crows approached from an adjacent field, soared past a white pine grove and began feeding on remnant corn left behind from the year's harvest.

Dozens followed the first crows, gliding past a narrow stream to join their comrades on the ground, chattering noisily among themselves. But all were not involved in the company's activity.

Two sentry crows sat on the topmost branch of a dead tree, guarding the group. At any given moment some member of the flock is alert and on the lookout for possible danger. It was the duty of these two sentinels to give an alarm at the slightest indication of an intrusion.

The birds continued foraging among the trampled stalks and husks for whatever corn might have been left behind. The two sentinels, assuming that their feeding site was free from danger, became careless in their vigil. But their inattention was not without consequence.

Another sound, the carefully placed steps of an intruder, blended with the chatter of the feeding birds as the afternoon sun extended lengthening shadows from the base of the forest. The intruder skirted the grove of white pine cautiously and then stealthily crept forward.

The threatening intruder drew closer and closer to the field, but the sentries were preoccupied and failed to notice his approach. The warning which should have been given was not, and the crows remained unaware of the unauthorized spectator.

Suddenly, the stranger was spotted by one of the birds on the ground, and a scream of alarm was taken up by one crow after another. Almost as a unit, the entire flock took to wing, but they did not fly away as the intruder had expected. To his amazement they began diving viciously in attack against the two sentries. The unreliable guards were torn to shreds by sharp beaks and claws in a brief but brutal battle. Justice was delivered swiftly for their failure to watch and warn. The flock could not afford to tolerate such irresponsibility, and to ensure that the sentries would never again be in a position to jeopardize their safety, they were swiftly eliminated.

CHARACTERISTICS AND PHYSICAL FEATURES OF THE CROW

The untrustworthy sentinel crows lost their lives because they casually regarded a very serious responsibility. As a rule, though, the crow demonstrates unusual reliability as evidenced in its cooperative communication and teamwork in warding off enemies.

HOW COMPLEX IS THE CROW'S COMMUNICATION SYSTEM?

Crows can express many ideas such as, "possible danger," "look out," "good food," or "be off at once." Their language is well-known to ornithologists. They communicate messages which are basically related to feeding or protection. A "mourning call" expresses sympathy and concern for a crippled or dead crow. Communication is so rapid that several crows may gather and attempt to aid a wounded comrade before it has fallen to the ground from a gunshot wound.

DO CROWS WARN EACH OTHER OF DANGER?

Yes. Crows do warn each other. They have a system of relaying messages and even assign a guard or sentry at a nearby post. A specific warning cry provokes an instant response by the flock if an enemy is spotted. Their dependence on each other for responsible communication may be one factor which explains their ability to survive despite man's encroachment. Within each flock, a high degree of loyalty binds the group into a cohesive unit of cooperation.

The elaborate communication system *of the crow is based on the single syllable, "Caw." With minor modifications entirely different meanings are expressed. For instance, "Caw-aw, caw-aw, caw-aw," assures the flock of safety. On the other hand, "Kawk, kawk, kawk," is a warning signal of danger, creating commotion as it sends the crows winging away. Over fifty such expressions have been distinguished by ornithologists.*

WHY IS THE OWL SUCH A DREADED ENEMY OF THE CROW?

Besides man, the crow fears enemies such as the hawk, the house cat or the fox, but the most dreaded is the horned owl. The owl can silently swoop down into a crow roost at night and kill an entire flock of sleeping birds, one at a time. It is for this reason that crows are so determined in their efforts to rout the owl from their territory. Hunters are aware of this and will employ a decoy or mounted specimen of the owl to draw crows to a particular area.

HOW DOES A CROW INTIMIDATE ITS ENEMY?

Crows use a specific harrassment technique against their noise-sensitive enemies. They will haze the owl as a group by making such an uproar that the intruder is put to flight. Intolerance for the noise of the raucous voices of this "loudmouth" will cause most to take to wing, quickly withdrawing their territorial rights.

ABOVE *Horned owl harrassed by crows as they work as a team to displace their enemy.*

LEFT *Typical owl decoy and gear used by crow hunters.*

HOW DO CROWS WORK AS A TEAM?

If an owl decided to fight against a hazing effort, teamwork would make the difference between life and death for the crows. The crows refine their defense and may even attack a superior enemy by employing a unique counterattack. Several crows will draw the owl's attention in a forward direction while a sneak attack from the rear is organized and executed. Each member of the attack team relies on the hecklers ahead to bewilder the victim while they approach from behind.

IS THE CROW EASILY DECEIVED?

The crow has keen eyesight and an ability to detect the unnatural. It has learned to cautiously keep its distance from suspicious surroundings and, once fired upon, will quickly learn to stay out of range of guns.

DO SCARECROWS REALLY WORK?

Not if their purpose is to keep the crows away from something they really want. If the crow does not see any movement of the figure, it will cautiously approach and become bolder, ignoring the lifeless guardian of the fields.

CAN A CROW TALK?

Like the parrot, a crow can learn to repeat words and even long phrases, word for word. Its ability to mimic indicates its high intelligence, enabling it to associate words with meaning. Although it is unable to talk in the same way we do, it can respond to commands.

IS THE CROW EVER FOOLED BY MAN'S IMITATION?

After learning to interpret various calls of the crow, man also learned to imitate them in order to lure the birds into a waiting ambush. For this reason, crows must learn to distinguish the genuine distress calls of their mates. Otherwise, they would be led to destruction. They also learn to discern false messages and will approach cautiously when called by hunters. Suspicious of the source, they circle the area hesitantly and then leave if they do not see their mate.

HAVE YOU EVER WONDERED WHY YOU OFTEN SEE CROWS BY THE ROADSIDE?

The crow is a scavenger. A major portion of its diet is carrion—dead or decaying meat. The crow is responsible for keeping the roads clear of many carcasses, consuming huge quantities of dead animals each year.

The scarecrow is an ineffective means *of deterring crows from raiding the farmer's corn field. In addition to grain, the crow's widely varied diet includes many destructive insects.*

WHAT DOES THE CROW EAT?

The crow's sturdy digestive system enables it to eat almost anything—grains, insects, eggs, fruit, even carrion. Their adaptability has enabled them to multiply because they are unlikely to face food shortages.

DO CROWS ALWAYS REMAIN WITH THEIR FLOCK?

No. A crow relinquishes flock loyalty and transfers that dedication to its mate during nesting season. It is believed that they mate for life and are considered model parents. Each knows where the other is at all times. In flight, the birds remain near each other and will wait for a slower mate to catch up so the two can fly as a team.

HOW MUCH ATTENTION DO THE YOUNG CROWS REQUIRE?

During incubation, the female has the responsibility of sitting on the three to eight greenish eggs. The male keeps within close range and provides her with food. Once the eggs have hatched, both parents feed their young at least eight full meals a day. Their rapid digestive system accounts for the enormous quantities of food required. It has been estimated that a single family could devour 40,000 harmful insects in one season.

ARE A RAVEN AND A CROW THE SAME BIRD?

No. They are members of the same order but differ in appearance. The raven is a larger bird, averaging 25 inches to the crow's normal 20 inches. It has a longer, thicker neck and a heavier bill than the crow. The raven also has a bearded feather structure on its throat and, in contrast to the crow's migration pattern, can remain in northern regions throughout the winter.

The crow's nest *is composed of neatly interwoven sticks and twigs. The eggs have an incubation period of 18 days. Within five weeks the young crows are able to fly.*

RAVEN
Corvus corax

COMMON CROW
Corvus brachyrhynchos

HOW DOES SCRIPTURE ILLUSTRATE RESPONSIBILITY IN PERFORMING A TASK?

The history of God's chosen people is interwoven with the failures and successes of those who were charged with difficult responsibilities.

As the young nation of Israel traveled from the land of bondage to the land of promise, a shocking report spread throughout the camp. A horde of wicked people was following close behind them waiting for those who became weak, sick or weary to fall behind the main group. Then the Amalekites would rush upon them, mercilessly slaughter them and steal their possessions.

God determined to destroy these wicked people but gave them many opportunities to repent. Years later the seer Balaam, hired by a neighboring king to curse the nation of God, looked toward the land of Amalek and predicted, "Amalek was the first of the nations to war against Israel, but its latter end shall be that it perish forever."

Four hundred years later, the time came for God to destroy them, and He sought a man who would fully carry out this grave responsibility. He gave the opportunity to a tall, handsome and courageous man. With him an army of two hundred and ten thousand men crept up to the valley next to the city of Amalek. At the given signal they made their attack; the defenses crumbled before them; victory belonged to the nation of Israel.

God had given His commander strict instructions. "Go and smite Amalek, and utterly destroy all that they have and spare them not." But the irresponsible leader did not fully obey the directive of God. Instead he spared the king and the best of the sheep and oxen.

God had given the task to this man as a test to determine whether or not he would be successful as the first appointed king of Israel, and he had failed. When approached by Samuel on his return the disobedient king said, "I have performed the commandment of the Lord." Confronted with the obvious evidence that he had not obeyed, he blamed the people for sparing the animals and assured the prophet that they were going to sacrifice them to the Lord.

Then Samuel uttered the famous words, "Behold, to obey is better than sacrifice, and to hearken than the fat of rams. . .Because thou hast rejected the word of the Lord, He hath also rejected thee from being king."

Years later this irresponsible king was mortally wounded in a fierce battle with another nation. After the battle a man returned to report what had happened. When he was asked how he knew that King Saul was dead, he replied, "I found him wounded, and he was afraid of being captured by the enemy. The arrow had not killed him, and he asked me to come over and help him drive his spear into his heart. I did what he asked. Then I took his crown and bracelet and fled." When asked who he was, he simply said, "I am an Amalekite."

From I Samuel 15

Gibeah *was Saul's birthplace and remained his residence after he became king.*

The Israelite altar *was a simple elevation made of earth, rough stones or turf. It was to have no engraved symbols common on altars used in pagan religions.*

SAUL'S DYNASTY CAME TO AN ABRUPT END BECAUSE HE FAILED TO REALIZE THE IMPORTANCE OF HIS TASK

The people wanted a man powerful enough to bring law and order to their confused situation. They pleaded for a warrior-king to lead them out to battle like other nations. God had ideally prepared Saul for his new responsibility as king, but with power came the danger of pride. It was Saul's responsibility to remain God's humble servant.

GOD HONORED HUMILITY

When Saul began his reign he humbly acknowledged his dependence on God. As a result he enjoyed success wherever he turned. He was God's instrument in inflicting judgment against Moab, the sons of Ammon, Edom, the kings of Zobah and the Philistines (I Samuel 14:47).

PRIDE BROUGHT FAILURE

In preparation for the campaign against the powerful Philistines, Saul's fatal tendency toward pride surfaced. The prophet Samuel told Saul to wait for him in Gilgal for instructions from the Lord before going out to battle. He predicted that he would have to wait at least seven days. When Samuel did not arrive after seven days and Saul saw his small army getting even smaller through desertions, he acted independently of the Lord's counsel and ordered the priests to present offerings to the Lord in preparation for the battle. Because of this dangerous attitude of indifference toward God's direction, Samuel predicted that Saul's dynasty would come to an end.

AN INCOMPLETE TASK ANGERED THE LORD

Later, the Lord gave Saul a mission which he did not fully understand. He was to destroy all the descendants of Amalek. He was to utterly destroy all their possessions and put to death both man and woman, child and infant, ox and sheep, camel and donkey. Because Saul did not understand the reasoning of the command of the Lord, he acted according to his own reasoning and decided to spare the best of the animals and Agag, the king of the Amalekites. Saul knew that the Amalekites had been the first nation to attack the Israelites after leaving Egypt and he knew that they had been continual enemies, but he still could not understand the reason for such severity.

THE KING'S DISOBEDIENCE WAS COSTLY

When Samuel heard of Saul's disobedience, he came and accused him of rebellion and insubordination. Saul's excuses were feeble and Samuel had to proclaim God's judgment. Because Saul had been irresponsible in accomplishing his assignment and had rejected the Word of the Lord, he was removed from the throne.

SAUL CHARACTER SKETCH

WHY DID GOD WANT SAUL TO DESTROY THE AMALEKITES?

One of the promises that Jacob received from his father was that those who cursed him would be cursed and those who blessed him would be blessed (Genesis 27:29). His brother, Esau, despised Jacob to the point of wanting to kill him when he learned that he was to be his servant (Genesis 27:40,41). Esau's grandson, Amalek, continued the family feud (Genesis 36:12). The descendants of Amalek and a group called the Kenites demonstrated the truth of the blessing which Jacob had received. The Kenites helped the nation of Israel to their new land by guiding them through their native land (Numbers 10:29-32; Judges 4:11). The Amalekites hindered the nation along their journey by making war against them (Exodus 17:8-13). As God's spokesman Moses promised to do good to the Kenites (Numbers 10:32) but to utterly blot out the memory of Amalek from under heaven (Exodus 17:14). It was Saul's responsibility to fulfill these promises by sparing the Kenites and destroying the Amalekites (I Samuel 15:3-6).

WHY DID SAUL DISOBEY SUCH CLEAR INSTRUCTIONS?

Saul's invalid excuse for sparing the best of the sheep and oxen was that the people wanted to offer them to the Lord (I Samuel 15:21). God had already banned all of the animals for destruction; they were not the people's animals to offer. It seems that Saul and the people were selfishly preserving the best of the animals to enjoy the sacrificial feast. Saul did not even offer an excuse for sparing King Agag, but it is possible that he was observing a common custom of increasing his prestige among surrounding nations by turning a powerful king into a royal servant. It was an act motivated by pride and an unwillingness to be the follower and servant of the Lord.

WHAT WERE THE CONSEQUENCES OF SAUL'S DISOBEDIENCE?

The punishment was severe. The Lord rejected him from being king over Israel and selected another to replace him (I Samuel 16:1). The Spirit of the Lord departed from Saul and an evil spirit terrorized him for the remainder of his life. Saul knew no peace during his reign, and he was finally killed by the Philistines with three of his sons. His body was disgraced even after death (I Samuel 31:8-10). One of Saul's remaining sons was assassinated by two of his own commanders (II Samuel 4:7). Two other sons and five grandsons were hung in revenge by the Gibeonites (II Samuel 21:9). Because Saul did not utterly destroy the Amalekites, they remained in the land for over three hundred years, and it was not until the reign of Hezekiah that God's judgment on them was finally completed (I Chronicles 4:43).

"**And Samuel said,** *What meaneth then this bleating of the sheep in mine ears, and the lowing of the oxen which I hear?"*

SAUL

IS TURNING ROUTINE TASKS INTO ENJOYABLE EXPERIENCES

LIVING LESSONS ON RESPONSIBILITY . . .

FROM THE PAGES OF SCRIPTURE

Unwilling to accept joyfully the task placed before him, a great leader in Scripture pleaded with God to remove the pressure. In his haste to secure relief from his responsibility, grave consequences resulted which handicapped his leadership and affected the future of his people.

ILLUSTRATED IN THE WORLD OF NATURE

THE RIVER OTTER *Lutra canadensis*

The frolicsome river otter inhabits watercourses throughout North America. This three-foot mammal averages thirty pounds in weight and is active at all times of the day and year. The only member of the weasel family with a webbed foot, it spends hours on end in spirited play.

The range and habitat of the river otter

RESPONSIBILITY

HOW DOES THE OTTER ILLUSTRATE RESPONSIBILITY IN MAKING WORK ENJOYABLE?

Talented acrobats, the otters are the most proficient swimmers of the weasel family. It is hard to believe that an animal which enjoys and is so competent in the water would be afraid of it at birth. But such is the case with the young otter pups. To introduce them to this threatening element the parents employ an involved strategy.

It was time for the otter, one of nature's most fun-loving creatures, to set aside its playful antics and settle down to the serious business of raising a family. But even this would be a pleasurable task. The responsibilities which it entailed necessitated a change in lifestyle for the perpetually on-the-move mammal. Rearing the young would mean confinement to one area and an underground den until the pups were old enough to travel.

In selecting her den site, the female requires that it be near the bank of a pond or stream. By choosing such a location, an underwater entrance can be made to facilitate her coming and going without exposing the pups to lurking predators. After the selection has been made and the den lined with soft vegetation, she gives birth to two to three pups.

The female waits until the pups' eyes are open before leading them out of their den. The young are afraid of water so she cannot use the underwater passageway and is forced to dig a hole above the chamber, allowing the pups to leave the den on dry land.

Once they leave, the female allows them to frolic and romp with each other, exploring their new surroundings with boundless energy. Both father and mother join in their play by scuffling with them and allowing the pups to ride on their backs. Periodically they slip into the water alone and return with morsels of food to meet the demands of the youngsters' growing appetites. This is their first exposure to water and the first step in a strategy to familiarize them with it.

The pups are not forced toward the stream but are allowed to play for several days until the parents feel they are ready to enter the water. Either one or both parents have the pups climb up on their back for a customary taxi-like ride. But this time, instead of running up and down the shoreline, they slip into the water's edge. The panicked pups cling to the fur in fright. This procedure is repeated until the pups gradually relax as they become more confident of their support and more accustomed to the water.

Soon after the young become comfortable in their riding position, the parent slips out from underneath, leaving them to experience their buoyancy for the first time. They frantically fight to stay above the surface. The parent then glides back underneath and supports them again. By extending these free-floating periods, the pups gradually learn the fine art of swimming.

The parents remain in the same area throughout the summer, concentrating on developing the skills of their pups, teaching them by example to fish and hunt for crayfish. By the end of the season not only will the pups have mastered their aquatic skills, but of even greater importance, they will have learned how to approach a routine task with the carefree abandon that characterizes this fun-loving mammal.

CHARACTERISTICS AND PHYSICAL FEATURES OF THE RIVER OTTER

Swimming skills which fearful otter cubs must develop are patiently taught them by their parents. But of even greater importance is the spirit with which they learn to approach each task. A joyful and adventuresome spirit transforms even the mundane jobs of survival into fun.

WHY DOES AN OTTER LIKE TO GO FISHING?

Although catching food is a serious matter for most wildlife, to the otter it is fun. Often the otter is more interested in the sport of the chase than in securing a meal and will play with a fish and release it after it is caught.

WHAT FISHING TECHNIQUES DOES THE OTTER USE?

Using its forepaws, the otter will slip up within 18 inches of an unsuspecting fish without making a ripple. It will then arch its back, dart forward, and seize the fish. The otter rarely misses. Another technique is for the otter to outswim a fish and then corner it along the shallower levels of water against a rock or bank.

HOW BIG A FISH CAN AN OTTER HANDLE?

Otter can catch fish up to 30 inches in length, and the species of fish doesn't make much difference. They have a fondness for trout but will eat muskellunge, northern pike, panfish or scavenger fish. The otter eats the fish as one would eat a hot dog, from one end to the other.

HOW SPEEDY IS THE OTTER?

The otter moves through the water at seven miles an hour. If it really wants to move quickly, it swims underneath the surface where it can achieve greater speed. Rather than steering with its tail as is popularly thought, the otter uses that broad surface to propel itself through the water.

The river otter, *an expert fisherman, teaches its young the skillful art of fishing.*

Beginning at one end, *young otters eat brook trout in hot-dog fashion as parent looks on. One of the mainstays of the otter's diet is fish. Proficient in securing its prey, the otter is capable of catching and eating fish up to thirty inches in length.*

Of all the aquatic life on which the otter feeds, *none is relished more than the crayfish, a relative of the lobster and shrimp. Crayfish hide beneath rocks or in burrows during the day and are active at night.*

The otter doesn't fish just for food. *Many times the captured fish becomes an object of sport and is released after the otter tires of play.*

Using its nose, *the otter dislodges crayfish from its hiding place. Sensitive whiskers and underwater vision enable it to locate this delicacy.*

WHAT DO AN OTTER AND A WEASEL HAVE IN COMMON?

They are members of the same family. In comparison to its other cousins, the fun-loving otter is the slowest on land but it is the fastest in the water.

ARE FISH THE OTTER'S FAVORITE FOOD?

The otter's diet is varied. It includes snails, turtles, snakes, eels, insects, crabs and even frogs. They will eat any kind of fish, but their favorite food is actually the crayfish. They learn to use their webbed feet to stir up the mud and then probe the bottom of the pond or river-bed, rooting out these succulent morsels. They catch fish with such skill that feeding does not occupy much of their time.

CAN AN OTTER SEE UNDERWATER?

Because the otter is so accustomed to probing along lake bottoms to feed, it has learned to recognize instantly the water life which it eats. Its short-range vision is excellent as well as its hearing and balance.

WHY DOES THE OTTER HAVE TWO COATS?

The otter's coat has two distinct layers. The under layer is fur-like, woolly and soft, providing insulation. An outer layer of long, coarser hair lies flat against the body when wet. These outer guard hairs protect the animal.

HOW DO WHISKERS AID THE OTTER IN FISHING?

The otter's stiff whiskers are connected to large nerve pads and are actually sensitive to water turbulence. When swimming in dark waters, they help in locating and following prey and in judging distance and depth. Whiskers are found on the nose area as well as on the otter's elbows.

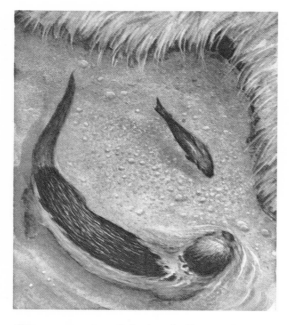

Otter cornering fish *in shallow inlet for easy capture*

HOW IS THE OTTER'S MOUTH EQUIPPED TO HANDLE FISH?

Each tooth has a specific function. Canines are able to pierce the fish's tough skin surface. Sharp incisors tear off small bits of fish. Molars are suited well for grinding fish bones or crushing the shell of a crayfish, and front shearing teeth aid in chewing.

DOES AN OTTER EVER GET "SWIMMER'S EAR?"

When an otter dives underwater, its ears are automatically sealed by a valve-like membrane. This membrane prevents water from entering. Its nose is also equipped with a similar membrane for the same purpose.

DOES AN OTTER MAKE WAVES?

You would think it impossible, but an otter can actually slide into the water without making a splash. It is able to stay beneath the surface for as long as four minutes since its pulse rate drops rapidly when it submerges.

HOW DOES AN OTTER BREATHE UNDER ICE WHEN THE LAKE IS FROZEN?

The otter's nose is flat, allowing it to get close to the ice and inhale the oxygen bubbles which may be found between the water and the frozen surface. An otter will create many holes in the ice by repeatedly exhaling its warm breath against the frigid surface, melting holes for passage and air. Such air holes are regularly maintained and used all season. By employing these methods, the otter is able to swim and catch fish throughout the winter months.

WHAT ARE THE OTTER'S FAVORITE PASTIMES?

Sliding and swimming. Otters are very playful animals and engage tirelessly in all types of impromptu games. They belly flop into the water, roll, play tag, tug-of-war, tumble, chase and generally enjoy themselves. Sliding is a year-round sport in which the entire family participates.

HOW DOES AN OTTER PREPARE A TOBOGGAN RUN?

A snow-covered slope leading to water's edge provides a perfect winter slide for an otter family. After a few downhill races, the path is packed and no further preparation is necessary. During the warmer months, more thoughtful steps must be taken. Again, the bank must be sloping, with water fairly deep at the edge, and the soil should be of clay-like composition. All obstructions—sticks, roots, and stones—are removed as soon as the site is chosen. Once the surface has been cleared, the otters climb the bank and skim down the hill at high speed. They tirelessly indulge in this activity for hours on end.

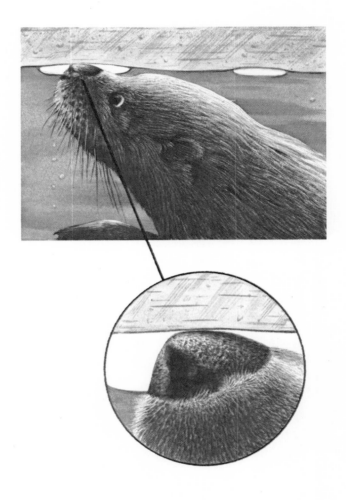

ABOVE *With its specially adapted nose the otter is able to utilize the small pockets of air between the water and ice for its oxygen supply.*

RIGHT *By continuously exhaling warm air the otter is able to bore through ice. Once a hole is made the otter will periodically free it from newly-forming ice.*

A popular winter pastime *for the otter is sliding down packed, snow-covered toboggan runs.*

Only when rearing young *will the otters live in a den. Because the den's only entrance is an underwater one, cold air is sealed out and protection from predators is afforded.*

IS THE OTTER ALWAYS ON THE RUN?

Yes. Otters rarely stay in one place for more than a few days. They travel definite pathways or watercourses which extend through chains of ponds, rivers and lakes and may complete a fifty-mile circuit in two weeks. They explore anything and everything that arouses their curiosity.

IF AN OTTER HAS A CHOICE, WILL IT GO UNDER OR OVER A LOG?

When traveling on land, the otters try to take the smoothest and easiest course that they can. If possible, they will slip under rather than jump over a log which is in their way.

WHAT ARE SOME HAZARDS OF TRAVELING?

If pursued on land, the otter is at a distinct disadvantage for its speed is best evidenced in water. In deep snow, the otter compensates for lack of speed with an elusive, burrowing run. It is difficult for its enemy to anticipate what direction it will go after surfacing, so by tunneling for short distances it is able to confuse potential attackers.

HOW CAN AN OTTER TELL FRIEND FROM FOE?

Rather than being aggressive, the otter is gregarious and friendly by nature and will assume, for example, that an advancing dog's intentions are friendly. If the otter is not able to approach with a "nose-to-nose" greeting, the dog will probably precipitate a fight and is likely to be the loser. But if the dog remains friendly, it is simply regarded as a new and unusual playmate for the carefree otter family and is in no danger of being attacked.

HOW LONG DOES THE FAMILY STAY TOGETHER?

The otter family stays together for at least a year. Their den or "holt" usually has a tunnel which leads to water. Both parents share responsibility for raising the young, and they are an openly affectionate, loyal unit. In fact, they have been known to mourn, even wail, for days when a mate or family member is lost or killed.

LEFT *The bond of loyalty between a pair of otters is very strong. When one of the partners dies, its mate has been known to mourn for long periods of time, going without food and refusing to be comforted by other otters. It may wander in search for its mate or remain by the lifeless body for days.*

HOW DOES SCRIPTURE ILLUSTRATE RESPONSIBILITY IN MAKING WORK ENJOYABLE?

Early one morning a large crowd began to gather around an empty wooden chair. Each one was in deep thought or in serious conversation with those standing around him.

Soon a hush came over the crowd. A dignified man with handsome features strode from his tent toward the chair. The assembly parted as he came and quickly closed in after him. There was a mood of reverence and eagerness as he sat on the chair and nodded to the one nearest him to begin speaking.

Soon he was listening to the details of a grievance which this man had against his neighbor. After hearing both sides, the revered leader explained statutes and laws of God which determined who was right and who was wrong.

Patiently the people waited their turn, but by the end of the day many had not yet been heard. A silent individual observed the leader and the group and devised what he thought was a better plan. His plan made sense, but it was destined to be a destructive force in the life of the leader and his people.

That evening he suggested to the leader, "You are going to wear yourself out as well as the people if you try to hear all their problems. It would be much better if you chose qualified leaders from among the people and let them hear small cases. If they have any difficult matters,

they will bring them to you. This will make it easier for you."

He knew that the plan would appeal to the leader because he sensed that he was weary and frustrated. Indeed, his desire to be free from part of his responsibility caused him to cry out to God for more help. God conceded by instructing him to gather together seventy other men. Then God spoke these revealing words. "I will take part of the spirit which is upon you and will put it upon them, and they shall bear the burden of the people with you that you bear it not yourself alone."[1]

The leader's request for less responsibility was granted, but the cost was far greater than he anticipated. He lost direct contact with many of the people, and they lost some of their respect for him. Confusion of leadership resulted and his most trusted friends began to challenge his authority. As a result, the goal which he had worked toward for eighty years suffered a setback that required forty additional years to overcome.

The responsibilities of his position were enormous, but Moses failed to realize that God had given him the power of His Spirit equal to the task to which he was assigned. By giving up part of that task, he lost part of that Spirit. And whatever became of the seventy who helped carry his load? They became the organization which years later voted to crucify the Son of God.

From Exodus 18

1. Numbers 11:17.

MOSES' FAILURE TO ACCEPT RESPONSIBILITIES JOYFULLY ULTIMATELY DEFEATED HIM

Moses is one of the great characters of the Old Testament. He is known as the meekest man who ever lived and appeared with Elijah and the Lord on the Mount of Transfiguration. But three times Moses shirked the responsibility God had given him. Three times the Lord conceded to his request for less responsibility, and three times the result was a decrease in his effectiveness.

RELUCTANT TO SPEAK

The first incident occurred when the Lord commissioned him to lead the nation of Israel out of slavery in Egypt to the land of Canaan. Moses argued that he was not capable, but God promised him that He would provide all the necessary resources. Then Moses said that the elders of Israel would neither believe nor follow him, so God gave him three miracles to convince them. Finally Moses said that he was not eloquent and could not be God's spokesman. God promised that he would be with him and teach him what to say. Moses still shrank from the task so God reluctantly consented to divide his responsibilities with his brother Aaron. From this position of authority Aaron later led the people into idolatry and challenged Moses' right to rule.

RELUCTANT TO JUDGE

The second incident took place shortly after Moses led the nation out of Egypt. The people began wearing him down with petty disputes until Moses cried out, "How can I myself alone bear your cumbrance, and your burden and your strife?" (Deuteronomy 1:12). At the advice of Jethro, his father-in-law, he allowed the people to elect their own judges and appointed them over thousands, hundreds, fifties and tens. This wholesale delegation of responsibility throughout the tribes was worse than ineffective. A year later, instead of the peace Jethro predicted, the people were complaining so much that God had to consume some of them with fire (Numbers 11:1).

RELUCTANT TO LEAD

The third time Moses complained about having too much responsibility was when the people of Israel actually wept aloud in complaint over the food God was providing for them. They wanted the fish, cucumbers, melons, leeks, onions and garlic they were used to eating in Egypt. Moses felt like a failure and cried for relief, "I am not able to bear all this people alone, because it is too heavy for me. And if Thou deal thus with me, kill me, I pray thee, out of hand, if I have found favor in Thy sight; and let me not see my wretchedness." (Numbers 11:14,15) Again God granted Moses relief and allowed him to share his authority with seventy men among the elders of Israel. Moses yielded his authority at a time in the young nation's history when they needed a strong individual to lead them in the way of the Lord. By abdicating his responsibilities at this critical time he merely compounded his burden and fostered the crisis of leadership which followed.

AN OLD MAN RECOGNIZES HIS TRUE STRENGTH

Moses had to learn the hard way that when God gives a responsibility He also provides the necessary resources to meet the responsibility. In the last verse of the ninetieth Psalm, the only recorded psalm written by Moses, he reveals the final prayer of his heart. "And let the beauty of the Lord our God be upon us: and establish thou the work of our hands upon us; yes, the work of our hands establish thou it."

Moses may have copied *the larger body of God's Law on paper made from the pith of the papyrus plant, a common reed. Sheets were pasted together to form a continuous scroll.*

When Moses was at Rephidim, *he was joined by his father-in-law Jethro who brought his wife and two sons from the land of Midian.*

MOSES CHARACTER SKETCH

SHOULD MOSES HAVE LISTENED TO JETHRO—A PRIEST OF A HEATHEN LAND?

Scripture tells us not to walk in the counsel of the wicked but rather to delight in the Law of the Lord (Psalm 1:1,2). But Jethro was not a wicked pagan priest and the full body of the Law had not yet been revealed. Jethro was the priest of Midian (Exodus 3:1) and hence, a descendant of Abraham (Genesis 25:1,2). His other name, Reuel, (Exodus 2:18) means "friend of God," and it seems likely that he was a worshipper of the God of Abraham. Furthermore, Jethro was Moses' father-in-law whom he had served for forty years. Jethro was sincerely concerned for Moses' welfare and the welfare of his daughter and two grandsons. He may have been worried that Moses' responsibility would only lead to further marital difficulties (cf. Exodus 4:24-26; 18:2). Moses was wise in giving attention to the instruction of his father-in-law in order to gain understanding (Proverb 4:1). He was wrong not to seek the Lord's more complete solution which would have answered Jethro's objections and would have prevented the unnecessary consequences which followed.

WHAT WERE THE CONSEQUENCES OF MOSES' PREMATURE DECISION?

There were over six hundred thousand men in the nation (Exodus 12:37). If Jethro's advice were taken literally there would have been six hundred judges over thousands, six thousand over hundreds, twelve thousand over fifties, and sixty thousand over tens—seventy-eight thousand and six hundred judges in all. Many of these judges would no doubt have felt privileged to a larger amount of Moses' time than otherwise would have been the case. So ineffective was this new system that a year later the Lord conceded to give Moses seventy additional men to share his position as final arbitrator. Immediately afterward his own brother and sister challenged his authority (Numbers 12:1,2). Then ten of the spies sent into the new land challenged his authority (Numbers 13:31,32). Finally the spirit of anarchy and rebellion broke out among the leaders who were supposed to have eased Moses' burden (Numbers 16:1-3).

WHAT WAS GOD'S SOLUTION?

If Moses had endured his responsibility for a few more months he would have been able to see God's perfect plan for the organization of the nation. Jethro spent only one evening explaining his plan to Moses, but God spent forty days and forty nights revealing His organizational plan for the nation. When Jethro gave his advice, the detailed Law had not been given and the people had few principles to follow. Every new shade of every situation needed a special decision. Jethro's advice would have amounted to the building of an extremely complex and unwieldly code of law which only a special group of trained men could understand (Exodus 18:19-22). God's method was to give a very compact set of laws which every individual could learn, meditate on and obey (Psalm 1:2; Psalm 119:1,2). Furthermore, it was not God's plan to separate the civil laws from the religious laws as Jethro's plan would have done. The Lord's plan was to give the tribe of Levi the responsibility of teaching and administering the Law to the other tribes and of objectively arbitrating inter-tribal disputes (Deuteronomy 17:8-13; 33:10).

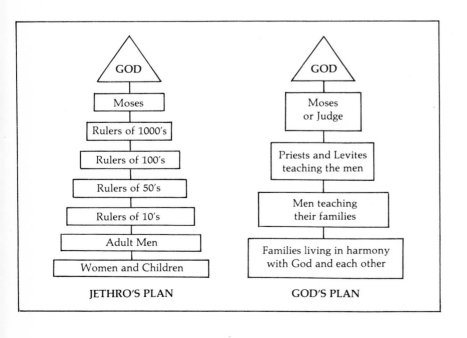

JETHRO'S PLAN

GOD'S PLAN

MOSES

Courage

PART THREE

RESPONDING TO DANGER WITHOUT THOUGHT OF RETREAT

APPLYING THE RESOURCES I HAVE IN CREATIVE WAYS WHEN FACED WITH OVERWHELMING ODDS

FOLLOWING DIFFICULT INSTRUCTIONS IN THE FACE OF DANGER

CONFRONTING AN OPPONENT WITH THE CONFIDENCE THAT I WILL ULTIMATELY SUCCEED

Courage

IS RESPONDING TO DANGER WITHOUT THOUGHT OF RETREAT

LIVING LESSONS ON COURAGE . . .

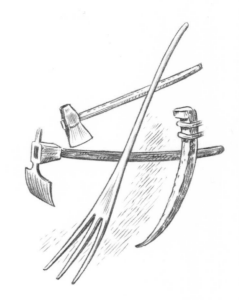

FROM THE PAGES OF SCRIPTURE

It would be difficult to find a more pathetic mismatch than that which occurred when two armies faced each other in battle. But it would be equally difficult to find a greater illustration of courage. Only one factor marred that courage, but that one flaw resulted in tragedy.

ILLUSTRATED IN THE WORLD OF NATURE

THE SHORT-TAILED WEASEL *Zmustela eriminea*

Pound for pound, the short-tailed weasel has earned the distinction of being one of the most courageous animals alive. This five-ounce mammal measures seven to fourteen inches in length. Although it is nocturnal by nature, it is not uncommon to see the solitary weasel during the day in the swamps, fields and farmlands which it inhabits.

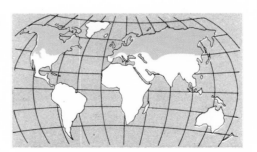

The range and habitat of the short-tailed weasel

COURAGE

HOW DOES THE WEASEL ILLUSTRATE COURAGE IN RESPONDING TO DANGER?

The wiry weasel picked up the scent of a white-footed mouse and began to tirelessly track it down. It scurried across an open field, its muscular body tense and alert. Making its way through underbrush and over surfaces of stone, it traced the trail to its end and after a brief skirmish captured the mouse.

The weasel had left six squealing offspring at its den whose eyes were not yet open. The furless young were kept warm with bits of grass and mouse hair. The male weasel had been bringing home mice and other small rodents to accumulate a storehouse of food. For in five weeks, the young weasels would be weaned from their mother's milk to a diet of meat.

Returning from its successful hunt, the weasel approached the den carrying the body of its prey. Concentrating on its burden, the weasel did not see a coiled king snake. A few yards from the burrow it glanced to the left. There was the snake, poised to strike.

The weasel could have dropped its catch and run, but that would have exposed its mate and young to an inevitable attack since the snake would follow the male weasel into the burrow. Instead, it turned to its attacker and with fierce courage initiated the battle.

The snake sprang forward as the weasel darted, narrowly escaping its sharp teeth as well as eluding the entrapping coils of the snake's muscular body. Quickly it recoiled and lunged for the weasel again, but with rapid movements the weasel bobbed and weaved, escaping its threatening attempts.

As the snake lunged a third time, the weasel was able to maneuver itself and clamp its powerful jaws low on its enemy's neck. It shook the snake, tightening its hold. Furious, the snake struggled and writhed wildly as it both bit and wrapped its muscular body around its assailant. The weasel's teeth sank deeper and deeper into its neck as the snake intensified its grip. After agonized thrashing, the struggle finally ended.

Although faced with the threat of a deadly enemy the weasel had responded to the danger without the thought of retreat. But the courage was costly. It had not protected it from the snake's crushing strength. Sharp broken bones had punctured vital organs. With fatal wounds, it painfully limped toward the bushes beyond its den to die.

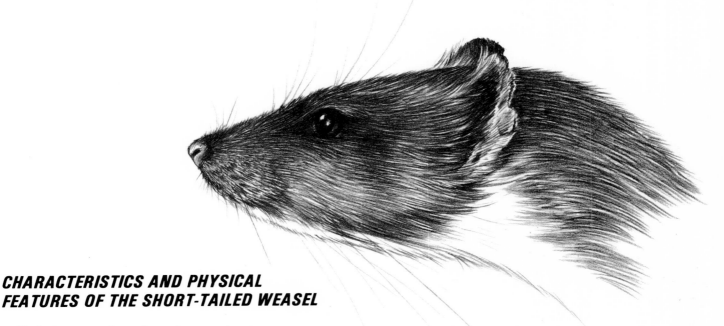

CHARACTERISTICS AND PHYSICAL FEATURES OF THE SHORT-TAILED WEASEL

Had the weasel made a hasty retreat into its burrow, it probably could have saved its own life. But in so doing it would have jeopardized its entire family. Fearless and bold, the weasel does not have a reputation for backing away from danger.

WHAT AIDS THE WEASEL IN WITHSTANDING LARGER OPPONENTS?

The weasel strategically employs speed of attack as one of its major weapons. Because of its small size, any hesitation on its part could mean defeat.

On one occasion an unsuspecting red-tailed hawk detected movement in the underbrush. It flew down to attack a small rodent on which it was accustomed to feed. Swooping down from a tree, the hawk seized the seven-inch animal. As it lifted it off the ground the weasel struck back with lightning speed, sinking needlepoint teeth into the hawk's neck.

With each effort of the surprised hawk to shake the animal loose, the weasel's teeth sank deeper until they reached their vital target. Pain shot through the body of the hawk as the bird plummeted to earth, killed not by size but by sheer swiftness of action.

WHY IS THE WEASEL KNOWN AS A "KILLING MACHINE"?

The body structure of the weasel enables it to be one of the most effective hunters of its size. It has been said that if a weasel were as large as a collie, it would be the most vicious animal on earth. The weasel is a bundle of finely-tuned, highly-coordinated muscles which respond swiftly and accurately. The power of its crushing jaws and needlepoint teeth make its mouth a deadly weapon. The sleek, low-slung body of the animal enables it to stealthily approach and surprise any victim.

The weasel's sleek structure, *highly developed muscles and speed make it effective in capturing food and in protecting itself from would-be predators. Because the weasel is such a highly effective killer its victims have been known to become paralyzed and even die from fright when faced with their assailant.*

Under normal conditions *the short-tailed weasel will not attack a man, but if the animal is cornered or pursued, it will boldly retaliate regardless of the size of its opponent. Because of its lightning speed, it is almost impossible to pick up the animal without being bitten.*

WOULD A WEASEL ATTACK A MAN?

Yes. It has been known to attack man. The weasel does not hesitate to use its needle-sharp teeth when man interferes by coming between it and the food it seeks.

On one occasion a man unknowingly interfered with the weasel's search for prey, and the determined animal lunged toward him. Surprised by the attack, the man tried to grab the animal, but the weasel clamped its teeth into the man's thumb. His attempts to dislodge the tenacious grip of the weasel were to no avail. Until it was killed, the weasel could not be removed.

WHAT IS THE MAINSTAY OF THE WEASEL'S DIET?

In regions where there is an abundance of mice and rats the weasel's diet consists almost entirely of them. It is not uncommon for the weasel to subdue prey as large as a rabbit, chicken or goose.

The weasel is carnivorous, eating both cold and warm-blooded animals. A nocturnal feeder, it searches open woodland areas, swimming and climbing trees in pursuit of its prey. Farmers are aware of the destruction a weasel can effect among their poultry and take great precaution to ensure that they do not gain entrance.

WHAT IS THE SMALLEST HOLE A WEASEL CAN FIT THROUGH?

A weasel is capable of slipping through a hole as narrow as one inch in diameter.

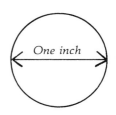

Could a weasel fit through this hole?

Piercing incisors and bone-crushing molars *allow the weasel to make quick work of its prey. The heavy bone structure of the jaw, sheathed in strong muscles, enables the weasel to establish and maintain a vice-like grip which is released only in death.*

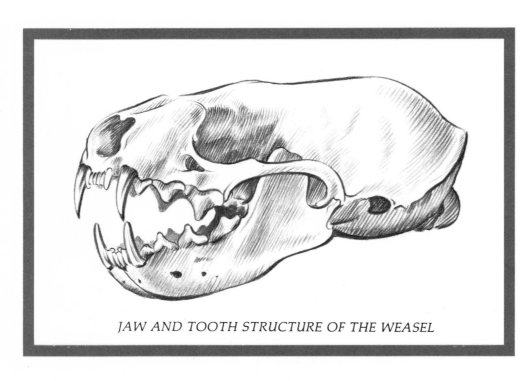

JAW AND TOOTH STRUCTURE OF THE WEASEL

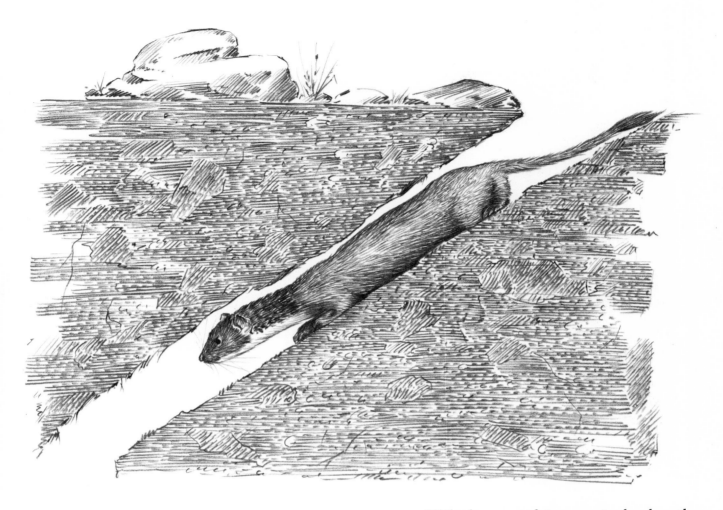

While larger predators must abandon the chase *once their quarry reach the safety of their burrow, the weasel with its sleek design is not hampered by size and continues pursuit.*

DOES THE WEASEL EVER GET STUCK GOING THROUGH A HOLE?

If a weasel is able to slip its head through an opening, it is assured that it will have no difficulty in getting the rest of its body through as well. If its head does not fit the opening, it will forego the attempt. Because the weasel is able to squeeze through such small spaces, few burrowing rodents are safe from its assault.

IS AN ERMINE RELATED TO THE WEASEL?

An ermine is a weasel. The name ermine refers to the weasel when it is in its winter's white coat. In late autumn when leaves begin to fall and rain turns to snow, the weasel sheds its summer coat of light brown and replaces it with lustrous white fur. The white coat helps the animal to blend with its surroundings, giving it an added advantage against predators during the lean winter months. The coat returns to its brown shade in early spring.

Centuries ago, use of the ermine was reserved for nobility. Members of royalty used the fur to accent their robes. Characteristic black flecks which dotted the trim were taken from the tail of the pelt.

Weasel, looking through knothole *to determine whether or not passage is wide enough.*

ABOVE *A golden eagle was found dead upon the shore. Close examination revealed a weasel embedded in its neck. Apparently the eagle, which was considerably larger, underestimated the ferocity and persistence of its foe.*

DOES A WEASEL EVER WALK AWAY FROM A FIGHT?

Once the weasel is engaged in a conflict, it will either persist until its opponent is subdued or it will be killed. The weasel does not consider retreat as an option.

DOES THE WEASEL USE ITS EYES TO HUNT?

Although the eyes are employed to a certain extent, the weasel does not depend on them as much as its nose. The sense of smell is predominantly relied on in hunting.

WHAT MAKES THE WEASEL SUCH A SUCCESSFUL HUNTER?

The weasel's endurance and determination ensure it a high degree of success. By sniffing the air with its sensitive nose, it will pick up the slightest scent, whether fresh or old. With this scent, the weasel begins a tireless pursuit of its quarry and doggedly unravels the trail. Its single-minded tracking has occasioned it to run past a downwind rabbit in clear view while following the scent of a trail which was made earlier.

BELOW *The weasel is benefited by the change in its coat from a pure white in winter, blending with the snow, to a golden brown during warmer months for a camouflage against its summer habitat.*

HOW DOES SCRIPTURE ILLUSTRATE COURAGE IN RESPONDING TO DANGER?

All that separated the two armies were two steep cliffs and a valley. One group, though, could hardly be called an army. For years the nation was not allowed to have any swords or spears. Even the sharpening of farm implements had been done by the nation that controlled them, whom they now faced in battle.

The prince beckoned to his companion, and they slipped away from the pathetic group of six hundred frightened and ill-equipped soldiers. They crept down the slope and looked toward the mighty army camped on the opposite cliff.

He said to his companion, "Let us attack the enemy. It may be that the Lord will work for us. For there is no restraint with the Lord to save by many or by few." His companion eagerly agreed. "I will be with you in whatever you want to do."

They devised a plan which involved a signal from the Lord. Then they exposed their presence to the enemy. The guards on the opposite cliff mockingly shouted, "Well! Our enemy is coming out of their holes. Come on up here and we will show you a thing or two."

That was the invitation they were waiting for! They both scrambled over the top of the cliff. After reaching the top, they sprang to their feet—one with a sword and the other with a shield to protect him. Their strength and fury so surprised their enemy that, within a few minutes, twenty of them had fallen within a half-acre of ground.

Then God shook the ground with a great earthquake. Those in the tents who were enjoying their plunder thought a mighty army was approaching. They rushed out of their tents in confusion, and in their haste they mistook each other for the enemy. The six hundred men, without the two who had precipitated the confusion, rushed to the edge of the cliff when they heard the rumbling. They were astonished to witness the slaughter taking place among their enemies.

Eagerly their leader gave a precise command, and they rushed in to join the battle. By the end of the day a great and unexpected victory was theirs. But the rejoicing of that victory soon turned to grief. The courageous hero of the day inadvertently acted in a way which placed him under the curse of the leader of the army.

The prince, although acting courageously, had done so without his father's knowledge, and so missed hearing a special command which was given in front of the other men. The king was bound by his word to punish this action and reaffirmed the curse, "Though it be my son who transgressed my command, he shall surely die." The heroic effort was marred. Years later the curse was fulfilled when Jonathan was killed with his father, Saul, in battle against the same enemy.

From I Samuel 14:1-46

After years of humiliating subjection to the powerful Philistines, Israel initiated their revolt for freedom under the leadership of their first king, Saul, and his son Jonathan. But things were not going according to plan. Saul's original army of three thousand had been reduced to six hundred. The other men were either in hiding, had fled the country, or had been forced to serve in the Philistine army. Only a deep ravine with steep sides separated the small, poorly-armed Israelite army from the powerful and sophisticated Philistines.

The Gorge at Michmash *which Jonathan so courageously scaled separated the Philistine and Israelite armies.*

A COURAGEOUS ATTACK

Jonathan and his armor bearer decided to single-handedly attack the outpost guard at the main pass across the ravine. Not believing that only two men would stand up against the mighty Philistines, the soldiers who were guarding must have been deceived into thinking that the entire Israelite army had scaled the cliff. At this time the Lord intervened with an earthquake and implanted fear in the hearts of the Philistines. Their courage melted away, and they left their defenses in a wild and unorganized retreat.

CONFUSION DEFEATS THE ENEMY

When Saul's watchmen reported what had happened, his soldiers quickly crossed the undefended pass in pursuit of the retreating Philistines. At the same time Israelites who had been in hiding and those who had been drafted into the enemy army rallied behind Saul against the Philistines. There was such a state of confusion that even the Philistine soldiers started fighting among themselves.

AN UNREASONABLE OATH BRINGS DEATH

Determined to capitalize on this sudden and unexpected turn of events, Saul unnecessarily put the people under oath, saying, "Cursed be the man that eateth any food until evening, that I may be avenged on mine enemies." (I Samuel 14:24) Jonathan was not present to hear this command, so when he found honey in the forest later in the day he naturally ate some. When Jonathan heard that his father had forbidden the people to eat anything until sundown he became frustrated. He knew the men were weary after a long day of battle and that they needed energy to continue effectively. What could be a quicker source of energy than honey? By dipping the end of their staffs into the honey they would not even have had to stop. Jonathan recognized that the command designed by his father to strengthen this victory was ironically destined to weaken it.

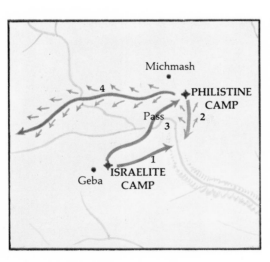

(1) Jonathan and his armorbearer crossed the gorge and (2) repelled the Philistine guards. (3) Saul and his army crossed at Michmash Pass and (4) routed the Philistines from the land.

A SORROWFUL VICTORY

When Saul inquired of the Lord that evening for direction whether or not to continue the battle, the Lord would not answer. Lots were thrown to decide what person was at fault, and to everyone's disappointment the hero of the day was singled out as the offender. Even though Jonathan's offense was unwillful, he still fell under the curse of his father and king. The people refused to allow Saul to carry out the curse against his son and the day ended in despair rather than celebration. What could have been a great victory from the Lord was a personal defeat for Saul and his son Jonathan.

JONATHAN CHARACTER SKETCH

WHY DIDN'T JONATHAN TELL HIS FATHER ABOUT HIS PLAN?

Jonathan was probably convinced that Saul would not have considered approving his daring plan. It would have been a suicidal mission apart from God's supernatural intervention. Saul remembered his son's last raid against the Philistine's garrison in Geba (I Samuel 13:3). That battle only succeeded in rallying the Philistines. As a result, Saul's army had dwindled from three thousand to six hundred (I Samuel 13:2,15) largely through desertions. The Philistines had ten horsemen to each one of Saul's men, and their foot soldiers were like the sand which is on the seashore in abundance (I Samuel 13:5). The last thing Saul would have wanted Jonathan to do was precipitate an attack before he could strengthen his reinforcements.

WAS JONATHAN TESTING GOD OR THE PHILISTINES BEFORE HIS ATTACK?

When the Israelites were thirsty for water at Massah they tested the Lord, saying, "Is the Lord among us, or not?" (Exodus 17:7). To test the Lord in this way was strictly forbidden later by the Mosaic Law (Deuteronomy 6:16). Jonathan was not testing God by demanding a miracle but was cleverly testing his opponent and looking for an indication from the Lord. The guards were surprised and had no idea how many more men were behind Jonathan. They did not know if they were outnumbered or not. When the Philistines refused to approach him, Jonathan and his armor-bearer made their courageous charge and killed about twenty men within a distance of roughly forty yards (I Samuel 14:14).

WHY DID GOD ALLOW JONATHAN TO BE SO SEVERELY REPROVED?

Although Jonathan's courageous act demonstrated a firm trust in the Lord and a strong jealousy for His name, two of his other actions revealed attitudes in his life which God had to reprove. The first is indicated in the short phrase, "But he told not his father." (I Samuel 14:1) Jonathan revealed the same attitude for which Samuel had just rebuked King Saul. He was taking things into his own hands without receiving direction or permission from the one to whom he was responsible. Because he left camp without informing his father, he missed hearing Saul's instruction not to eat until sundown. Even though his disobedience was unintentional he nevertheless fell under the curse (I Samuel 14:24). The other attitude was revealed when he justified himself and publicly denounced his father's judgment in prohibiting the people from eating (I Samuel 14:29,30). He dishonored his own father (cf. Exodus 20:12) and spread seeds of disloyalty and rebellion against the Lord's anointed (cf. II Samuel 1:14-16). The people saw Jonathan's outward courage and spared his life, but God saw his heart and gave his throne to one more worthy than he (I Samuel 13:14; 16:7).

"But Jonathan heard not *when his father charged the people with the oath: wherefore he put forth the end of the rod that was in his hand, and dipped it in an honeycomb, and put his hand to his mouth; and his eyes were en-lightened.*"

JONATHAN

Courage

IS APPLYING THE RESOURCES I HAVE IN CREATIVE WAYS WHEN FACED WITH OVERWHELMING ODDS

LIVING LESSONS ON COURAGE . . .

FROM THE PAGES OF SCRIPTURE

One of the most courageous men who ever lived devised a bold plan that collapsed. He was left with two choices—give up and face death or use the resources he had in a creative way. His astonishing tactic not only changed the course of events but later won the admiration and friendship of his former enemy.

ILLUSTRATED IN THE WORLD OF NATURE

EASTERN HOGNOSE SNAKE *Heterodon platyrhinos*

A gentle and harmless snake that does well in captivity, the eastern hognose is heavily built and measures two to three feet in length. It inhabits sandy, dry and wooded areas and lays approximately twenty-four eggs in the summertime.

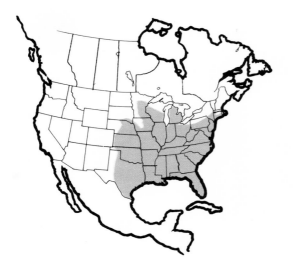

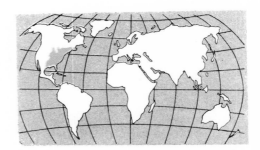

The range and habitat of the eastern hognose snake

COURAGE

HOW DOES THE EASTERN HOGNOSE SNAKE ILLUSTRATE COURAGE IN CREATIVE RESOURCEFULNESS?

As the boys set up their campsite in the woods, the youngest of the group questioned his older companions about Indian lore and the wildlife that might be lurking in the forest. His imagination returned to the many stories he had heard about wild animals.

A few hours later he began searching for firewood and discovered a large, dried out tree that had fallen to the ground during a storm. He busily began to break off branches which would make excellent tinder for their campfire.

Suddenly he heard a fluttering noise beneath him. He stood motionless and listened more carefully, but the sound did not repeat itself. Shrugging his shoulders, he turned back to the tree. Then he heard the noise again. It sounded like a rattlesnake! It appeared to be coming from among the dry leaves on the far side and to the left of the fallen tree—only a few feet away from where he stood.

Lifting a long, heavy branch, he cautiously moved toward the sound. Suddenly he spotted it—a coiled, well-camouflaged snake. It was a thick, three-foot monster with a fierce face. Its tail beat against the leaves as it began its vicious hissing. The upraised head seemed ready to strike as it weaved in the air, mouth open.

Mustering all the courage he could, the boy stepped toward the snake, swung at the deadly-looking creature and grazed its head with the branch. The snake slumped to the ground. It rolled over and lay limp and motionless in the leaves. Surprised at the effectiveness of the blow, the boy cautiously approached it, poked it with his stick and flipped it in the air, testing the lifeless form. Satisfied that it was dead, he ran back to the campsite.

Returning to the clearing, he quickly called his friends, blurting out the story of his valor. Before he had time to finish, they all rushed over to see the vicious snake which the young boy had killed all by himself. When they came to the tree, to the amazement of all, the snake was gone. The boys searched the area around the fallen oak, but no trace of it was found.

Meanwhile, a safe distance away, the bruised hognose snake curled up under another log watching the search. When first faced with the threat of the boy, it had attempted to frighten him away. When that tactic failed, it skillfully feigned the appearance of being dead. As soon as the young boy ran away to tell the others his story, it had slipped away and carefully hid among some leaves, safely concealed away from the encounter.

CHARACTERISTICS AND PHYSICAL FEATURES OF THE EASTERN HOGNOSE SNAKE

When endangered, the hognose snake demonstrates its ability to be courageous with limited resources. The snake is equally bold when searching for food, utilizing its unusual assets in unique ways.

HOW CAN A SNAKE EAT WITHOUT CHEWING ITS FOOD?

As is common with most snakes, the hognose is not equipped with teeth designed to tear and chew its food. Instead the snake must swallow its prey whole and then depend on digestive juices within its stomach to dissolve and use the food it has eaten.

HOW MUCH CAN A SNAKE EAT AT ONE TIME?

If a snake were to kill a rabbit it wouldn't be able to eat it. The rabbit is too large to get into its mouth, and the snake is unable to tear it into smaller, manageable pieces. Its food, therefore, is limited to what it can swallow whole. So the size of its mouth actually determines how large an animal can be eaten.

HOW CAN THE HOGNOSE SNAKE EXPAND ITS MOUTH?

Rather than limiting itself to very small prey, the three-foot snake is equipped with a unique jaw structure which enables it to increase considerably its mouth opening. When the hognose approaches an animal much larger than its mouth, it unhinges its jaw at two points. This disconnects its lower jaw from the base of the skull and expands the mouth cavity.

DOES THE SNAKE HAVE A RUBBER JAW?

The hognose snake does not have a rubber jaw, but it does have an elastic muscle in the front of its mouth. This rubbery muscle connects the two sides of the lower jaw, enabling the snake to expand its mouth much wider than it normally would.

WHAT IS THE PRINCIPAL FOOD OF THE HOGNOSE SNAKE?

The snake eats birds, mice, chipmunks, frogs, salamanders and other snakes. But in particular, it favors the toad.

The hognose snake's diet *encompasses a wide variety of food, but its favorite meal is the toad.*

Closed jaw of the snake

Distended jaw of the snake

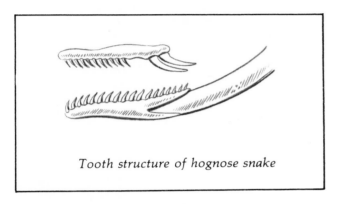

Tooth structure of hognose snake

The teeth of the hognose snake *are designed in such a way that they curve into the mouth, making it virtually impossible for prey to slip out. The snake's saliva chemically breaks down the tissues of the prey so that the solution can be absorbed through the walls of its intestines.*

IS THE TOAD CAPABLE OF DEFENDING ITSELF AGAINST THE SNAKE?

The toad has the ability to inflate its body with air, increasing its size far beyond normal proportions. This defense is usually effective. After capturing a toad, most snakes are forced to release it as the once-small body expands. In contrast, a pair of large curved teeth located in the back of the hognose snake's mouth serves two purposes. First, they puncture the skin, deflating the toad. Then the saliva, which is a digestive agent, seeps into the puncture wound and causes a chemical breakdown and damage to the tissues of its prey.

WHY IS IT ALMOST IMPOSSIBLE TO ESCAPE THE GRIP OF A HOGNOSE?

The hognose snake is equipped with uniquely structured teeth. They are very sharp and curve inward, pointing into the mouth. Once the snake has its mouth around its prey it is very difficult, if not impossible, for it to escape. The curved teeth prevent the victim from slipping back out. Two sides of the lower jaws work independently. Alternately, one side holds the prey and the other works the body farther and farther into the mouth.

HOW DOES THE HOGNOSE SNAKE DISGUISE ITSELF?

The snake has a blotchy, diamond-backed design on its skin of olive, brown, orange and black tones. This pattern blends well with the dry, sandy areas of the hognose's home. Such coloration gives the snake an advantage both offensively when hunting and defensively when avoiding predators. When lying still, the snake is indistinguishable from its background.

HOW DOES IT UTILIZE ITS BODY STRUCTURE IN HUNTING?

With rhythmic, steady movement, the hognose snake glides along the stony surface of the ground. It stealthily approaches its unsuspecting prey lying low against the earth. The snake is able to slip quickly in and out of rocks, burrows and crevices in search of food. With its subtle coloration, low-slung body structure and agile maneuverability the snake is well-suited for hunting.

TOP LEFT *Toad employs a built-in inflation defense making it difficult for the hognose snake to maneuver it into its mouth.*

BOTTOM LEFT *The snake injects venom into the toad, puncturing the air sac and paralyzing the victim.*

146

HOW DID THE SNAKE GET ITS NAME?

The hognose was named because of the strong similarity between its nose and that of a hog. But the nose by which it is identified is not the most important organ to the snake. Instead, the snake depends on its eyes for hunting.

WHAT FUNCTION DOES THE NOSE HAVE IN ADULT LIFE?

In soft or sandy ground, a toad could quickly burrow to safety if pursued by the eastern hognose. Such an escape tactic would be effective were it not for the bony snout of the snake. Using its head as a shovel it digs down after its prey, nullifying one of the toad's defenses.

IS THE HOGNOSE SNAKE POISONOUS TO HUMANS?

The hognose is considered harmless—that is, it does not bring death or serious illness to people. However, the bite of even a harmless snake will cause local damage to the tissue should the snake's saliva be injected into the wound because the digestive qualities of the saliva cause irritation and a degree of swelling.

HOW DOES A HATCHING SNAKE USE ITS HEAD?

An oviparous reptile, the hognose lays eggs which hatch outside its body. After covering them with sand, it leaves the nest and relies on the warmth of the sun to incubate the eggs.

When the egg is ready to hatch, it would be difficult for the snakelet to emerge were it not for the sharp protrusion or "egg tooth" on the end of its nose. This edge cuts through the thick, leathery shell. After it hatches, the snake will lose its special tooth.

CAN THE SNAKE USE ITS TEETH FOR DEFENSIVE PURPOSES?

No. They are positioned too far back in the mouth to be used as weapons.

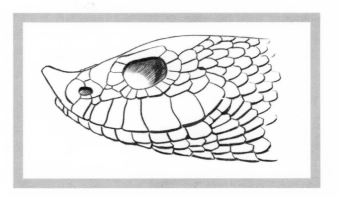

The protrusion on the snout *of the snake is not really its nose but rather a bony structure designed for the purpose of digging. With remarkable skill and speed, the hognose snake is capable of digging out burrowing toads.*

Newly-hatching hognose snakes *freeing themselves from the confines of the leather-like shell. They are aided by a bony cutting device located on the tip of their nose. Once the snakes are free from the egg, this cutting device will gradually disappear.*

The hognose snake's ground-hugging form *and subtle coloration enable it to move quickly, silently and unnoticed through the underbrush as it searches for its prey.*

HOW MANY DIFFERENT WAYS DOES A SNAKE CRAWL?

Very few animals have the task which has befallen the snake; that is, learning to get along without legs. Perhaps it is for this reason more than any other that it has been forced to use the resources it does have in creative ways.

There are four basic ways in which a snake propels itself. Among the larger snakes such as the constrictors, the caterpillar movement is common. The snake moves straight ahead by means of pulling together and then expanding sections of its body.

Snakes which coil their bodies and shoot their head in the direction they plan to travel use the concertina movement. They anchor their head on the ground and pull the rest of their body forward returning to a coiled position for the next forward movement.

A sidewinding movement is characteristic of the rattlesnake which bears its name. It consists of a series of sideward loops. The snake begins by reaching over with its head and holding it to the ground. Then it sends a winding movement through its body which is only touching the ground at two points.

The serpentine movement is the method which the hognose snake uses as well as most other snakes. It involves moving in a forward motion by putting pressure against various objects on the ground and sliding its body against them in a winding motion.

BELOW *Four basic forms of locomotion by which the snake propels itself. The first, the serpentine movement, is the method which the hognose snake uses.*

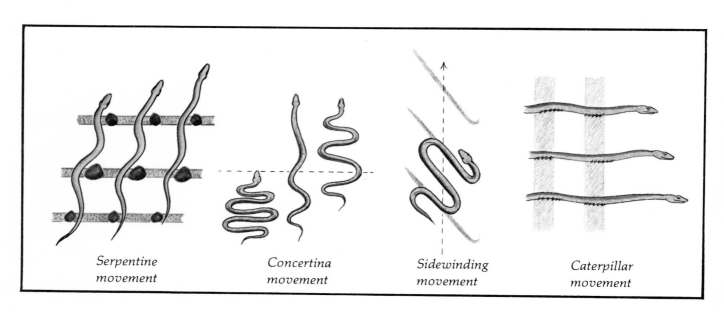

Serpentine movement   Concertina movement   Sidewinding movement   Caterpillar movement

HOW DOES SCRIPTURE ILLUSTRATE COURAGE IN CREATIVE RESOURCEFULNESS?

The small group of men despairingly reviewed the bleak options which were open to them. They could remain where they were. That meant certain death at the hand of their angered and jealous king. They could go to a friendly nation and seek asylum there. That involved a great risk as well. They could hide in the rugged hills. That involved additional dangers. It would require constant vigilance and expose them to their pursuers and to the wild beasts which roamed the region.

There was only one other option, risking death because of their citizenship by going to an unsympathetic foreign nation, a former enemy. It seemed unthinkable and required a great measure of courage, but that was the course of action they chose to take.

The men turned to the west and fled for their lives. When they reached the city, their leader went directly to the king. He was intercepted by officers of the royal court. When he told them who he was, their eyes widened in astonishment and they willingly agreed to take him to King Achish.

As he waited to see the king, he overheard these officers excitedly tell Achish many stories about him from the past. He was amazed that they knew so much about him. As he listened to their words and their tone of voice, he realized the desperate nature of his situation.

This king had more reasons to kill him than the one from which he fled. He had killed their chief warrior in battle and caused them to suffer a massive defeat. In fact, he even had the sword of that great warrior with him.

Fear overtook him. He knew he was helpless to escape. Well-armed soldiers of the king stood all around him, and others were quickly summoned to join them. The officers explained to the king how they could use this unexpected visitor to their own advantage.

Then the leader's courage took a new avenue of expression. When he entered the king's presence he would do something he had never done before. He would do it so well that it would be sure to throw their plans into confusion.

The door opened and he was ushered into the room. Rather than walking in, he staggered to the door post and began to claw at it. His mouth hung open and low, guttural sounds came from his throat. Spittle ran out of his mouth and dribbled down his beard.

Seeing this, the king turned to his shocked officers and angrily rebuked them for mocking him by bringing a madman into his presence. Then he ordered them to take him out and let him go. The tactic had worked! Once outside, he fled to the wilderness.

When King Achish realized the extent of courage and creativity in this young man, he formed a deep friendship with him. He invited him to live under his protection. In later years when this man whose name was David became the king of his own nation, six hundred men from the city of King Achish came to help him in a special time of need.

From I Samuel 21:10 through I Samuel 22:1

Madmen were thought to be possessed *by powerful supernatural spirits. King Achish was afraid to kill David for fear that this spirit would attack him.*

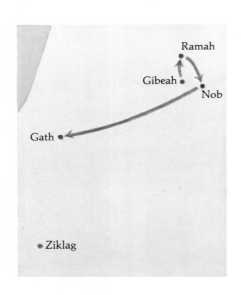

After David's meeting with Jonathan *at Ramah, he refreshed himself at Nob and proceeded to the Philistine city of Gath.*

USING LIMITED RESOURCES IN A CREATIVE WAY, DAVID ESCAPES CAPTURE

Ever since the women chanted, "Saul has slain his thousands, and David his ten thousands," King Saul regarded David with jealous suspicion. God had rejected him from being king and he must have been increasingly convinced that David was the one chosen to be his replacement.

FOUR ATTEMPTS AT MURDER

Four times Saul tried to kill David—twice by hurling his spear at him, once by sending him after the Philistines and once again in his own home. In a fit of rage Saul had even attempted to kill his own son because of his alliance with David. Now David was convinced that these attempts on his life were not temporary fits of uncontrolled jealousy but were part of a plan to prevent him from replacing Saul as king.

THE LAST RESORT

David knew that his life and the lives of his loyal companions were in constant danger as long as they remained within reach of King Saul. The reason David chose to go to the city of Gath is not given in Scripture, but it is almost the last place one would expect him to choose. Gath was one of five Philistine strongholds, the former home of the giant Goliath whom David had killed in addition to many other Philistine soldiers. David was probably hoping that he would be able to convince King Achish that he was a fellow enemy of King Saul and could be received as an ally on that basis.

A DEFENSE OF INSANITY

It seems that news did not travel as fast as David hoped. The Philistines had heard that he had become a national hero because of his exploits against them, but they were not aware of his disfavor with King Saul. Realizing that his plan was going to fail, he ingeniously feigned insanity. By so doing he removed himself as a military threat in the eyes of the king and lost his appeal as a captive to kill for revenge. The king wanted no part of a madman and ordered his immediate release.

A BENEFICIAL ALLIANCE WITH THE ENEMY

Years later when King Achish was convinced of the great hostility between Saul and David, he confidently welcomed him into his city with his band of six hundred men. He was impressed with David's former exhibition of courage and creativity and hoped to use his knowledge of the land and customs of Israel in his war against Saul. David had placed himself in a very awkward position, but with the Lord's help he lived out his exile in safety, avoided conflict with his own people and even protected his homeland from foreign raiders. At the same time he learned the land and culture of the nation of Philistia—an understanding that would be of great help when he became king of Israel in God's proper time.

150

DAVID AND KING ACHISH CHARACTER SKETCH

WHY DIDN'T DAVID OVERTHROW KING SAUL RATHER THAN RUN?

David would not lift his hand against the Lord's anointed (cf. I Samuel 24:6; 26:8-11). It would not have been completely presumptuous for David to rebel against Saul at this time. The Lord had already rejected Saul and chosen David as the new king (I Samuel 16:1,13). David had become a national hero by defeating the Philistine giant. He was the commander of a thousand men and all the nation loved him (I Samuel 18:13,16). Furthermore, he could have made a convincing case that Saul was mentally unfit to rule (I Samuel 16:14-16). But David was not impatient in waiting for the Lord's perfect timing. He was not willing to force the Lord's will by doing it in his own way as Saul had done (I Samuel 13:11-14).

WAS DAVID BETRAYING HIS OWN PEOPLE BY SURRENDERING TO ONE OF THEIR ENEMIES?

David's intentions in submitting to Achish, the Philistine king of Gath, were far from traitorous. His strategy was revealed when he successfully accomplished the same plan years later. After winning the confidence of King Achish, he obtained control of the city of Ziklag. From there he launched raids against the enemies of Saul. By warring against a mutual enemy of Israel and Achish and giving him part of the spoil, he successfully contributed to his own nation's protection (I Samuel 27:8-12).

WAS IT COWARDICE RATHER THAN COURAGE FOR DAVID TO ACT INSANE?

David had already been anointed by Samuel to be the next king. The circumstances which he now faced did not warrant laying down his life. He weighed the alternatives of his perilous position. Overhearing the guard's conversation, he realized that if he maintained his pride and dignity and was taken prisoner as a famous war hero, his fate would be certain death at the hands of the Philistines. On the other hand, if he were willing to humble himself and feign insanity, David knew that they would not kill him for fear of reprisal from the evil spirits which supposedly indwelled the insane. He therefore took this humbling but creative role in order that he might fulfill the mission which God had in store for him.

"And David arose, and fled *that day for fear of Saul, and went to Achish the king of Gath.*"

DAVID

Courage

IS FOLLOWING DIFFICULT INSTRUCTIONS IN THE FACE OF DANGER

LIVING LESSONS ON COURAGE . . .

FROM THE PAGES OF SCRIPTURE

God called him "a great and honorable man," and because of his high position he was more accustomed to giving commands than receiving them. But God used an insurmountable problem and a faithful prophet to teach him to follow difficult instructions.

ILLUSTRATED IN THE WORLD OF NATURE

THE WOOD DUCK *Aix sponsa*

An inhabitant of freshwater marshes and swamps, the drake wood duck is one of North America's most brilliantly colored waterfowl. This eighteen-inch migratory bird makes its nest in the hollow of a tree near a body of water. Its lifespan is approximately eleven years.

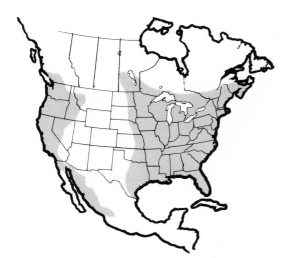
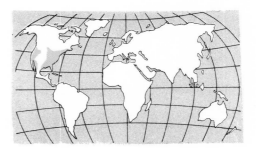

The range and habitat of the wood duck

COURAGE

HOW DOES THE WOOD DUCK ILLUSTRATE COURAGE IN FOLLOWING DIFFICULT INSTRUCTIONS?

The female wood duck perched motionless in the four-inch opening of her tree nest. Beneath her in the rotted hollow of the oak, six day-old ducklings huddled together. Once again her alert eyes scanned the landscape which she had investigated carefully that morning. She studied the tall grass for any movement which would betray the presence of a mink or raccoon. She listened to the water of the nearby pond for the splash of a large turtle or the croak of a bullfrog. She searched the sky for a circling hawk or owl.

Satisfied that the area was free from immediate danger, she fluttered to the ground. Then she looked up to the small opening forty feet above her and quickly gave a signal.

There was an immediate response from above. The ducklings jumped up and scrambled toward the opening above them using the claws on their feet and the hooks at the end of their bills to maintain a foothold. When they reached the opening, they took their first glimpse at a new world. Far below their mother waited.

They could not yet fly, but their mother urged them to jump. This would be a huge leap—the equivalent of a man jumping about 400 feet, but it had to be done. It would determine whether the ducklings would live or die.

The first duckling pushed its body out from the perch and leaped. Its webbed feet and downy wings helped break the impact of the fall. Seconds later it safely bounced on the soft grass at the base of the tree. Then it wobbled awkwardly to its mother and waited for the rest of the ducks to follow. One after another they reached the opening and jumped down. As each duckling descended, the mother increased the tempo of her call.

Within a short time five huddled close to their mother. She continued urging and calling to the last duckling remaining in the tree. Finally, when she felt she could no longer expose the vulnerable ducklings to danger, she gave one last call and then walked away with her young to the safety of the nearby brood pond.

The five that obeyed the difficult instruction had a good chance of survival. Death would come to the one who either could not or would not jump.

CHARACTERISTICS AND PHYSICAL FEATURES OF THE WOOD DUCK

The day-old ducklings courageously obeyed the command of their mother by making a leap which could have proved fatal. The female's thorough preparation and awareness of possible danger made it easier for them to follow these difficult instructions.

WHAT IS THE MORTALITY RATE OF A WOOD DUCK BROOD?

It is estimated that of an average family of six to eight offspring, only half will reach maturity. For this reason the parent birds take every precaution to assure a successful hatch.

WHERE DOES A WOOD DUCK LOOK FOR A NEST SITE?

The wood duck most often makes its nest in wooded areas near a river or quiet lake; however, this is not an absolute rule. They have been known to make their nests great distances from bodies of water. One precaution the wood duck usually takes is ensuring that the area in front of the nest is clear from obstructions which might injure the departing young.

WHAT IS UNIQUE ABOUT THE WOOD DUCK'S NESTING HABITS?

The wood duck is one of the few of its species which builds its nest in the hollow of a tree. The male will accompany the female wood duck in scouting out various cavities in trees. These have usually been created by woodpeckers, squirrels or decay. The male does not inspect the nest but remains at watch outside the area while the female surveys each location's possibilities. She will check and recheck many holes and is very particular about making her final choice.

Male stands by as female inspects potential nesting site.

Young wood duck heeding the call *of its mother as it prepares to jump to the ground from a high tree nest.*

SEQUENCE OF HATCHING EGG

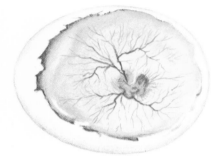

Developing embryo

Duckling breaks through shell with the aid of sharp "egg tooth"

When the hole is large enough, the duckling uses its body to crack the shell

Duckling dries off after emerging

WHAT REQUIREMENTS DETERMINE WHETHER OR NOT A NEST IS SUCCESSFUL?

Two factors which determine the survival of a brood are the height of the hollow from the ground and the depth of the recess itself.

Predation is a major threat to the survival of the ducklings. Because of this the nest must not be too low to the ground, accessible to animals such as raccoons or weasels which might feed on the eggs.

In addition to proper height from the ground, the wood ducks require a specific depth for the hollow itself. The deeper the hollow, the greater the difficulty the frail ducklings will have in scaling the wall. But the hollow cannot be so shallow that the eggs are exposed to predators. If the female is able to successfully raise her brood, she may return to the same nesting site year after year.

HOW HIGH WILL A WOOD DUCK BUILD ITS NEST?

Wood ducks have been known to build their nests in tree hollows as high as sixty feet or as low as five feet from the ground. The average is usually a moderate ten to twenty feet above ground level.

HOW DOES A FEMALE APPROACH HER NEST?

The wood duck is cautious not to reveal the location of its nest and will very seldom fly directly to it. Instead it lands by a nearby tree, surveying the area for possible danger. Only after satisfying itself that the area is free from would-be attackers will it return to the nest.

WHY CAN ALL THE WOOD DUCK'S EGGS HATCH ON THE SAME DAY?

Once the nesting site has been selected, the female begins plucking down feathers from her breast, forming a soft insulated area for as many as twelve eggs. She lays one egg a day. After an egg is laid, she carefully covers it and returns the next day to lay another. The day after the last egg is laid, she begins incubation. In this way she ensures that the eggs all hatch at approximately the same time.

DOES A MOTHER WOOD DUCK TALK TO HER EGGS?

Two to three days before the ducklings break out of their creamy-white shells, the female does something unusual. She listens for the faint "peeping" inside of the eggs, and she communicates back to them. This ritual familiarizes the ducklings with the sound of her voice even before they hatch.

DOES IT MAKE ANY DIFFERENCE WHETHER SHE TALKS TO THEM OR NOT?

Experiments have been conducted to determine whether or not the communication a female has with her eggs is really important. In cases when communication was not established, the ducklings would either not respond to her direction or would require greater time and coaxing to follow her commands.

HOW DOES THE DUCKLING BREAK ITS TOUGH SHELL?

The female will not assist her young in breaking out of their shells; however, the duckling is equipped with a sharp protrusion on the end of its bill for this purpose. This protrusion is known as an "egg tooth" and the unhatched duck uses it to scrape against the shell. Beginning at the large end of the egg, it continues chipping until the hole is enlarged. Then it uses its body to crack the surface. When it emerges its wet feathers are dried in the air.

HOW SOON AFTER HATCHING WILL THE DUCKLINGS LEAVE THE NEST?

Usually the young ducklings leave the nest within twenty-four hours after hatching. The female will not give the signal to leave, though, unless the area is free from danger. She waits as long as necessary to guarantee their safety.

Female perched at the entrance *of her nest, scouting the land for possible enemies that might endanger her young on their way to the brood pond.*

Young ducklings *struggling to climb the steep interior wall of the nest will use their egg tooth protrusion and tiny claws to reach the opening.*

Wood ducks require a body of water *at least ten acres in size in which to rear their young.*

Above: *Proper cover from aquatic plants such as the arrowhead is necessary for protection.*
Below: *An adequate food supply including pond weed, nuts and insects is essential in the choice of a brood site.*

Wood ducks in direct flight *as they wing their way in family groups from the brooding area to their warmer winter quarters.*

WHAT IS A BROOD POND?

Before the ducklings leave the nest their mother will have chosen a pond or lake in which to rear her young. The area is usually at least ten acres in size with sufficient food for the family and adequate cover protection. Water life such as arrowhead plants, cattails and reeds are used as a refuge by the wood ducks.

WHAT DANGERS CAN DUCKLINGS EXPECT TO FACE?

Brood ponds can be up to a mile away from nesting sites. The young duckling's journey to the brood pond initiates it into a world of potential danger. It will need to be aware of such enemies as bullfrogs, turtles, snakes, owls, hawks, mink and raccoon. Throughout the training period of several months, the ducklings stay close to their mother as she remains in continual communication with them, guiding and instructing.

HOW DOES SCRIPTURE ILLUSTRATE COURAGE IN FOLLOWING DIFFICULT INSTRUCTIONS?

He was a very influential man, accustomed to giving orders rather than taking them. But when he discovered that he had a desperate problem which he could not solve, he was open to any kind of counsel.

The advice he received resulted in a long trip for a possible solution. The power of his position and the favor he had with the king were obvious in the elegant procession that pulled up to a small house on the outskirts of that foreign city.

He climbed out of his royal chariot and knocked at the door, expecting the prophet who lived there to go through elaborate religious procedures to solve the problem. Then he planned to show his appreciation by giving him twenty thousand dollars worth of silver, sixty thousand dollars worth of gold and ten handsome suits of clothing.

The door opened and Gehazi, the prophet's servant, stood there. "I have instructions from the prophet for you," he said. "If you follow them completely, all traces of your problem will vanish."

He was greatly disappointed and offended that the prophet had not met him in person, and he was sure that following these instructions would only worsen his condition.

He angrily climbed back into his chariot, shouted at the horses and rode away in a rage. As he began the long journey home, his assistants reasoned with him. "If the prophet had told you to do some great thing, you would have done it. Why not follow the simple thing he has instructed you to do?"

The man knew that the instructions were difficult to follow because they spelled death to his pride and disregard for his power and prestige. But after reconsidering the situation, he turned his chariot around and carried them out.

To his amazement and overwhelming joy, they worked! Excitedly he drove back to the prophet's house, urging him to take the gifts he had brought. But the prophet refused because the Lord had given him instructions not to take the gifts. He then affirmed his belief in the God of the prophet and returned to his home.

The great dignitary, Naaman, was humbled by washing himself in a muddy, filthy river, but because he was willing to follow difficult instructions which seemed contradictory to common sense, he was healed.

From II Kings 5:1-19

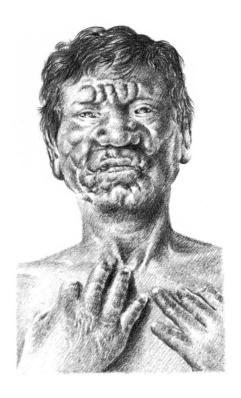

Leprosy is a long-lasting, *frequently painful and fatal disease when left untreated. The advanced state leaves grotesque patches of spongy, tumor-like swellings on the face and body. Today's effective medicines were not available to Naaman's physicians.*

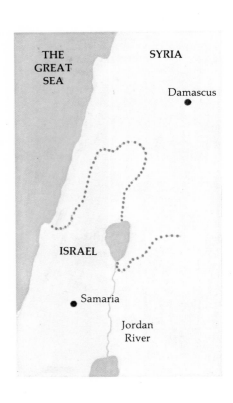

THE GREAT SEA

SYRIA

Damascus

ISRAEL

Samaria

Jordan River

Although neighbors, Syria and Israel *were seldom friendly and border wars were frequent. Naaman's visit to the king was met with suspicion and alarm.*

162

A DIFFICULT INSTRUCTION WHICH NAAMAN HAD TO FOLLOW IN THE FACE OF DANGER

The Lord had used the nation of Syria to discipline the nation of Israel for their continued rebellion against Him. Naaman, the captain of the Syrian army, had been one of the men God used to reprove the people.

GOD USES AN ENEMY TO PUNISH HIS PEOPLE

Naaman was a highly repected man because of his central role in the previous Syrian victories over King Ahab of Israel and King Jehoshaphat of Judah. He had led successful raiding parties into Northern Israel and brought back much spoil to the Syrians. Because of his military success over the nation of Israel, it would have been easy for Naaman to believe that the Syrian god Rimmon was more powerful than the God of Israel. God wanted to show Naaman the real reason for his success.

A GENERAL DEFEATED BY LEPROSY

In order to teach Naaman, the Lord afflicted him with leprosy, an incurable disease which eventually would have cost him his career, his respect and his life. When Naaman heard about the prophet of God in Israel who supposedly had power to heal, he could have refused to humble himself by seeking help. He decided instead on a compromise. He would go on the condition that he maintain his dignity. He had no intention of begging and took ten talents of silver, six thousand shekels of gold, and ten changes of clothes.

THE HUMBLING PRESCRIPTION

When Elisha merely sent out his messenger who told Naaman to wash himself seven times in the Jordan River he became furious. He had taken this journey prepared to pay for a great exhibition, not to humble himself before what he considered to be another foreign god. Naaman may have even thought that Elisha was mocking him by telling him to wash in the turbid Jordan as opposed to the water of Syria's beautiful Abanah River which was clear and transparent.

A SERVANT LEADS A GENERAL

Finally, the objectivity of Naaman's servant convinced him to submit to the prophet's instructions. When he did his flesh was restored like the flesh of a little child, and he was clean. When Elisha refused to accept Naaman's very generous present, he learned that there was no God in all the earth but in Israel, and that the God of Israel neither required work nor accepted money for his mercy (cf. Ephesians 2:8,9; Titus 3:5-7).

NAAMAN CHARACTER SKETCH

WAS IT DANGEROUS FOR NAAMAN TO VISIT THE KING OF ISRAEL WITH SUCH A REQUEST?

Israel and Syria had been enemies for years. During the previous reign of Israel's King Ahab, Ben-hadad of Syria provoked him to war and one hundred thousand Syrian foot soldiers were killed in one day (I Kings 20:29). In an attempt to recapture the city of Ramoth-gilead, Ahab was defeated by the Syrians and died in battle (I Kings 22:34,35). Jewish tradition states that on this occasion it was Naaman who drew his bow at random and struck Ahab in a joint of the armor (Josephus Antiquities viii 15.5; cf. II Kings 5:1). Naaman was responsible for leading raiding parties into the land of Israel and bringing back captives to be used as Syrian slaves (II Kings 5:2). Since the prophets of the land were subject to their rulers, Naaman's request for healing had to be directed to the King of Israel. His unreasonable request to be healed from an incurable disease could have been interpreted by the Israeli king as a provocation to war (II Kings 5:7; cf. I Kings 20:7-9). If the prophet Elisha had not rebuked the king and called for Naaman, it is possible that a war would have been precipitated.

WHY DIDN'T ELISHA DEAL DIRECTLY WITH A MAN AS IMPORTANT AS NAAMAN?

The Lord not only desired to cure Naaman of his leprosy, but He desired to cure him of his pride as well. Unaware that his former accomplishments were from the Lord (II Kings 5:1), Naaman had become a very proud man. He did not approach Elisha humbly but as an important captain in the Syrian army (II Kings 5:9). He regarded Elisha, a prophet of the Lord, as his inferior when he said, "... he will surely come out to me." The "to me" is in an emphatic position meaning "to a person like me." (II Kings 5:11) His refusal to follow Elisha's directive indicates that he was not used to humbling himself before another's instructions (II Kings 5:11,12). To humble Naaman the Lord arranged for him to be afflicted with leprosy, directed to a solution by his servant girl, treated in a manner uncommon for a man of his position, and forced to wash in a muddy, foreign river. The treatment was effective and Naaman learned that "God resisteth the proud, but giveth grace unto the humble." (James 4:6)

HOW WAS NAAMAN USED AS AN EXAMPLE TO THE ENTIRE NATION OF ISRAEL?

When Jesus was teaching in the synagogue at Nazareth, one of the examples He used was that of Naaman the Syrian. He told His people that there were many lepers in Israel in the time of Elisha the prophet, but only Naaman was cleansed (Luke 4:27). The inference is that the Israeli lepers were too proud to humble themselves before the Lord as Naaman finally did. Jesus went on to warn them that if they would not receive Him, he would leave them for those outside of the nation of Israel—like Naaman—who were willing to receive Him.

"And Elisha sent a messenger *unto him, saying, Go and wash in the Jordan seven times, and thy flesh shall come again to thee, and thou shalt be clean."*

NAAMAN

Courage

IS CONFRONTING AN OPPONENT WITH THE CONFIDENCE THAT I WILL ULTIMATELY SUCCEED

LIVING LESSONS ON COURAGE . . .

FROM THE PAGES OF SCRIPTURE

Because he had unwavering confidence in the Lord and in his ability to use two skills, one young man was able to courageously face an opponent who had terrified and immobilized an entire army.

ILLUSTRATED IN THE WORLD OF NATURE

THE STRIPED SKUNK *Mephitis mephitis*

A nocturnal hunter of the woods and meadows which it inhabits, the striped skunk attains a length of 24-30 inches. In early spring the female gives birth to three to five young in an underground den or log which she has lined with vegetation.

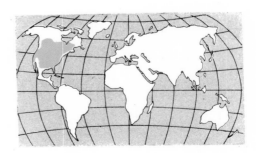

The range and habitat of the striped skunk

COURAGE

HOW DOES THE STRIPED SKUNK ILLUSTRATE COURAGE IN ITS CONFIDENCE OF VICTORY?

Two wounded and weary soldiers stumbled into a clearing as dawn began to brighten the sky. The shoddily clad men had escaped from the enemy's encampment, and they were now within a few days' journey to freedom.

Worn out from battle, imprisonment and a two-day chase by a Union patrol, the men were near exhaustion. Now they needed to rest. Beyond the next wooded ridge the fugitives spotted a small clearing and an old, weather-beaten barn. The barn would make an excellent place to sleep, and it could also serve as a hideout from the Union patrol which was in pursuit.

Approaching warily, they entered the barn, pulled themselves up to a pile of hay, and concealed themselves in the damp, musty straw as well as they could. Their quarters were crowded by an unusual abundance of field mice which scurried along the floor, feeding on remnant grain. After several hours of restless sleep they were startled by a noise. Both men instinctively reached for the one musket which they had managed to grab during their escape. Looking in the direction of the noise, they saw a family of skunks wander into the barn. The soldiers breathed a sigh of relief.

This was the friendliest sight they had seen for a long time. The two men had come from the farmlands of Tennessee and knew the ways of skunks. They remained motionless so they would not startle the visitors. Then quietly they began talking to them. The skunks looked at them curiously and then resumed their search for mice.

Several minutes later, as they lay amused by the skunks, they heard the dreaded sound of the Union patrol. As the hoof beats grew louder, one of the soldiers had an idea. He knew that the skunks would not be intimidated by the patrol because of their confidence in their effective weapon. He also realized that if he could get the skunks to go out of the barn when the soldiers arrived, then they might possibly turn the patrol away. This would mean escaping inevitable recapture. He knew that the skunks' weapon might be more effective than the one shot they could get off with their ball and cap musket.

As the horses of the Union patrol stopped outside of the barn, the soldier nudged his partner and motioned him to be silent. He searched among the hay for a mouse, grabbed it and threw it toward the opening of the door. The stunned mouse lay there. The skunks spotted it and began pursuing it. The wounded soldiers held their breath.

A long and tense moment passed. Finally there came that reassuring commotion—the sound of the Union men noisily and quickly trying to get themselves and their horses out of range of the skunks. Their commotion frightened the skunks into positioning themselves to spray. The men quickly mounted their horses and rode away. Relieved, the men flopped back against the straw with a sigh. They had been saved by an unexpected friend in enemy territory.

CHARACTERISTICS AND PHYSICAL FEATURES OF THE STRIPED SKUNK

The Confederate soldiers were quick to rely on the skunk's effective weapon. The powerful potency of its scent glands lends confidence to the skunk which is reflected in its bold and fearless lifestyle.

HOW MANY KINDS OF SKUNKS ARE THERE?

On the North American continent there are four species of skunk—the hooded skunk, the hognose skunk, the spotted skunk, and the striped skunk. Of the four species, the striped is the most widely distributed.

WHAT DOES THE SKUNK EAT?

The eating habits of the skunk are of great value to the farmer. It consumes large quantities of mice, rats, chipmunks, shrews and many harmful insects such as squash bugs, grasshoppers, and potato beetles. The skunk also feeds on carrion—the carcasses of larger animals such as squirrels or woodchucks supplement its diet.

DOES THE CARNIVOROUS SKUNK EAT FRUITS AND VEGETABLES?

Yes. Thirty percent of the skunk's food consists of vegetable matter. Wild plums, grapes, blackberries and cherries are consumed during the summer months. In winter, the skunk feeds on grass, buds, and remnant grain.

In a warning position, *the spotted skunk dances on its two front feet, threatening to discharge its potent spray. If the threat were to actualize, the skunk would drop to all four paws before releasing its weapon. The spotted skunk is a North American cousin of the striped skunk. This agile member of the family will even climb trees if pursued.*

169

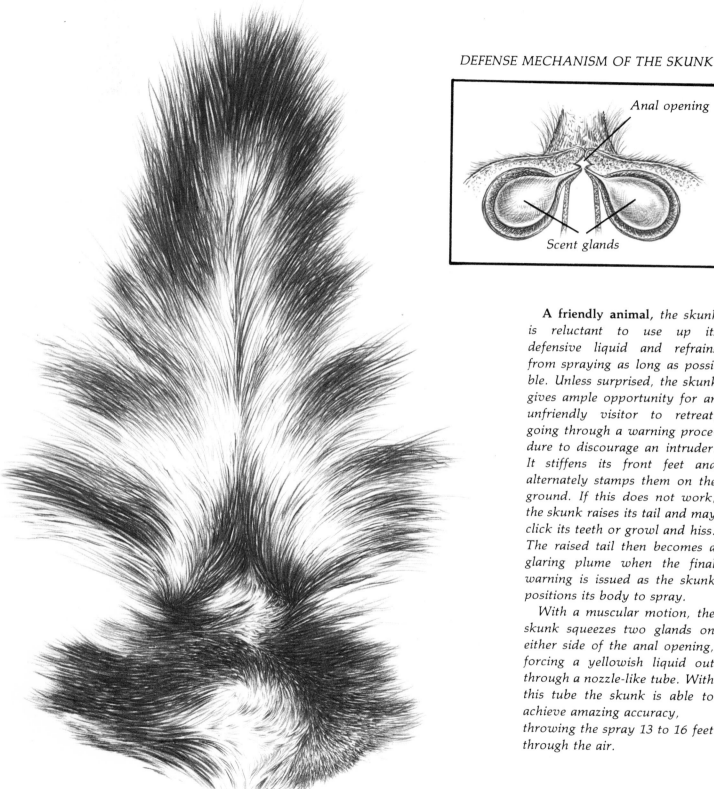

DEFENSE MECHANISM OF THE SKUNK

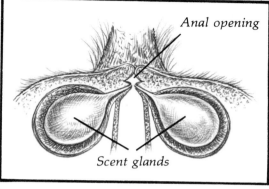

Anal opening

Scent glands

A friendly animal, *the skunk is reluctant to use up its defensive liquid and refrains from spraying as long as possible. Unless surprised, the skunk gives ample opportunity for an unfriendly visitor to retreat, going through a warning procedure to discourage an intruder. It stiffens its front feet and alternately stamps them on the ground. If this does not work, the skunk raises its tail and may click its teeth or growl and hiss. The raised tail then becomes a glaring plume when the final warning is issued as the skunk positions its body to spray.*

With a muscular motion, the skunk squeezes two glands on either side of the anal opening, forcing a yellowish liquid out through a nozzle-like tube. With this tube the skunk is able to achieve amazing accuracy, throwing the spray 13 to 16 feet through the air.

The plumed tail of the striped skunk *must be in an upright position in order for it to emit its scent. The skunk is very careful not to contaminate its own fur with the smelly liquid.*

DOES THE SKUNK HAVE DIFFICULTY IN SECURING ITS FOOD?

Securing its live food does not come as easily for the skunk as it does for its carnivorous relatives. The skunk is not swift-footed so it is unable to chase down its intended victim. Instead, it digs out nesting mice and insects with its claws. Another method it employs is that of slowly stalking or even patiently waiting for its prey. Once the victim reaches striking range, the skunk quickly pounces to secure its meal.

WHAT IS THE TEMPERAMENT OF A SKUNK?

The skunk is really a friendly animal, and it doesn't like to use its spray unless it has to. It peacefully goes about its business with little or no concern for an enemy. Because of its docile personality, skunks have made excellent pets.

HOW ACCURATE IS THE AIM OF THE SKUNK?

The skunk is not entirely without its predators, especially during a time when food is scarce. When molested, the skunk is able to look its opponent in the eye and swing its body around at the same time. With tail raised it protrudes a tube out through the anal opening, aiming for the eyes of its enemy. The skunk is amazingly accurate from distances of thirteen to sixteen feet.

WHAT EFFECT DOES THE SPRAY HAVE?

The nauseous yellow spray penetrates the fur of an animal, and only time will remove this foul odor. But of greater detriment to the animal is the burning sting of the eyes, causing the victim discomfort for hours. Temporary blindness may even result. When this liquid reaches a human eye, it causes equal discomfort which may be relieved by bathing in clean, lukewarm water.

Occasionally a young and inexperienced predator such as this young bobcat mistakenly regards the skunk as a possible meal. The consequences of such an encounter are a lasting reminder that this striped animal is to be treated with caution and respect.
ABOVE *Skunk warns the young bobcat by assuming a ready position.*
RIGHT *Skunk ready to release powerful fluid.*
BELOW *Bobcat in agony as it tries to wipe eyes and fur clean of nauseous smell.*

WHAT ARE THE NATURAL ENEMIES OF THE SKUNK?

The skunk's weapon is effective against most would-be predators. Two enemies, though, which are undaunted by the odor are the barred and horned owls. The scent seems to have no effect on these birds, and they consume the skunk with great relish.

DOES THE SKUNK HAVE A PERMANENT HOME?

The skunk is on the move most of the year, making a home wherever it can. It may cover up to five or six miles on its nightly hunting expeditions. In the morning it finds a suitable residence and beds down for its sleep. When winter comes, the skunk locates a den which it can use for three to four months, during which time the female will raise her young. Born with their ears and eyes sealed shut, the cubs will neither be able to see, hear nor use their defense mechanism until they are a month old.

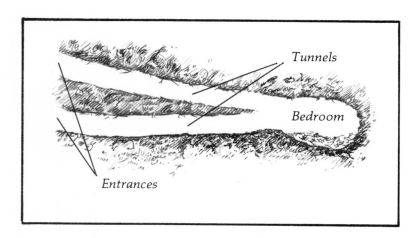

Before the heavy snows begin, the skunk looks for a permanent winter residence. It either uses another animal's abandoned den or digs its own. Two tunnels six to twelve feet in length converge two feet underground in the bed-chamber which is lined with leaves and grass. Once the skunk is in the den for the winter it plugs the holes to lock out the cold.

172

HOW DOES SCRIPTURE ILLUSTRATE COURAGE IN CONFIDENCE OF VICTORY?

It would have been easy for the young shepherd to become discouraged. He was the youngest of eight boys and had been given a responsibility which none of his older brothers wanted.

Not only did his job require constant exposure to the heat of the day and the cold of the night, but if he lost even one of the sheep under his care he faced the displeasure of his father and the scorn of his brothers. Rather than becoming discouraged, though, this young man turned his job into a special classroom, learning two skills which brought success to his life and instilled in him true courage—based on the confidence that God was with him.

First, he purposed to do a better job in protecting and caring for his sheep than anyone. Second, he purposed to delight in God and in His Word more than anyone or anything else. This skill involved learning how to meditate on Scripture day and night. He turned his long hours into a classroom as he strove to perfect these two skills.

One night he had an opportunity to put his courage to the test. A vicious lion smashed through the brush and lunged at one of his lambs. Quickly the young man put a stone in the pouch of a long leather thong. In an instant the stone went sailing directly to its mark. Long hours of practice enabled him to hit his target with great accuracy. He rushed toward the stunned lion and with all his might ripped open its mouth and released the bruised lamb. Later, a similar incident occurred with a bear, and this gave him the confidence he needed to face a giant.

But his second weapon, the skill of meditation, gave him an even greater advantage than his skill with a sling. In learning this he discovered a new way of looking at any enemy.

On the day he faced the great adversary, the young shepherd demonstrated his unwavering courage. All the soldiers of Israel heard the vile threats of this foe and thought, "He's defying the army of Saul." But this young man heard the boastful cursings and because of his meditation on Scripture, realized instead that this adversary was defying the armies of the living God.

The army of Saul looked at the giant and thought, "He's too big to hit." The young man regarded the giant in an entirely different way, thinking, "He's too big to miss."

Knowing that God was on his side, young David could boldly approach his enemy with the confidence that he could only succeed.

From I Samuel 17:1-54

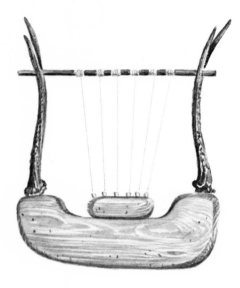

David's skill on the harp was the result of long hours of practice while tending his father's sheep.

The lion and Syrian bear were menaces to sheep and goats and were feared by all Judean shepherds.

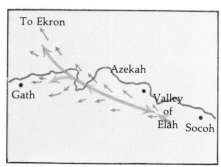

After David killed Goliath in the valley of Elah, Saul chased the Philistines back to Ekron and Gath in Philistia.

DAVID, CONFIDENT OF SUCCESS, COURAGEOUSLY FACED HIS OPPONENT

The nation of Philistia had been a continuing rod of discipline to the Israelites ever since God instructed Moses to detour inland around them. "Lest peradventure the people repent when they see war, and they return to Egypt." (Exodus 13:17)

SUPERIOR EQUIPMENT GIVES THE ENEMY A DECIDED ADVANTAGE

The Philistines controlled the distribution of ore and had learned the secret of making iron weapons. Their monopoly of this industry gave them a decided military advantage. The common soldier of Israel, armed with only his crude agricultural implements or a sling shot, lived in daily fear of his Philistine counterpart with horse, chariot of iron, sharp two-edged sword, dagger, spear, helmet and protective armor.

A DEFENSE OF GIANTS

The Philistines did not only possess superior armament. They employed men in their army of huge stature and strength, possibly descendants of the Rephaim who had made the spies of Moses feel like grasshoppers. In full battle array these men were practically invulnerable to the average Israeli soldier. In the past, the five independent city-states of Philistia had been satisfied with enlarging their borders at the expense of Israel. But now that Saul was leading an organized resistance, the five lords of the Philistines had also organized and were intent on subjecting the entire nation to slavery. If the Lord had not supernaturally intervened during the battle at Michmash, Israel would already have been overtaken.

BLASPHEMY ANGERS A YOUNG MAN

By the time David brought supplies to his older brothers who were fighting in Saul's army, the Philistines had gathered and camped across a shallow brook in the valley of Elah. While he was talking with his brothers, a huge Philistine named Goliath taunted the entire army of Israel, daring any one to hand-to-hand combat. When David expressed concern that Goliath's mocking of the army of the living God was unchallenged, he was severely rebuked by his oldest brother. Nevertheless, he pressed for more information. Convinced that no one was going to oppose this mocker, he persuaded King Saul of his capability and was permitted to represent the army.

EQUIPPED WITH A STAFF, A SLING AND HIS GOD

After refusing a set of armor offered him by King Saul, he armed himself only with a sling, his shepherd's stick, five smooth stones and a confident trust in his God. David did not even consider defeat that day. He knew exactly what he was going to do. He had no doubt that the Lord would give him the necessary skill with his sling, and he even foretold Goliath of the outcome. When the Philistines realized that their champion was dead, they fled. Saul's army won a great victory that day, and the Lord's reputation was magnified because of the courage of one godly young man who was confident of success.

DAVID AND GOLIATH CHARACTER SKETCH

WHY WAS DAVID REBUKED BY HIS OLDEST BROTHER ELIAB?

When David expressed concern that no one would oppose Goliath, Eliab angrily accused his brother of neglecting his duties and said, "I know thy pride, and the naughtiness of thine heart; for thou hast come down that thou mightest see the battle." (I Samuel 17:28) Eliab is an illustration of the hypocrite who seeks to remove the speck out of his brother's eye without first removing the log out of his own (Matthew 7:1-5). Eliab was guilty of the very things for which he was accusing his brother (cf. Romans 2:1). Eliab had not been chosen for leadership because God saw the condition of his heart (I Samuel 16:6,7). David no doubt had pricked his brother's conscience by reminding him of his responsibility to defend the Lord's reputation. Now Eliab was trying to justify his actions by condemning his brother.

WHAT WERE THE RESULTS OF DAVID'S COURAGEOUS ACT?

The immediate result was victory in this critical battle. If the Philistines had won they would have reduced Israel to a slave state. A more lasting result was the nation of Israel's new respect for the power of their God. No longer would Saul's men need to shrink in fear at the sight of their ironclad enemies.

WHY WAS DAVID SO CONFIDENT THAT HE WOULD WIN?

Psalm 106 reveals David's understanding of the working of God through the history of the nation of Israel. It is certain that he knew these things before his battle with Goliath. His deep concern and disgust for an uncircumcised Philistine who taunted the armies of the living God was an indication of many hours of reflection on the power of God, His past deliverances, and His commands to possess the land. It was the responsibility of the father to teach the Law and the history of Israel to his children, (Deuteronomy 4:9,10) but it was the responsibility of the child to learn his lessons. Not only did David learn the Law, but he obeyed it, memorized it, loved it and meditated on it (Psalm 119:10, 11, 97).

"And David put his hand in his bag, *and took thence a stone, and slang it, and smote the Philistine in his forehead, that the stone sunk into his forehead; and he fell upon his face to the earth.*"

DAVID

Determination

PART FOUR

REALIZING THAT MY PRESENT STRUGGLES ARE ESSENTIAL FOR FUTURE ACHIEVEMENT

BREAKING DOWN A SEEMINGLY IMPOSSIBLE TASK BY CONCENTRATING ON ACHIEVABLE GOALS

EXPENDING WHATEVER ENERGY IS NECESSARY TO COMPLETE A PROJECT

REJECTING ANY DISTRACTION WHICH COULD HINDER THE COMPLETION OF A TASK

Determination

IS REALIZING THAT MY PRESENT STRUGGLES ARE ESSENTIAL FOR FUTURE ACHIEVEMENT

LIVING LESSONS ON DETERMINATION . . .

FROM THE PAGES OF SCRIPTURE

A proud group of religious leaders engaged a wise man filled with spiritual power in a debate. A crowd witnessed the event; a city witnessed the retaliation, and a world witnessed the far-reaching impact of the events following the debate. The history of the world was reshaped during those days because the principal factors of determination were understood and implemented.

ILLUSTRATED IN THE WORLD OF NATURE

THE CECROPIA MOTH *Samia cecropia*

The cecropia moth is a member of the silkworm family. Like many other species in the order Lepidoptera, it transforms from a pupa to a colorful velvet-winged moth. Few realize the stages through which it passes before achieving its splendor. The moth is five to six inches wide and has four major stages of development.

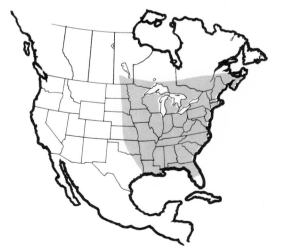

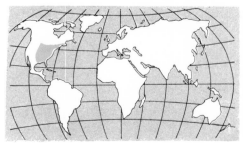

The range and habitat of the cecropia moth

DETERMINATION

HOW DOES THE CECROPIA MOTH ILLUSTRATE DETERMINATION IN USING STRUGGLES FOR FUTURE ACHIEVEMENT?

The wealth of the ancient Chinese city could be attributed to one industry—silk. As early as 2600 B.C. the people of this country had developed the technique of softening the cocoon, locating the filament end and unwinding the delicate material. They then combined several strands together to form a single, stronger thread of silk.

So important was this trade to these people that to maintain their monopoly they imposed the death penalty on anyone who tried to take the eggs or silkworms out of the country.

In spite of this harsh penalty, the silkworm industry gradually became dispersed. In the fourth century a Chinese princess carried some eggs out of the country in her headdress when she married a man in Buchara, a medieval Islamic center of culture and trade. From there the eggs spread to other nations.

A North American species of the silkworm is the cecropia moth. Their cocoons may be seen in trees and bushes during the winter months. They are often carried into homes for observation and study where the fascinating events of the emerging moth are attentively watched.

On one such occasion a young viewer watched with awe as the top of the cocoon broke open and the moth struggled to release itself. As he watched the moth struggle to exert its newly-formed muscles, he observed that its progress was very slow. In an effort to help, he reached down and widened the opening of the cocoon to make it easier for the moth to get out. Within a few minutes it was free from its prison. Its shriveled wings were wrapped close to its body. Soon the wings would fill out, and it would be able to fly. But as the boy watched, the wings remained shriveled. Something was wrong.

What he did not realize was that the struggle to get out of the cocoon was an essential means of developing the muscle system of the moth's body. The pressure of these muscles working together was necessary to push the blood into the wings and fill them out to their full dimension.

In an effort to relieve a struggle, the boy had crippled the future of this creature. He realized at the expense of the cecropia moth that present struggles are essential for future achievement.

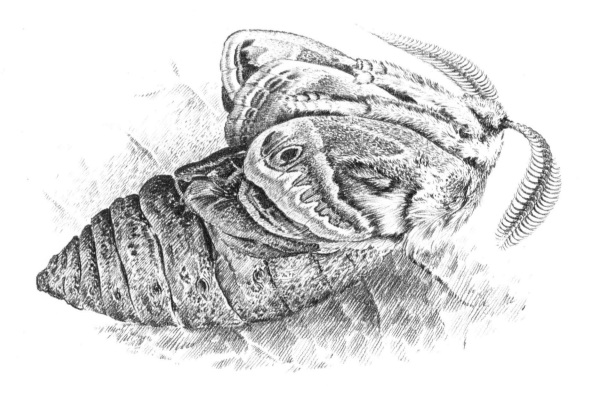

CHARACTERISTICS AND PHYSICAL FEATURES OF THE CECROPIA MOTH

The cecropia moth experiences intense struggle in its brief life. In order for the pupa to emerge from its cocoon to become a beautiful winged moth, it must first pass through three successive stages of development.

WHEN DOES THE CATERPILLAR GET ITS START?

Life for the caterpillar begins when the adult female lays a large cluster of eggs. Depending on the species of moth, the eggs may be spherical, hemispherical, cylindrical or lentricular. The moth egg is constructed similarly to that of a bird in that its shell varies in color from white or pale green shades to a bluish-green or brown. The shell contains a live embryo, surrounded by a liquid which serves as its food. The embryo eventually becomes the colorful caterpillar.

WHEN DOES THE FEMALE MOTH LAY HER EGGS?

Although the time of year when the moth lays her eggs varies from species to species, this timing is not haphazard. Some eggs hatch almost immediately after they are laid while others lie dormant for many months. An egg that is laid during summer days of longer and more intense sunlight hatches immediately. Eggs which are laid in late summer or early fall do not hatch until the following spring. If they were to hatch right away, the larvae would not survive the cold winter. By remaining in the shell, the embryo subsists on the liquid nourishment which surrounds it. With food and protection it is able to withstand severe cold, even to the point of being frozen solid. Months later when spring arrives and the sunlight hours lengthen, the embryo emerges from its confinement as a caterpillar or larva.

TOP *Female cecropia moth lays her eggs on a food plant.*
BELOW *When the food substance within these eggs is consumed by the embryo, it breaks out of its shell and emerges as a beautiful green caterpillar.*

STAGES OF CATERPILLAR DEVELOPMENT

Capterpillars grow rapidly, feeding on leafy plants.

New growth is possible when larva emerges from its thick epidermis.

As it begins the pupa stage, *the caterpillar spins a silken chamber to protect it during its transformation.*

DOES IT MATTER WHERE THE FEMALE MOTH LAYS HER EGGS?

Absolutely. When the female lays her eggs on leafy structures, the choice of plant is very important. As the caterpillar emerges from its egg, it immediately begins a search for food. Since the parent has already chosen the location and laid the egg on the proper food source, the larva's initial struggle of survival is eased. If moths are being raised in captivity and the proper food plant is not provided, the caterpillar cannot survive.

DOES THE CATERPILLAR OUTGROW ITS SKIN?

As the caterpillar feeds on vegetation, a phenomenal struggle of growth occurs within it. The epidermis or outer skin becomes too small for it to continue growing, and it is forced to shed the confining surface. This process of shedding is called molting.

HOW DOES THE CATERPILLAR SHED ITS SKIN?

A new covering is formed underneath the surface skin. After this occurs, the outer surface becomes hard, resembling a coat of armor. Under this outer shell is a third covering. During the time the inner layer is being formed, special glands secrete a fluid which dissolves the middle layer, leaving a hard outer shell and a larger, pliable covering underneath. To free itself from the confining outer skin, the caterpillar splits the old shell from the head to the thorax and fights its way free, emerging with a new covering.

HOW OFTEN WILL A CATERPILLAR SHED ITS SKIN?

After the caterpillar has emerged from the armor-like outer skin, a sudden spurt of growth occurs, and in a short time its new pliable covering is once again too small. It must then repeat the process of recreating an exact cast of its irregular, spiny body. Molting is controlled in the head of the insect and will take place four times during the life of the larva. In some species, it will occur as many as ten times.

WHEN DOES THE CATERPILLAR SPIN A COCOON?

During the previous stage of the caterpillar's life, it was free to move about on leaves and trees in search of food. But the next stage of development is characterized by immobility. The larva spins a cocoon, completely encasing itself with fiber. During the period it spends in this confined position, a transformation takes place and the caterpillar emerges as a beautiful moth.

HOW DOES THE CATERPILLAR MAKE SILK?

Two glands emerge from a single opening located on the caterpillar's head. From these glands the larva emits a liquid which, when exposed to air, hardens into two silk strands. A second pair of glands in the head secretes a gummy substance which cements the two threads together. Because the cecropia's cocoon is large and requires massive production of silk, these glands comprise one-fourth of the total body weight of the mature caterpillar.

HOW MUCH SILK CAN THE CECROPIA PRODUCE?

The cecropia larva chooses a convenient branch or stick on which to build its cocoon. It begins by wrapping a few cemented strands around its body to hold it in place, continuing until it is completely encased in a silken structure. The silk glands in its head are capable of secreting two to three thousand feet of silk in order to construct the cocoon.

WHAT IS A PUPA?

When the larva is in the cocoon its skin forms a ringed, sheath-like covering which is dark brown or black in color, providing the insect with an additional protective layer. This period is known as the pupa stage, and in appearance it varies very little among species.

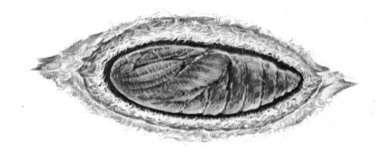

The caterpillar spends the season *in its silken cocoon. Inside it hardens its covering and takes on a dark appearance. The picture above shows a portion of the cocoon cut away, exposing the pupa.*

Moths and butterflies *are members of the order Lepidoptera. These insects pass through four distinct stages of life. Beginning as an egg, the cecropia develops into a larva or caterpillar. During this stage it sheds its skin approximately four times to allow room for growth. Once the caterpillar matures, it spins a cocoon and when so encased passes into the pupa stage. Finally, it emerges from the cocoon as a beautiful cecropia moth.*

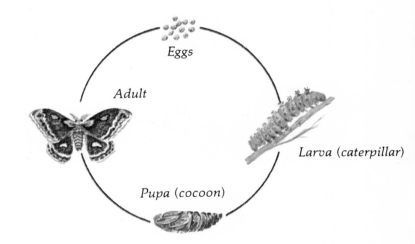

Eggs

Adult

Larva (caterpillar)

Pupa (cocoon)

185

The final function *performed by the cecropia is that of reproduction. After mating, the male moth dies. The female looks for a proper food-bearing plant on which to lay her eggs. Once this is accomplished, her life, too, comes to an end.*

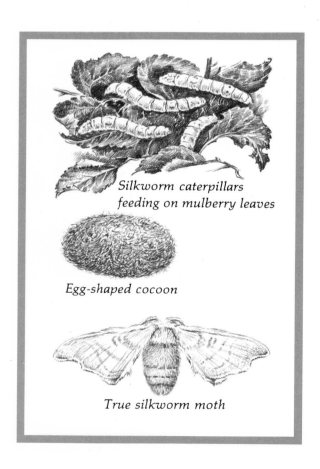

Silkworm caterpillars feeding on mulberry leaves

Egg-shaped cocoon

True silkworm moth

HOW DOES THE PUPA PREPARE FOR ITS ROLE AS A MOTH?

Although the pupa appears dormant within its cocoon, great internal changes are taking place beneath the outer covering. Adult legs, wings and a new type of mouth are being formed. A vital new muscle system is also developing. These muscles force blood and other fluids necessary for proper development into the wings. Reproductive organs are formed. All these structures equip the moth to carry out its final stage of life.

HOW DOES THE MOTH ESCAPE FROM ITS CHAMBER?

When the moth is ready to emerge from its cocoon, it secretes a liquid which softens the silken end of its chamber. Poking its head out, it uses its legs to free the rest of its body. Once free from the chamber, the moth rests—its wings undeveloped. But within minutes the muscle system begins forcing fluids through the vessels. Twenty minutes later, the wings reach their full size. After a brief exposure to the air, they dry and become firm. The other parts of the body become stronger, and it soon tries its wings and flies away. The moth has now reached full maturity. Each stage was achieved only through struggle, and each was necessary for the insect to attain full growth.

A relative of the cecropia moth, *the Asian silkworm, produces one of the finest fibers in the world. The qualities of this remarkable material make it superior among all natural fibers. Warmer than cotton, stronger than an equivalent thread of steel, light in weight and with a high degree of elasticity, this resilient material dyes beautifully and is easily pressed.*

HOW DOES SCRIPTURE ILLUSTRATE DETERMINATION IN USING STRUGGLES FOR FUTURE ACHIEVEMENT?

The angry faces of those who had come to debate stood out in the crowd. Their pride was fortified by years of study in the disciplines of their teachings.

As they observed the honor and attentiveness which the crowd gave the speaker, their anger intensified. Then these men assumed facial expressions feigning humility and respect and began to lay their verbal traps. The role of the crowd changed from learner to jury.

The speaker studied the faces of these unfamiliar visitors. His piercing eyes became uncomfortably distracting to them, and the debaters found it necessary to look into the distance to maintain their train of thought and finish their well-rehearsed questions.

They were quite skilled in debate. For years they had reacted to the strict disciplines under which they lived. They spent long hours discussing with their friends and teachers the inconsistencies of their teachings and the merits of greater freedom in fulfilling their natural desires. Their manner of life and related philosophies had molded them into a cohesive and respected religious group. It was important to them that people understood their ideas and respected their way of living.

All attentively waited as the speaker organized his thoughts to answer their questions. Then with remarkable insight, he exposed the folly of their thinking and living. He spoke with such practical wisdom and spiritual power that they were reduced to shame, and they left in humiliation.

They had never been exposed to such an opponent, and they realized that their future depended on their ability to discredit him. To this end they gave their full attention. Hiring men to accuse him falsely, they united with others who also wanted to see him and his colleagues silenced.

Their contrived accusations were serious, and he was brought before city officials. His defense was so convincing and convicting that the mob which these men had stirred up covered their ears and ground their teeth at him in a rage. Their next action was destined to fan the fires of the greatest spiritual upheaval the world has ever known.

They rushed against him, dragging him out of the council to the outskirts of the city. There they picked up any rock they could find and flung them at him until he died.

That scene was indelibly imprinted in the mind of one young man who watched. He saw how the face of that martyr became more and more radiant as the pain from the final assault intensified. That bystander was the apostle Paul. The triumph of this determined martyr whose name was Stephen became a motivation for his life and an example for his death.

From Acts 6 and 7

The Theodotus inscription *from a Jerusalem synagogue may be from the same Greek-speaking synagogue whose members persecuted Stephen.*

Even though the above shekel of Tyre *portrayed the head of the Tyrian god Baal Melkart, it had received official approval by the Jewish priest for the payment of the annual temple tax.*

The Capernaum Synagogue *from the third century A.D. was very similar to the synagogues which existed in Jerusalem during Stephen's time.*

THE STRUGGLES STEPHEN WENT THROUGH WERE ESSENTIAL FOR THE FUTURE OF THE EARLY CHURCH

A crisis had arisen in the early church. Because of the powerful preaching of the Apostle Peter and the other disciples, thousands of men, women and children were being added to their fellowship.

A MAN FULL OF THE HOLY SPIRIT

Many of the new believers were Greek-speaking Jews who had been born outside of Israel. It happened that the needs of the widows among these Hellenistic Jewish believers were not being adequately met. Church leaders recognized the need for wise and unprejudiced men who could meet the practical needs of all the believers regardless of their language or background. Stephen was one of seven men chosen for this task. It is said that Stephen was a man full of faith and of the Holy Spirit.

ORGANIZATION EXPANDED HIS MINISTRY

So successful were Stephen and his colleagues in their new responsibility that Peter and the other disciples could continue spreading the Word of God. So impressive was the new harmony of the young church that even a large number of the Levitical priests became obedient to the faith. In fact, things were running so smoothly that Stephen was able to expand his ministry to meet the spiritual as well as the physical needs of the people. We learn that Stephen was full of grace and power and performed great wonders and signs among the people.

SLANDER TO REMOVE A THREAT

Because Stephen was familiar with the Greek language, his ministry centered around Greek-speaking Jews. God blessed his ministry, and a large number of people began leaving the Greek-speaking synagogues. A conflict between Stephen, considered the spokesman and organizer of the Hellenistic believers, and the leaders of the Hellenistic synagogues was inevitable. Because they were not able to cope with the wisdom and Spirit with which Stephen spoke, they induced men to slander him with charges of blasphemy. Then they stirred up the people, brought him before the Sanhedrin, and resorted to using witnesses who accused him falsely.

EVEN IN DEATH THE MESSAGE LIVED ON

As was the custom of the Sanhedrin, the officiating high priest allowed Stephen to testify in his behalf. It is possible that if Stephen had just slightly compromised his convictions before this more objective assembly of native Jews, he would have escaped with his life. But when he condemned them for the very crime of which they accused him—blasphemy and disobedience of the Law—this was more than they could tolerate. Without even obtaining permission from the Roman authorities, they illegally murdered him by stoning him just outside the city. The crowd left that day with his final words ringing uncomfortably in their ears, "Lord, do not hold this sin against them." So ended the life but not the influence of the Church's first martyr.

STEPHEN CHARACTER SKETCH

WHY WAS STEPHEN'S MINISTRY SO EFFECTIVE?

The clue to the secret of Stephen's effective ministry is given in his address to the Sanhedrin. The address indicates a comprehensive knowledge of the Scriptures. Stephen had evidently mastered the record of God's great acts from the time of Abraham to his present day. In addition, he quoted from memory passages of Scripture from the books of Genesis, Exodus, Deuteronomy, Isaiah and Amos. Stephen was a responsible man of good reputation, full of the Spirit and of wisdom (Acts 6:3). He was also willing to serve and demonstrated faith, grace and power (Acts 6:5,8). His ministry was successful because Stephen's mind was saturated with God's thoughts.

WHY WAS A MAN LIKE STEPHEN PERSECUTED?

Stephen was persecuted because he spoke out against the corruption of temple worship. By so doing, he provoked the anger of officials who were profiting from these fraudulent practices. The priest's livelihood depended on the lucrative business of temple worship. "Pre-approved" sacrificial animals were sold at exorbitant prices. A fifteen percent fee was charged for changing foreign money into the required Galilean shekel for the temple tax (cf. Matthew 21:12, 13). These men formally accused Stephen of blasphemy against God, the temple in Jerusalem, Moses the Law-giver and the Law itself (Acts 6:11,13). Stephen was also accused of saying that Jesus would destroy the temple and change or destroy the customs handed down from Moses (Acts 6:14).

WHAT WERE THE EFFECTS OF STEPHEN'S DEATH?

Because of Stephen's martyrdom, the message of the Gospel was given a great impetus throughout the world. The Lord had commissioned His disciples to go to every nation with the Gospel (Matthew 28:18-20; Acts 1:8), but Christians had not as yet even left Jerusalem. Stephen's speech indicates that he may have been the first one to catch this larger vision for the whole world (cf. Acts 7:46-50). After his death, the first organized persecution was directed primarily against Hellenistic believers (cf. Acts 8:1). As a result, the message of salvation spread throughout all of Judea, Samaria and eventually the entire world (cf. Romans 1:8).

"And they chose Stephen, *a man full of faith and of the Holy Spirit . . . and when they had prayed, they laid their hands on them.*"

STEPHEN

**IS BREAKING DOWN A SEEMINGLY IMPOSSIBLE TASK
BY CONCENTRATING ON ACHIEVABLE GOALS**

LIVING LESSONS ON DETERMINATION . . .

FROM THE PAGES OF SCRIPTURE

The report of spies had discouraged the people from even attempting their mission. But they failed to realize that nothing was impossible with God's help and their own determination. As a result, God had to wait until a leader was able to break down the seemingly overwhelming task into achievable goals.

ILLUSTRATED IN THE WORLD OF NATURE

THE ARCTIC TERN *Sterna paradisaea*

The graceful arctic tern inhabits both large and small bodies of water along ocean coastlines. This small bird, just fifteen and one-half inches in length, accomplishes a remarkable migration. The long trek between its summer and winter ranges is completed many times during its twenty-year lifespan.

The range and habitat of the Arctic tern

DETERMINATION

HOW DOES THE ARCTIC TERN ILLUSTRATE DETERMINATION IN ACCOMPLISHING A SEEMINGLY IMPOSSIBLE TASK?

The delicate features of the arctic tern give little hint to the extraordinary feat which it accomplishes each year of its life. Its name suggests a rugged bird, able to endure severe cold and privation. But such is not the case. Despite its size, the tern has adapted an awesome schedule of activity which has earned it the reputation of being the champion of migratory birds.

In autumn the tern leaves its nesting grounds in the Arctic Circle near the North Pole and begins its journey to the opposite end of the earth. Each year it covers a distance of 22,000 miles in its migratory flight. Considering all side trips for food and other purposes, the actual number of miles it flies is undoubtedly greater than this.

On its flight to the Antarctic Ocean near the South Pole the arctic tern will choose one of two routes. It either flies along the western coast of Alaska, Canada, the United States and Central and South America, or it chooses the alternate route along the western coasts of Europe and Africa.

These flight courses are chosen because they include food-bearing currents. By the time the tern reaches the Antarctic, snow has begun to melt with the approach of spring. A few short months later the tern begins its long journey home.

When it returns to its breeding grounds near the North Pole, it has literally flown around the world. To accomplish such a feat the arctic tern clearly demonstrates a significant aspect of determination.

The tern completes this seemingly impossible task by concentrating on smaller, achievable goals. Each day it covers approximately 150 miles, and by so doing, flies around the world in twenty weeks.

Severt
Andrewson

Extended daylight affords the tern longer hours in which to secure its food.

CHARACTERISTICS AND PHYSICAL FEATURES OF THE ARCTIC TERN

The fragile arctic tern flies thousands of miles each year by breaking its long journey down and pacing itself. Its amazing migratory flight is one of several unusual aspects in the life of this determined bird.

WHAT DOES THE TERN ENJOY THAT NO OTHER LIVING CREATURE DOES?

Constant sunlight. For approximately eight months of the year the arctic tern lives in almost continual daylight. In its migrational pattern it arrives at each of the poles just in time to enjoy their long summer days of twenty-four hour sunlight. During the remaining four months it also enjoys more daylight than darkness.

HOW DOES DAYLIGHT BENEFIT THE TERN?

Because the tern is a small bird and flies long distances, it uses tremendous amounts of energy and so requires a great deal of food. Long daylight hours afford the bird more opportunity to catch the right amount of food and to store extra fat which it utilizes on its demanding journey.

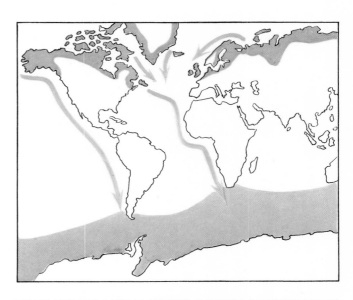

MIGRATION AND RANGES OF THE ARCTIC TERN
- ▢ *Winter range*
- ▢ *Spring and summer breeding range*

WHY DO TERNS BUMP EACH OTHER?

The energetic arctic tern is a dedicated parent. Both participate in raising the young chicks. Each sits on the nest and assumes this responsibility with such enthusiasm that the other bird must bump its mate off the nest to have an opportunity to incubate the eggs. When the eggs hatch, the parents also share the task of feeding the young. A successful nest is usually not achieved by birds under three years of age.

WHERE DOES THE ARCTIC TERN MAKE ITS NEST?

The tern breeds in the North Polar Basin region and may nest as far south as Massachusetts and the New England states. Nests of the arctic tern have been found in locations as remote as seven degrees from the North Pole.

ABOVE *Closely spaced colony of nesting terns*
LEFT *Studies have shown that a combination of silver and red stimulates a response in the chick to beg for food. When these colors are substituted for others the chick does not respond as quickly.*
BELOW *Intent on incubating eggs, the tern is "bumped" by partner.*

Arctic tern fights off the larger herring gull *to protect its young from the predation of these scavenging birds.*

HOW ELABORATE IS THE TERN'S NEST?

Crude in structure, the tern's nest is built by making a hollow in either sand, gravel or rocks. The bird uses a few building materials around the perimeter to contain the two or three brownish or greenish spotted eggs.

IS THE TERN A SOLITARY BIRD?

No. In fact, terns seek others of their kind and form colonies during breeding season. The birds even allow other species of terns and gulls to join their community. The nests are built near each other, sometimes as close as two feet apart.

IS THE HERRING GULL WELCOME TO JOIN THE COLONY?

A nesting tern regards the herring gull as a major threat. These larger gulls prey upon their eggs and young chicks. When predators approach the vicinity of the nest, the arctic terns resist with such a spirited fight that they usually succeed in driving off older gulls and may even inflict fatal wounds on younger birds.

The survival of the young terns *is threatened by many dangers. Ants may enter and kill the bird before it has a chance to get out of its shell. Sudden changes in water conditions may drive aquatic life from the area and force parent terns to desert their nests. Predatory animals are also a threat, but the greatest hazard is sudden high tides which can destroy thousands of eggs and young terns.*

ENEMIES OF YOUNG TERNS

Destructive insects

Rising tidal waters

Predatory animals

Changing water conditions

Fishermen may look *to the tern for a clue to where the fish are feeding.*

HOW DOES THE TERN AID FISHERMEN?

Those who make their living from the sea have benefited from closely observing this bird. Commercial fishermen who search for mackerel and other schooling fish may set their nets by the tern as it dives for minnows which are surfacing to escape the paths of larger predatory fish.

HOW DOES A TERN CATCH ITS FISH?

As it skims along the ocean using its telescopic eyes, the bird is able to see small fish breaking the surface of the water. It dives down and snatches them up in its bill with a high degree of accuracy. The tern prefers to put as little of its body under water as possible.

WOULD A TERN EVER GET LOST IN THE FOG?

Even in foggy weather, the tern will continue fishing. As soon as the bird finishes feeding, it heads for shore—its sense of direction unerring, direct, and unaffected by the fog.

LEFT *In addition to small fish, the arctic tern also eats shrimp, grasshoppers and flying insects.*
BELOW *The tern's remarkable ability to navigate is unaffected by the fog.*

HOW DOES SCRIPTURE ILLUSTRATE DETERMINATION IN ACCOMPLISHING A SEEMINGLY IMPOSSIBLE TASK?

The nation of Israel had grown in strength and number and was now preparing to conquer the land. Through unmistakable evidence God had led them to this point in their development. This accomplishment would be the greatest in their history. Nothing hindered them from completing the task—nothing, that is, except a strange decision which their leader had recently made.

Rather than taking God at His word, he listened to the people and decided that it would be wise to exercise one caution before taking this next step. Accordingly, he selected twelve men to go in and spy out the land. The nation waited anxiously for their return.

Ten of the twelve spies lacked determination and brought home a bleak report. Two other men returned with them, but their report was in sharp contrast to that of the others. Their great faith and desire to accomplish this national dream gave them the determination to assure the people that with God's help, the land could be theirs. But the two were outnumbered and the people, deciding that the task was too large for them, chose not to go into the land.

As a consequence, God sent a series of tragic events which plunged the nation into despair. Because of their disobedience and lack of confidence in Him, the Lord crushed their hopes of ever personally achieving this goal.

One of the two men was sickened by his nation's lack of faith. He carefully reviewed what he would have done had he been the leader. A few years later this very man was chosen to assume leadership. Now he had his opportunity to put into operation the plan of action that would allow the nation to conquer the land as God intended.

He called two trusted men and gave them instructions. They were to do what the original group of twelve had done many years earlier, but from a different perspective. The men did their job well and returned with the information. The Israelites moved ahead. In the years that followed they conquered and subdued all the nations which occupied the land God had given to them.

What was the factor which caused the first leader to fail and the second to succeed? The first group of twelve made their mistake when they spied out the entire land. The total job of conquering these nations overwhelmed them. The second leader, Joshua, learned to complete a seemingly impossible task by concentrating on smaller, achievable goals. He sent his two men out to spy on only one area and one city at a time.

From Deuteronomy 1:19-38 and Joshua 11:15-23

Jericho was possibly the first fortified city in Canaan. Parts of the massive stone wall extended to thirty feet in thickness. Its collapse struck fear into the hearts of neighboring kings.

Although the mission of the two spies was limited, it was also very dangerous. They escaped through a city wall.

JOSHUA ACCOMPLISHED AN IMPOSSIBLE TASK BY REDUCING IT TO ACHIEVABLE GOALS

Joshua had waited forty long years to reenter the land God had promised to give His people. Each year of the forty-year delay represented one day of an earlier spying mission when the nation had been discouraged from claiming God's promise.

A LEADER FAILED TO GIVE SPECIFIC INSTRUCTIONS

Joshua remembered when Moses commanded the people to take possession of the land. But Moses failed to give them specific instructions. As a result, his directive overwhelmed the tribal leaders, and they insisted on sending a representative from each tribe to search out the land. Then the representatives could advise the leaders on strategy for attack. God permitted the plan but did not approve it. Joshua had been chosen to represent the tribe of Ephraim as a member of the reconnaissance mission.

ALL WERE DEFEATED—EXCEPT TWO

As a spy, Joshua had seen the fertile land, lush pastures, beautiful fruit trees and abundant springs of fresh water in the land God had promised His people. He remembered that the other spies became discouraged after visiting fortified cities with strong, fighting men. All of the men except for him and Caleb were convinced that the mission was impossible. Rather than discussing strategy, they began to talk about returning to Egypt and how they would convince the rest of the people to do so.

A NEW LEADER WITH A DIFFERENT TACTIC

Forty years later, only his friend Caleb from the original group was alive to reenter the land with him. Joshua knew that it would be crucial to give the people specific and achievable goals without overwhelming them or allowing others to discourage them. After a word of encouragement, he told the people to prepare their provisions. In three days they would cross the Jordan River and begin an invasion. Now he needed information about the land which surrounded the first city they would attack. He wanted to know where the water supplies were, where there would be a safe place to keep the women and children, the design of the city and the attitude of its inhabitants.

A LESSON LEARNED—A VICTORY WON

This time, Joshua would send only two spies to one city. They would be given a definite time limit and their mission would be kept secret. Even if they came back with a bleak report they would not be allowed to discourage the people.

The spies returned from their brief mission, and after their report Joshua became more determined than ever to conquer the land. The people, busily engaged in the project Joshua had assigned them, had confidence in their new leader because his determination to obey God was contagious.

JOSHUA CHARACTER SKETCH

WHY DIDN'T JOSHUA BECOME DISCOURAGED AS THE OTHER TEN SPIES DID?

Joshua had learned to look at things differently from most other men. He saw the same strong armies and the same fortified cities as the others. The ten spies saw a human impossibility. Joshua and his friend Caleb saw an opportunity to see God work another miracle.

Joshua had been the leader of the Israeli defense against the attack by the Amalekites at Rephidim. He had learned there that victory belongs to the Lord. On that day, when Moses held his rod toward heaven, the Israeli army advanced; when the rod dropped, they were forced to retreat (Exodus 17:8-13). As an aide to Moses he learned from firsthand experience of the power and reality of God (Exodus 24:13). Nothing was too hard for Him.

WAS IT NECESSARY FOR JOSHUA TO SEND TWO SPIES INTO THE LAND?

Joshua did not intend for the spies to search out the entire land. Neither did he ask them to return with feasible strategy. Instead, they were required only to obtain detailed information on the city itself. God had not yet given Joshua specific details on how Jericho was to be taken (cf. Joshua 6:1-5). It was not a lack of faith which prompted him to send out the spies but rather the proper fulfilling of his responsibility as leader to learn all the available facts.

HOW SUCCESSFUL WERE JOSHUA'S METHODS?

Joshua had learned to look at things differently from most other men. He saw the same mission. His determination to achieve God's goal for His people impressed upon him the necessity of breaking the task they faced into smaller, achievable efforts. From his experience, Joshua established the criteria for the second spying effort. Their mission would be a secret one and their efforts were confined to information-gathering during a prescribed length of time in one city only. Joshua's method of taking one step at a time was so effective that the people were able to conquer and inhabit the land which God had promised them.

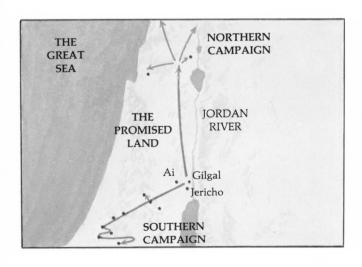

"So Joshua took the whole land, *according to all that the Lord said unto Moses; and Joshua gave it for an inheritance unto Israel according to their divisions by their tribes. And the land rested from war.*"

JOSHUA

Determination

IS EXPENDING WHATEVER ENERGY IS NECESSARY TO COMPLETE A PROJECT

LIVING LESSONS ON DETERMINATION . . .

FROM THE PAGES OF SCRIPTURE

A king's lack of spiritual discernment robbed him of the full potential which God had in store for him. His unwillingness to expend sufficient energy to maximize victory deprived him of the opportunity of winning back his kingdom. God used the puzzling instructions of a prophet to measure this man's determination.

ILLUSTRATED IN THE WORLD OF NATURE

THE KING SALMON   *Oucorhynchus tshawytscha*

The sporting challenge and excellent flavor of its meat have made the king salmon one of the most highly prized game and commercial fish. A mature salmon will range in weight from twenty to one hundred pounds, inhabiting both fresh and salt waters. The fish shows remarkable determination in its effort to complete its hazardous migrational run.

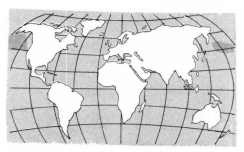

The range and habitat of the king salmon

DETERMINATION

HOW DOES THE SALMON ILLUSTRATE DETERMINATION IN EXPENDING WHATEVER ENERGY IS NECESSARY?

In a determined effort to return to its spawning grounds upstream, the king salmon encounters overwhelming obstacles. A strong urge which compels the mighty fish to return is instilled at birth and serves as a driving force throughout its life.

Equipped with a highly developed sense of smell, the salmon is indelibly impressed with the unique scent of its spawning grounds. Now, triggered by instinct, the great fish leisurely begins moving upstream from the ocean waters in which it spends its adult life. The scent of its destination is the compass which unerringly directs the fish back to its place of birth.

Moving downstream was relatively simple. Going upstream involves not only rushing rapids and waterfalls but also the threat of predatory animals and birds. In addition to natural hazards, there is also the risk of failing to distinguish the guiding scent and so swimming down the wrong tributary—requiring an exhausting and time-consuming backtrack.

As the days pass and the salmon progresses upriver, it gradually increases its speed until it is traveling at the rate of twenty-five miles per day. Even at this speed many days pass before reaching its destination, perhaps hundreds of miles away.

After an absence of four years the salmon actually locates the exact area of gravel in the riverbed where it was hatched. During its long journey it performs unbelievable feats of determination, overcoming obstacles that seem physically impossible, leaping fifteen feet up the side of a waterfall and then, with skillful flops of its powerful tail pushing itself over the top. Often many attempts must be made before clearing these formidable barriers. But the fact that the salmon is willing to expend whatever energy is necessary to achieve its goal distinguishes it as a magnificent example of determination.

Severt Andrewson

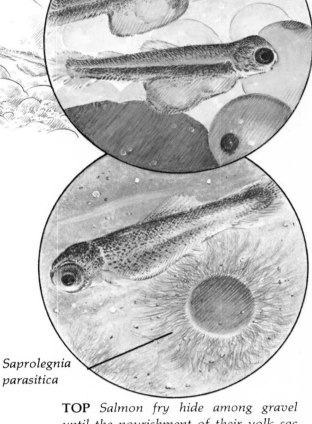

CHARACTERISTICS AND PHYSICAL FEATURES OF THE KING SALMON

Facing overwhelming odds, the king salmon doggedly fights its way upstream, returning to the spawning grounds where it was hatched years ago. This is the dramatic climax of a pattern of determination which has repeated itself all through life. The eggs which it deposits are the beginning stage of the continuing life cycle of the salmon.

WHAT IS THE MORTALITY RATE OF THE SALMON EGGS?

Each February, pale orange salmon eggs hatch after lying on the bottom of the riverbed during the winter. But tens of thousands of these eggs, one-quarter of an inch in diameter, never emerge. Lying along the gravel of the river bottom, the eggs are vulnerable to many destructive forces and the staggering mortality rate is between ninety and ninety-five percent under natural conditions.

WHAT ARE THE HAZARDS THE EMBRYONIC FISH FACES?

The battle of survival is probably greatest during the embryonic stage of the salmon. Destructive forces during this time are over exposure to light, extreme cold, exposure to air, sedimentation and menacing parasites. In addition to these dangers, spring runoffs cause strong currents to wash away the protective gravel, and thousands more are swept downstream for waiting birds and fish to devour.

Saprolegnia
parasitica

TOP *Salmon fry hide among gravel until the nourishment of their yolk sac is consumed.*

ABOVE *Underwater parasites such as the Saprolegnia parasitica attack the eggs of the salmon.*

Actual size of salmon fry

207

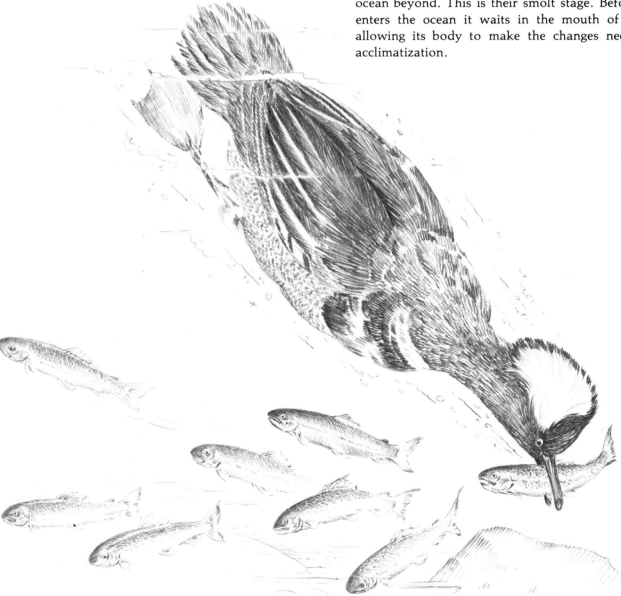

ABOVE *Migration routes of the adult king salmon*
BELOW *A hooded merganser captures two-year old salmon in parr stage*

HOW DOES THE NEWLY HATCHED FISH FEED AND PROTECT ITSELF?

Now in their fry stage, newly hatched salmon remain under protective gravel until the yolk sac attached to their stomach is emptied of its nourishment. As soon as they emerge from beneath the gravel, they are swept by a current into a lake where they mature.

WHEN DO SALMON LEAVE THE LAKE?

The period which the salmon spends in the lake is called the parr stage. The lake affords a refuge in which the young salmon develops before swimming to the ocean. During this period it feeds on plankton and insects, growing four to eight inches in length.

IS THERE AN ADJUSTMENT THE YOUNG SALMON MAKES BEFORE ENTERING SALTWATER?

When the parr leave their lake and enter the stream, they begin a journey to the mouth of the river and the ocean beyond. This is their smolt stage. Before the fish enters the ocean it waits in the mouth of the river, allowing its body to make the changes necessary for acclimatization.

Female king salmon

Male king salmon

ABOVE *The male is neither as large nor as heavy as the female.*

RIGHT *Comparative changes during the reproductive cycle. The male's jaw develops a hook-like structure. Its expanded body turns a deep red. The female's body cavity also swells, but physiological changes are not as extreme as those of the male.*

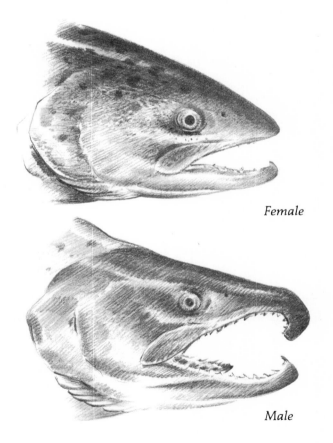

Female

Male

HOW DEEP CAN A SALMON DIVE?

Once the king salmon moves out into the ocean, it travels in all directions. During the day it dives to depths of over one hundred feet. It swims closer to the surface during the night. In the summer the fish gain their greatest weight as they feed on herring and other ocean fish.

HOW LONG DOES THE SALMON STAY IN THE OCEAN?

Salmon spend from one to four years in the ocean. A fish that returns to freshwater streams prematurely is called a "jack."

HOW DOES A SALMON FIND THE MOUTH OF THE RIVER?

During its ocean life, the salmon travels hundreds of miles, sometimes swimming from twenty to sixty miles each day. When the urge to return to freshwater occurs, the salmon relies on the rays of the moon and sun to navigate back to the mouth of its river. Along the way it eats all the food it can for once it returns to freshwater, it no longer eats.

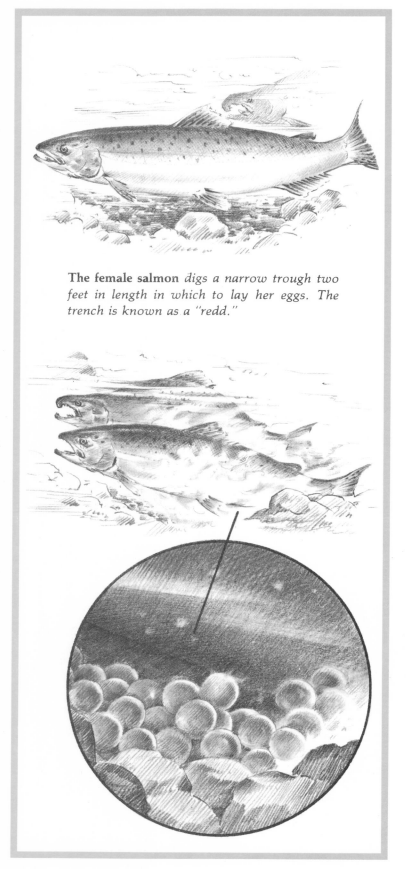

The female salmon *digs a narrow trough two feet in length in which to lay her eggs. The trench is known as a "redd."*

WHAT CHANGES TAKE PLACE IN PREPARATION FOR REPRODUCTION?

When the salmon re-enters its native river, its body once again experiences several changes—this time in preparation for reproduction. Changes in the male are more drastic than those of the female. The lower jaw grows larger and turns up at the end. The upper jaw also lengthens, turning into a curved hook. Its body color deepens to a dull red.

HOW LONG WILL IT TAKE FOR THE FISH TO REACH THEIR DESTINATION?

The tedious upstream journey may take as long as six months. All the way the salmon struggle against the current and go without food. When they arrive, the males battle against each other to establish territorial rights. Damage caused in these struggles is often more devastating than anything suffered during their dangerous return.

HOW MANY EGGS ARE LAID AT ONE TIME?

The female sets the stage by scraping out a broad trench two feet long. When the temperature of the water is just right, 45° - 50° F., the paired fish turn into the current and the female begins laying her 30,000 eggs, one thousand at a time. As the male fertilizes the eggs, the female covers them with sand and gravel. After fertilization, the parents drift downstream to die.

The paired salmon *face into the current as the female deposits her eggs, and the male quickly milks them. Fertilization must take place within fifteen seconds after the eggs are laid.*

HOW DOES SCRIPTURE ILLUSTRATE DETERMINATION IN EXPENDING WHATEVER ENERGY IS NECESSARY?

The admiration and affection of the king of Israel for the prophet Elisha were clearly visible when he came into the chamber where he lay dying. The king leaned over, looked into his face and wept.

"Oh my father, my father, You were the strength of Israel." Little did the king realize the importance of what was to happen next.

The prophet told him to get a bow and some arrows. After the king took them the prophet placed his hands over them, adding to his strength to pull back the arrow. Then he pointed at the open window and said to the king, "Strike!"

They carefully pulled back the shaft string and shot the arrow. Fervently the prophet proclaimed, "This is the arrow of the Lord's deliverance from your enemy."

Hope filled the king's heart. Here was promise that deliverance was possible from the bitter oppression that he and his people suffered at the hand of their enemy. But then the prophet gave one more instruction. He told the king to strike the ground with more arrows.

Earnestly the prophet watched as the king took his bow and arrow. One arrow hit the ground—then a second and a third. He stopped and straightened himself.

A great emotion of disappointment and rebuke swept over the prophet. He spoke angrily to King Jehoash.

"You should have shot the ground at least five or six times. Then you would have overcome your enemies until they were consumed. But now you will only have three victories over them."

God exposed the king's lack of true determination through the simple instruction of the dying prophet. The incident revealed the kind of determination that is required to conquer enemies. We often fail in a task because it requires more energy than we were expecting to give. In order to accomplish a task we must determine to expend whatever energy is necessary to complete the project.

From II Kings 13:14-25

A contemporary portrayal of Jehoash's grandfather, Jehu, kissing the ground in submission to the king of Assyria.

The strings of ancient bows were made of leather, hair or catgut. The arrows were tipped with metal or horn and sometimes feathered.

JEHOASH'S INABILITY TO EXPEND THE NECESSARY ENERGY CUT HIS POTENTIAL FOR VICTORY IN HALF

The famous prophet Elisha was soon to die. Jehoash, king of the war-torn nation of Israel, hurried to pay his last respects. When he came into the presence of the aged and weakened prophet of God, he wept as he recalled the miraculous deeds the Lord accomplished through him which more than once saved the nation from destruction.

"THE CHARIOT OF ISRAEL AND ITS HORSEMEN"

Jehoash knew that Elisha had predicted the defeat of Moab for one of his predecessors. He knew that when the Syrians and Israelites were at war, Elisha had saved the Israelite king several times by revealing the location of their enemy. He had been told that Syrian soldiers were struck blind in their attempt to capture the prophet and were single-handedly marched into the capital city of Samaria. He had learned that Elisha predicted the failure of the Syrians' seige of Samaria. The people had been miraculously delivered. Now this man who was called "the chariot of Israel and its horsemen" was soon to die. Who would be left to call down the favor of God upon Israel? What man could replace Elisha's ability to bring about the miraculous deliverance of Israel from the invading Syrian armies which had so recently paralyzed the nation?

A BLEAK OUTLOOK FOR A DEFEATED NATION

When Jehoash took over the throne from his father Jehoahaz, Syria controlled practically the whole country. His grandfather Jehu had lost control of all the land east of the Jordan River, and his father had performed just as poorly. Beaten and conquered, Jehoash was allowed a bodyguard of only ten chariots and fifty horsemen and a standing army of a mere ten thousand men. Although the powerful Assyrians were occupying the attention of the Syrian armies, thus relieving him of the constant pressure that his father and grandfather had faced, he still had no reason to be optimistic about the future.

A BOW AND ARROW PREDICT THE FUTURE

On his deathbed, Elisha proclaimed his final prophecy, hoping to stimulate the faith of the weeping king. After symbolically helping Jehoash shoot an arrow through the east window in the direction of Syria, he predicted the Lord's deliverance from the Syrian occupation. At the command of the prophet, Jehoash continued to shoot arrows into the ground nearest Syria. When he stopped shooting after only three arrows, Elisha angrily rebuked Jehoash and told him that he would defeat the Syrians only three times.

THREE VICTORIES AS THE PROPHET FORETOLD

Elisha died. His prophecy was fulfilled. Three times Jehoash fought against Syria, and three times the Israeli army prevailed. He succeeded in recapturing all of the cities west of the Jordan River which his father Jehoahaz had lost. But he was not able to regain possession of the land east of the river which had been captured from his grandfather Jehu. This task would be left to his son Jeroboam who completed the fulfillment of the prophecy and regained control of the entire land which had formerly been occupied by Syria. The deliverance which Elisha had foretold was accomplished at last.

The enemy of Jehoash's father and grandfather—Hazael, king of Syria.

JEHOASH CHARACTER SKETCH

DID JEHOASH SEEK GOD'S POWER OR ELISHA'S MIRACLES?

When Elisha died, Jehoash wept over the loss of a man he considered to be his personal magician, not his godly counselor. Although Jehoash respected the power he saw in the life of the prophet, he did not obey nor love the God whom the prophet served (cf. John 14:21). It seems that he viewed Elisha as a great seer with a mysterious ability to reveal his enemies' war plans or cast spells to cause their defeat. The source of his power to perform such acts was not a concern to Jehoash.

WHY DID JEHOASH STOP AFTER SHOOTING ONLY THREE ARROWS?

Jehoash did not have the spiritual discernment to understand the real significance of what Elisha was asking him to do. As was characteristic of his life, Jehoash performed only the bare minimum in fulfilling the commands of God. His haphazard attempt to satisfy the Law of God in the worship of golden calves is similar to his half-hearted effort to obey Elisha's commands. When Elisha plainly told Jehoash that the arrow they shot together signified "the arrow of deliverance from Syria," it should have been evident that there was military significance in shooting the other arrows (II Kings 13:17,18).

WHAT WAS THE REAL REASON FOR ELISHA'S ANGER TOWARD JEHOASH?

When Jehoash revealed a lack of concern and determination in ridding the nation of its physical enemies, he indicated a lack of concern and determination in ridding the nation of its spiritual enemies. We read that "He did that which was evil in the sight of the Lord; he departed not from all the sins of Jeroboam, the son of Nebat, who made Israel to sin, but he walked in them." (II Kings 13:11) The chief sin of Jeroboam was his use of golden calves to prevent the people from leaving to worship God at the temple in Jerusalem as commanded in the Mosaic Law (I Kings 12:28; Deuteronomy 12:5). Jehoash's irreverence for the Lord was climaxed when he looted all the gold, silver and vessels that were found in the house of God in Jerusalem (II Chronicles 25:24). A final commentary on his failure came when rather than destroying the idolatrous altars which Jeroboam established, he named his eldest son in honor of him (II Kings 14:16).

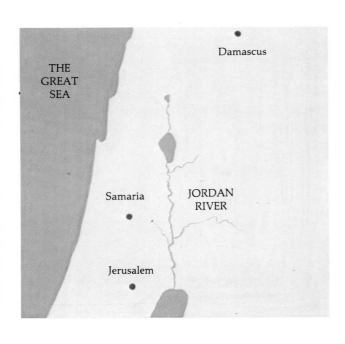

THE GREAT SEA

Damascus

Samaria

JORDAN RIVER

Jerusalem

In three successful battles (*II Kings 13:25*) *Jehoash regained cities which had been lost by his father Jehoahaz. He did not recover the cities east of the Jordan River which had been lost by his grandfather Jehu.*

JEHOASH

Determination

IS REJECTING ANY DISTRACTION WHICH COULD HINDER THE COMPLETION OF A TASK

LIVING LESSONS ON DETERMINATION . . .

FROM THE PAGES OF SCRIPTURE

God was grieved with the sin of a ruler and sent an unnamed prophet to rebuke him. The prophet courageously completed his dangerous task but failed to exercise determination on his return. Tragedy resulted because he allowed himself to be distracted.

ILLUSTRATED IN THE WORLD OF NATURE

THE WOLVERINE *Gulo luscus*

Early trappers and Indians had a healthy respect for the legendary wolverine. This fierce animal will fight any opponent, regardless of size or strength. Bears and mountain lions will even back away from this ferocious member of the weasel family. Averaging only thirty-five pounds in weight, the wolverine will eat anything it can kill in the brushlands and forests of its home.

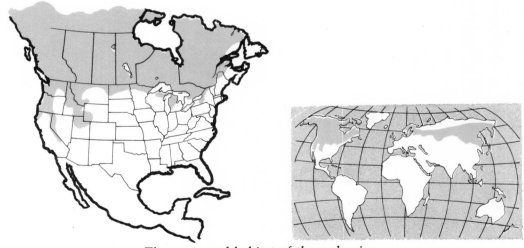

The range and habitat of the wolverine

DETERMINATION

HOW DOES THE WOLVERINE ILLUSTRATE DETERMINATION IN REJECTING DISTRACTIONS?

Satisfying its voracious appetite, the wolverine dined on a freshly-killed marmot. This rocky stream shoreline had provided it with many such meals.

The river was also a feeding area for bears. They feasted on salmon returning from ocean waters to their spawning grounds. Some salmon had already begun swimming by but the empty streams made them elusive. Later, when the streams filled with fish, there would be less difficulty catching them.

There had been no sign of bear near the stream today, but their presence would have made little difference to the wolverine. This fierce, determined animal turns aside for nothing and fights any challenger.

As it gorged itself on the marmot, the aroma of fresh blood was picked up by a hungry bear disappointed after a fruitless search of the stream. It lumbered toward the source of the scent and approached from the wolverine's back. Hearing a noise, the wolverine turned and faced a four-hundred pound grizzly. Moving toward the marmot, the bear growled a warning, but the wolverine refused to surrender its meal.

The wolverine sprang first, but with one powerful swipe the four-inch claws of the grizzly slashed through its tough skin and sent it sprawling to the rocks. The wolverine leaped again aiming for the back of the neck, but it only managed to sink its sharp teeth into the shoulder muscles. In a wild fury of fangs and claws new wounds opened on each contestant. But the powerful grizzly soon overcame its tenacious opponent. It clamped its large jaws around the wolverine's back, lifted it high into the air and flung it against the rocks.

The wolverine's body lay motionless where it had fallen. The grizzly was clearly the winner and

might have walked away with the marmot, but its rage had been aroused. It triumphantly stepped forward to pour out more fury on its victim. As it bent down, the wolverine mustered all its remaining strength and lunged at the bear. Its sharp teeth sank into the bear's throat and reached their mark. The stunned and surprised grizzly felt the fiery pain of vital cords being severed. Then a strange numbing seized its body and it slumped to the ground.

Exhausted and badly wounded, the wolverine managed to drag itself over to a crevice in the rocks. There it would wait for healing to come to its body. The determination which made retreat unthinkable would now be used to recover from the near-fatal wounds.

Severt Andrewson

CHARACTERISTICS AND PHYSICAL FEATURES OF THE WOLVERINE

With sheer determination, the tenacious wolverine defeated a grizzly bear over three times its size. By using the abilities it does have in single-minded concentration, the wolverine overcomes several handicaps.

WHAT ARE THE WOLVERINE'S HANDICAPS?

The wolverine is not endowed with physical traits which are common to other members of the carnivore family. The eyesight of the wolverine is very poor and the animal cannot rely on it in its pursuit of food. Its specially designed gait causes the animal to be slow and clumsy on dry terrain. These major drawbacks of speed and sight force the animal to use the assets it does have to the optimum.

HOW DOES THE WOLVERINE ATTACK ITS PREY?

The wolverine is the largest member of the weasel family and, like the rest of its relatives, has partially retractable claws. These claws are not only useful for tearing but help the wolverine in climbing as well. Because the animal is slow, it will climb to an overhang and wait for an unsuspecting animal to pass. Leaping from its perch, it tries to jump squarely on the back of the animal in order to sever vital organs.

Because it is a slow animal, the wolverine usually resorts to ambushing its prey.

HOW DOES A WOLVERINE LOCATE ITS SOURCES OF FOOD?

The only sure method that the wolverine has in locating its prey is to rely on its sense of smell. Once it picks up a scent, it doggedly tracks it down until it overtakes and captures its quarry.

WHAT ARE THE TWO SPEEDS OF A WOLVERINE?

If the wolverine is not running full speed ahead, it is at a complete stop. It does not have an intermediate pace, and it is not characteristic of the animal to simply walk. Great reserve strength is packed in its low-slung, muscular body. It may hunt for three or four hours and then rest for the same amount of time.

WHAT IS THE RANGE OF THE WOLVERINE?

A member of the *Mustelinae* or true weasel sub-family, the wolverine is equipped with musk glands. Traveling an area which may vary in size from fifty to seventy-five thousand acres, it stakes out vast sections for its exclusive use by spreading its distinctive scent over mounds. This serves as a warning to other wolverines not to intrude on the hunting territory which it has claimed.

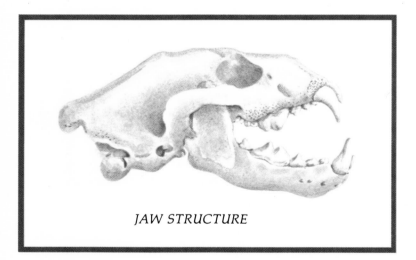

JAW STRUCTURE

ABOVE *Wolverine tearing apart cached food.*
LEFT *The massive jaw structure of the wolverine gives the animal tremendous crushing power.*
Heavy, wide teeth enable it to penetrate thick hide and bones.
BELOW *Relying on its sense of smell, the wolverine tirelessly tracks a deer.*

HOW IS THE WOLVERINE SPECIALLY EQUIPPED FOR SNOW?

The large wilderness area which the wolverine roams is usually covered with deep snow. Snow and cold weather do not bother this animal, and it is active throughout the most severe winter. For this climate, the wolverine has two distinct advantages. First, its fur does not collect frost or snow. Since the wolverine is built low to the ground, its fur would become matted and heavy were it not for its resilient quality. Secondly, the wolverine has the ability to move quickly over deep snow without sinking. By using its strange gait, all four feet hit the snow at the same time. Large foot pads distribute the weight evenly and prevent it from sinking. This advantage and its determination more than compensate for its lack of speed when hunting deer or caribou. Their sharp hooves sink deeply into the snow and eventually cause them to become exhausted long before the wolverine tires.

HOW DO THE WOLVERINE'S EATING HABITS HELP IT SURVIVE THE WINTER?

Because the wolverine inhabits northern regions, there are many times during the winter months when deep snow makes food totally inaccessible. Animals who are dependent on their hunting ability will starve. Although the wolverine has a tremendous appetite, it can abstain from eating when necessary. When food is available it eats all that it can, but it is able to go for days and weeks without eating anything at all.

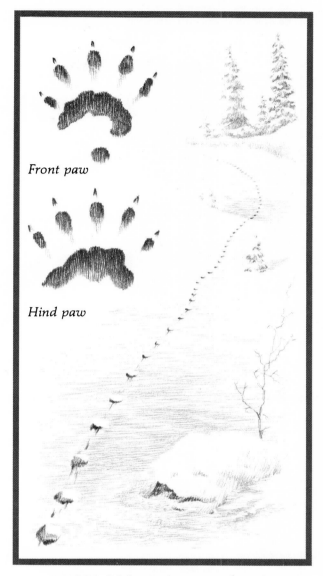

Front paw

Hind paw

BELOW *Wolverine's unusual gait enables it to move swiftly over snow.*

221

The female wolverine is more protective of her kits than even a mother bear. The color pattern of the young wolverine is exactly reversed from that of the adult.

HOW DOES THE WOLVERINE USE ITS SCENT TO PROTECT ITS FOOD?

Because of the tenacious nature of the wolverine, it is not unusual for it to pull down game much larger than itself. A moose or caribou, for example, could be the victim of a persistent attack. The wolverine's powerful and efficient digestive system enables it to eat all of its prey without waste. When a large prey is taken, the wolverine could not possibly make use of the entire animal. It will either camp in the area for several days in order to eat as much as possible, or it will tear the carcass into large hunks and store them in separate places for future use. In order to prevent other predators from stealing the food, the wolverine spreads the repulsive scent of its musk gland over it, discouraging even the hungriest of animals.

DOES THE WOLVERINE LIVE UP TO ITS REPUTATION OF CUNNING?

Indians and trappers feared and respected the wolverine. Following their traplines, the wolverines would spring traps and devour the animals. They would even eat the bait in unsprung traps without getting caught and then hide or destroy the traps. The Indians felt certain that only a reincarnated hunter would know all their techniques. The wolverine has been the source of many legendary stories. Whether or not the animal is as clever as the accounts portray is debatable, but one thing is certain—its single-minded determination distinguishes the animal from all others.

Even in sub-freezing weather the fur of the wolverine will not frost. For this reason Eskimos use the fur to line their parkas.

Legendary myths *about the wolverine have earned it a reputation for intelligence and cunning.*

HOW DOES SCRIPTURE ILLUSTRATE DETERMINATION IN REJECTING DISTRACTIONS?

The crowd watched as a proud king approached a golden calf which rested on a newly-constructed altar. Suddenly a man boldly stepped in front of the king and proclaimed, "God's curse is upon this altar and all who would worship here." The king was furious. He shook his fist and shouted to his guards, "Arrest that man!" Instantly the king's arm became paralyzed. Then the altar broke apart.

Horrified, the king cried out to the prophet, "Please pray to your God to heal my arm." The prophet prayed, and the king's arm was healed immediately. The grateful king invited him to his palace to have some food and receive a reward.

But the prophet refused his invitation. God had given him strict instructions not to eat any food or drink any water and to return home a different way than he had come.

As he got on his donkey to ride away, two young men slipped out of the crowd and ran home to their aged father. They reported all that had happened. He listened with eager interest, for he, too, used to be a prophet. "Quick! Saddle the donkey for me," he said, "and point me in the direction the prophet went."

He found him resting under the shade of an oak tree. The older man then invited him to a meal.

"No," refused the younger prophet, "for God has instructed me not to eat or drink and to come home by a different way." The old man explained to him, "I, too, am a prophet, and an angel gave me a message from the Lord that I am to take you home with me and give you food and water."

He was hungry and thirsty and it was a long ride home. He thought about how refreshing the food and water would be. Distracted from obeying God's clear direction, he agreed to have a meal with the old prophet.

But as they were eating, he received a message from the Lord through the old prophet. "The Lord says that because you have disobeyed His command and have had food and water you will not be buried in your home country."

After the meal the unnamed prophet resumed his journey. Just outside the city he was brutally and fatally attacked by a lion. The old prophet brought his body back and buried him in the foreign land as prophesied.

The brave prophet had courageously carried out the most difficult part of his mission, but by not swiftly completing it, he exposed himself to an unnecessary consequence.

From I Kings 13

Jeroboam may have patterned his golden calf *after the bull-calf of the god Apis which he saw being worshipped in Egypt.*

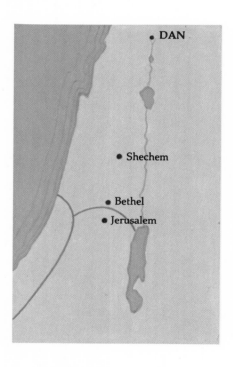

To prevent the people from worshiping in Jerusalem *under the influence of the king of Judah, Jeroboam established counterfeit centers of worship in Dan and Bethel.*

THE UNNAMED PROPHET FAILS TO REJECT A FATAL DISTRACTION

The nation of Israel was divided. The northern ten tribes were under the rule of Jeroboam, and the southern tribe of Judah was under the leadership of Solomon's son, Rehoboam. The Law of Moses did not make provision for a divided kingdom but designated only one temple and one spiritual center. Since the temple was located in Jerusalem, the capital of his rival, Jeroboam could foresee the danger of his people wanting to return to Jerusalem for worship.

A RELIGIOUS FESTIVAL JEOPARDIZES A KING'S REIGN

The annual Feast of Tabernacles which was celebrated from the fifteenth to the twenty-first of the seventh month was approaching. It was required in the Law that all men throughout the nation attend this feast at the Temple in Jerusalem. Jeroboam feared that these religious festivals would lead to the desire of national unity under the rule of his rival, Rehoboam. To counteract this threat he decided to create his own hybrid form of worship which would satisfy the majority and not endanger his rule. Solomon had already set a dangerous example by mingling the pagan rites of idolatry with the true worship of God.

FALSE WORSHIP ESTABLISHED

Jeroboam established two new centers of worship, Bethel and Dan, both conveniently located. To substitute for the Ark of the Covenant located in the temple at Jerusalem, he set up two golden calves and claimed that Aaron himself had set the precedent for this type of worship on the journey from Egypt. To replace the popular Feast of Tabernacles which was also held in Jerusalem on the seventh month, he designed a counterfeit feast to be held the same time on the eighth month (I Kings 12:32,33). He also opened the priesthood to all tribes rather than excluding membership to the tribe of Levi. He no doubt had convinced himself and hoped to convince the people that they were not really worshipping another god but merely adopting new methods because of the new situation.

A KING IMMOBILIZED BY THE REBUKE OF A PROPHET

On the opening day of the counterfeit feast the man of God from Judah came to Bethel to deliver his unpopular message. Jeroboam was standing at the altar with many of the people present when the prophet cried against the illegal altar with his prediction of doom. Jeroboam discerned the tenseness of the crowd and decided to demonstrate his superior strength by seizing the intruder. When Jeroboam's outstretched hand dried up and his altar split apart according to the prophecy, he begged the prophet for healing. He then tried another tactic in order to salvage the situation. He invited the man of God to eat with him and tried to bribe him with a gift. If the prophet had agreed it would have indicated to the people that Jeroboam's actions were really not intolerable and that it was possible for a compromise to be reached. But the prophet refused, explaining the commandment given him by God not to eat bread, drink water, or return by the way he came.

A DISTRACTED PROPHET DOESN'T MAKE IT HOME

As the man of God returned to Judah he had no way of knowing that his real test of obedience was just beginning. An old prophet living in Bethel had refused to attend Jeroboam's feast. But his sons were not as scrupulous and informed him of the events of the day. He craved the spiritual fellowship he had experienced in his youth and resorted to a lie to achieve his purpose. By claiming that he had received new revelation from an angel, the man of God was deceived by the older prophet into going back to his home. Punishment for disobedience was death at the mouth of a wild beast. The day had begun in a mighty spiritual victory for the Lord but ended in a pathetic spiritual defeat for the man of God because he allowed himself to be distracted before his task was complete.

THE UNNAMED PROPHET CHARACTER SKETCH

WHY WAS THE PROPHET NOT TO EAT OR DRINK ON HIS MISSION?

Because of the natural inclination to refuse food during a time of severe personal grief, fasting was considered a sign of mourning or deep distress (cf. Judges 20:26). On the other hand, eating and drinking with another person was normally the occasion for happiness and signified the desire for friendship (cf. Matthew 9:14,15; I Corinthians 5:11). For the prophet to fast was completely appropriate with the somber message he delivered to Jeroboam. To stop and enjoy the fellowship of even a godly friend would have completely misrepresented the message with which God had entrusted him.

HOW COULD THE PROPHET HAVE BEEN SO EASILY DECEIVED?

This man of God had just stood alone against an entire nation and its king. He had walked many miles and still had to make the return trip home. He was so tired that he felt it necessary to rest, and it must have been hot because he sat under an oak tree (I Kings 13:14). He was probably thirsty, hungry and very lonely after his recent physically and emotionally exhausting mission. After refusing Jeroboam's invitation to eat at his home he may have felt that this exhausted the reason for the command to fast. His physical desire for nourishment and his emotional desire for fellowship with an old prophet overpowered his knowledge of God's specific command. He had become lazy in spirit and allowed the Adversary entrance (cf. Genesis 4:7; I Peter 5:8). When the old prophet reached him, he was already in a compromising position. In disobedience to the Lord, the unnamed prophet was found resting underneath a tree. Had he been determined to complete his mission he would not even have stopped to rest, and it is likely that the older prophet would never have caught up with him.

WHY DID GOD PUNISH THE YOUNGER PROPHET SO SEVERELY?

The sin of the prophet was deeper than just his natural desire for food and fellowship. As a spiritual leader, his duty was to protect the people from false religion and erroneous doctrine. His guiding principle was to be the fact that God does not contradict Himself. The sin of Jeroboam which the prophet condemned was the sin of modifying and disregarding God's commands because of changing circumstances and personal conveniences. Now he was doing the exact same thing by disregarding what God had commanded and believing instead that the word of another prophet could annul a former command.

"**Thus saith the Lord,** *Forasmuch as thou hast disobeyed the mouth of the Lord. . .but camest back, and hast eaten bread and drunk water in the place. . .thy carcass shall not come unto the sepulcher of thy fathers."*

THE UNNAMED PROPHET

Orderliness

PART FIVE

ORGANIZING AND UTILIZING MY RESOURCES TO THEIR GREATEST EFFICIENCY

MAINTAINING CLEANLINESS AND GOOD GROOMING

REMOVING ITEMS THAT COULD HINDER ACHIEVEMENT

PROVIDING SPECIFIC AREAS FOR DIFFERENT FUNCTIONS

Orderliness

IS ORGANIZING AND UTILIZING MY RESOURCES TO THEIR GREATEST EFFICIENCY

LIVING LESSONS ON ORDERLINESS . . .

FROM THE PAGES OF SCRIPTURE

The thoughtful planning of the leader in gathering and assembling a myriad of materials—metals, timber and precious stones—was a remarkable example of precision and orderliness. It took years to finish, but when it was completed it was the most magnificent structure ever built.

ILLUSTRATED IN THE WORLD OF NATURE

THE WOODCHUCK *Marmota monax*

This sixteen to twenty-inch rodent makes its home in fields and open spaces throughout North America. Active in the early morning and late afternoon, it is a visitor of local gardens and feeds chiefly on vegetation. This burrowing animal is known by many names: woodchuck, marmot, ground hog or varmint.

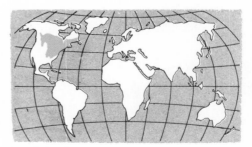

The range and habitat of the woodchuck

ORDERLINESS

HOW DOES THE WOODCHUCK ILLUSTRATE ORDERLINESS IN ORGANIZING ITS RESOURCES?

When early English settlers came to this country they saw for the first time a little animal which for lack of a better name they called, "chuck," meaning, "little pig." From all outward appearance the name was aptly chosen.

Spending much of its time digging and living the rest of the year in an earthen den, the woodchuck would appear to be a dirty animal to the casual observer. But such is not the case. The woodchuck is, in fact, extremely fastidious both in its personal grooming and in the care of its surroundings.

The woodchuck takes great care to remove burrs from its fur with its teeth and has a regular program of licking its paws and the fur on its body. Rarely will one see any substance such as dirt, burrs or grass on the woodchuck.

But the feature that distinguishes the woodchuck from most other animals is the way it keeps its surroundings perfectly clean. It is very unusual to see the excrement of this animal. When the tidy woodchuck must eliminate its waste, it looks for a spot some distance from the den and digs a hole two to three inches deep. Afterward, it carefully covers the hole with dirt. This practice alone is more than is normal in the animal world. But even this is not sufficient for the woodchuck. Using its head, it hammers the earth to compact the loose dirt around the deposit to ensure that it will not be uncovered.

When it is not convenient for the marmot to go outside, improvisation is necessary. Digging a chamber to provide its own indoor plumbing, it takes care to construct this compartment for waste well below the sleeping chamber. The waste is buried with great care and is periodically removed and reburied outside the den.

The woodchuck is also tidy in its sleeping quarters, especially when the female is rearing her brood. When the chucklings are young, the mother routinely replaces soiled nesting material with clean, dry grass. Hot summer days are pleasant because pesky insects are not attracted to the odorless area. The diligence with which the woodchuck maintains cleanliness in its surroundings makes it the model housekeeper of the animal world.

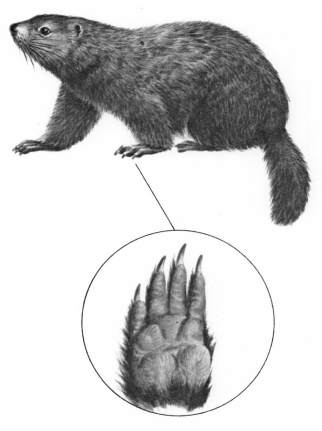

CHARACTERISTICS AND PHYSICAL FEATURES OF THE WOODCHUCK

Just as the little woodchuck is meticulous in its personal grooming and the maintenance of its surroundings, so it is also precise in the way it constructs its living quarters, taking great care to organize and engineer an elaborate dwelling.

HOW MANY DIFFERENT WAYS DOES A WOODCHUCK DIG?

The woodchuck's ability to move tremendous amounts of earth efficiently and quickly may be its most distinctive characteristic. This animal can literally dig itself out of sight in a matter of minutes. The woodchuck loosens the earth with its front feet and then with a spring-like action uses its hind feet to fling the soil backward in a spray of earth. When a mound builds up, a special double-footed backward kick—which leaves the woodchuck sprawled flat—is employed. If the tunnel is so deep that the earth cannot be tossed out, the woodchuck loosens the earth with both front and hind feet. Then it pushes the soil out of the hole using the top of its head as a ram.

HOW MUCH DIRT CAN A WOODCHUCK MOVE?

This amazing ten-pound rodent can move 700 pounds of earth in a single season.

HOW DOES A WOODCHUCK KEEP DIRT OUT OF ITS EARS?

The animal has a unique muscular structure which actually brings down the upper portion of the ear. The sides of the lower portion of the ear press against each other so completely that the smallest particle of dust cannot enter. By using this special apparatus, the woodchuck's ears remain clean despite the most furious digging.

The woodchuck removes huge amounts of earth *with its long powerful claws to engineer an elaborate burrow. But the next year will find it on the move again.*

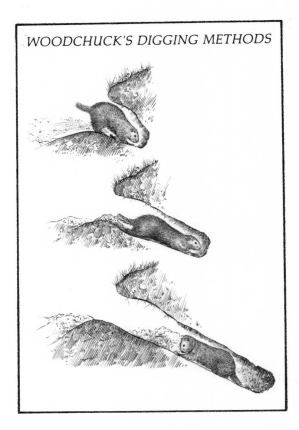

WOODCHUCK'S DIGGING METHODS

233

WHERE DOES THE WOODCHUCK DIG ITS BURROW?

The woodchuck or marmot usually selects its homesite on the side of a hill or near a fence or stone heap. Once the burrow is constructed, the animal rarely ventures farther than one hundred yards away from its home. Each year it may construct two or three burrows which it occupies at different times.

WILL IT EVER MAKE ITS DEN IN A TREE?

No. The woodchuck never nests in a tree, although it can climb and may scamper up a trunk if surprised and chased by a dog. In late summer, the animal may be lured to climb for the reward of ripe fruit in lower branches.

WHAT'S INSIDE A WOODCHUCK'S HOME?

The woodchuck's burrow is a maze of tunnels. The den begins with a two to three foot slanting entrance. At this point a small mound of earth is carefully pounded in place. No enemy can see beyond this barricade which is used as a "look-out" point by the little engineer. Then the main tunnel, which may be as long as forty-five feet, becomes narrow and takes a gradual turn. Branching off from this main tunnel are many compartments such as a brood chamber where the female has her young, a sleeping chamber and an excrement chamber. Several lateral tunnels lead to other exits.

WHAT HAPPENS TO THE DEN WHEN THE YOUNG WOODCHUCKS ARRIVE?

When the den becomes crowded, the chucklings are moved from the main nest to separate burrows which have been prepared in advance. The entire family area is usually limited to a one hundred fifty yard square, and the mother simply cares for each chuckling in its separate den.

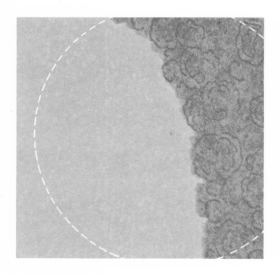

TOP *Having stored its food in fat, the woodchuck takes advantage of the warm days before winter. Perched on its haunches, it suns for hours, keeping a wary eye open for predators.*

ABOVE *The woodchuck usually confines itself to a one hundred yard radius, rarely venturing beyond these boundaries.*

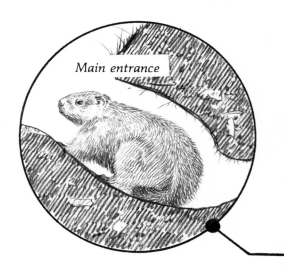

Main entrance

HOW DOES A WOODCHUCK MAKE ITS HOME FLOOD-PROOF?

The woodchuck's choice of a side hill for its home enables it to eliminate the danger of floods. After constructing the entrance, the woodchuck makes a sharp upward turn followed by an eight to ten-foot tunnel extending parallel to the surface of the ground. This construction guards against the possibility of flooding.

HOW DOES THIS CLEVER ENGINEER OUT-FOX THE FOX?

The woodchuck constructs its burrow with at least two exits. One, easily distinguishable, has a mound of earth heaped in front of it. The other serves as an escape route and is rarely used. When predators such as the fox pursue the animal to its front door, the woodchuck uses this point as a lookout. Taking great care not to leave any tell-tale signs of excavation in digging this secondary exit, it even avoids disturbing the surrounding vegetation.

The woodchuck's den is composed of tunnels, chambers and escape routes. It keeps its environment clean, periodically changing bedding material and either plugging up the excrement chamber or removing its contents from the den.

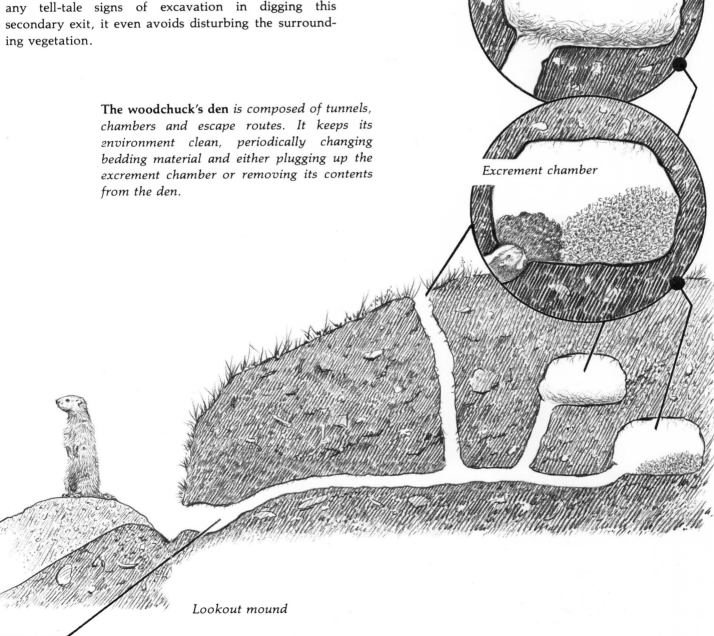

Concealed escape exit

Sleeping chamber

Excrement chamber

Lookout mound

IN WHAT WAY IS THE WOODCHUCK A MASON?

Always in close proximity to its den, the woodchuck runs at the slightest sign of danger. Retreat to the burrow is usually enough to discourage predators; however, there are some animals that try to pursue beyond this point by attempting to dig the animal out. In case of such pursuit, the woodchuck plugs its burrow behind it and closes the hole with earth as hard-packed as a cement wall.

DOES THE WOODCHUCK LIKE TO PLAY IN THE RAIN?

No. During a rainfall the woodchuck scampers to its dry, comfortable burrow and remains there until the storm passes. In fact, it dislikes water so much that it doesn't even drink in the conventional way. Instead, it relies on plant juices and morning dew for its liquid supply.

WHERE DOES THE WOODCHUCK STORE ITS FOOD?

Like other hibernating animals, the woodchuck stores large quantities of food throughout autumn, especially favoring clover. But instead of hiding food in warehouses which might be found, the woodchuck stores its winter food supply as fat in its body. This lining of fat serves as an insulation against the low temperatures of winter and a source of food for the early days of spring after it emerges from its hibernation.

IS THE WOODCHUCK AN ACCURATE WEATHER FORECASTER?

According to legend, the woodchuck determines the arrival of spring by the appearance of its shadow on February 2. If the day is cloudy and the woodchuck fails to see its shadow, one can expect spring to be well on its way. On the other hand if the woodchuck spots its shadow, six more weeks of cold weather are to be anticipated. The story is entirely without basis. In fact, it is unlikely that the woodchuck even leaves its den at that time of year.

WOODCHUCK IN ITS SLEEPING POSITION

HOW DOES SCRIPTURE ILLUSTRATE ORDERLINESS IN ORGANIZING MY RESOURCES?

Determined to fulfill the dream of his father, a wise young man undertook a project. His father would have liked to accomplish this task personally, but because he was a man of war he was unfit for the job. He was allowed to gather the materials necessary for the construction and did this until the end of his reign.

After his death, his son assumed leadership and resolved to fulfill the dream of his father—building the temple in Jerusalem to house the ark. This phenomenal feat would require all of his energies and organizational abilities in coordinating vast quantities of material and thousands of men of diverse nationalities and skills.

He began organizing the project, maintaining order in every aspect. First he secured stone and lumber from different countries. He made an alliance with a neighboring king to employ men skilled in woodworking. He established a rotational working program with thirty thousand men to help cut giant cedar trees of Lebanon. He sent an additional eighty thousand masons to cut and finish stones from the hills.

After four and a half years of collecting materials, actual construction began in the spring. Seventy thousand laborers at the construction site directed by over three thousand foremen began building the temple—ninety feet long, thirty feet wide and forty-five feet high. Constructed on an expensive stone foundation, the cedar-paneled walls were beautifully decorated with hand carvings and overlaid with gold.

The quantity of materials and the scope of coordinated effort were staggering, but even more remarkable is the fact that because the leader followed the plan so precisely, neither hammer nor chisel could be heard at the site. The prefinished stones and beams were so exactly cut that they fit perfectly together. After seven years of hard work, this sacred building was completed—hundreds of years after the nation left the slavery of Egypt.

Why was it so important for Solomon to complete his father's dream? His motivation to complete the project with such precision and order is revealed in his prayer during the dedication ceremonies, "But will God indeed dwell in the earth? Behold, heaven and the highest heaven cannot contain thee; how much less this house which I have built! Yet have thou respect unto the prayer of thy servant . . . That thine eyes may be open toward this house night and day, even toward the place of which thou hast said, My name shall be there." The Lord had given his father the promise that upon completion of the temple His glory would fill it. The temple would be the scene of His presence in Israel.

From I Kings 6:1-14

SOLOMON'S INTRICATE BUILDING PROGRAM
REQUIRED MAINTAINING ORDER IN ITS HIGHEST FASHION

Solomon's **Phoenician-built trading ships** *returned to Red Sea ports every three years loaded with cargoes of ivory, gold and other riches.*

The temple was about ninety feet long, *thirty feet wide and forty-five feet high. There was a fifteen-foot entrance porch and storerooms lined the sides.*

Solomon's temple *was built of stone and cedarwood from Lebanon. Cedar is a beautiful red-colored wood which is free from knots and remarkably durable.*

The life of Solomon is one of the most puzzling in all Scripture. He excelled all the kings of the earth in riches and in wisdom. Rulers from all over the world brought him gifts in exchange for the privilege of hearing the wisdom which God had given him. He was an expert on subjects ranging from human nature to natural science. He was responsible for writing a significant portion of the Old Testament Scripture—Psalms 72 and 127, a large section of the book of Proverbs, the book of Ecclesiastes and the Song of Solomon. He also wrote three thousand proverbs and one thousand and five songs (I Kings 4:29-34). Yet with all his wisdom, knowledge and understanding, his life ended in spiritual ruin. Unlike his father David, not even one of his sons was capable of preserving his great empire.

A SON FULFILLS THE DREAM OF HIS FATHER

The young prince Solomon did not resort to force in order to seize his father David's throne like his older brothers Absalom and Adonijah. He patiently waited for his father to fulfill the promise he had made to Bathsheba that their son Solomon would succeed him as king. With his parents' blessing, he assumed his father's position with hardly a struggle. After King David's death, Solomon moved swiftly to strengthen his hold on the throne. He very wisely obeyed his dying father's instructions to dispose of a few key enemies. He then turned his full energies toward fulfilling the life-long dream of his father which was to build a permanent temple in Jerusalem to house the sacred ark and hence establish a central place of worship.

HIS OWN AMBITIONS LACK LASTING PURPOSE

After Solomon dedicated the temple, he began work on his own ambitious building campaign. He spent thirteen years building his own house which was large enough to accommodate his huge family and army of servants. He built a huge fortress to protect the temple, military defenses and fortifications for cities throughout his kingdom.

Solomon's grand plans, though, were not accomplished without cost. To secure an adequate construction force he reduced the former Canaanite occupants of the land to slaves. Since this number of people was insufficient, he compelled free-born Israelites to work in groups of ten thousand every third month. In addition to men he also needed money for importing materials and food for feeding all of the state employees. The provisions needed for just one day by Solomon's court alone were one hundred eighty-eight bushels of fine flour, three hundred seventy bushels of meal, ten fat oxen, twenty pasture-fed cattle, one hundred sheep, besides hart, gazelles, roebucks and fatted fowl.

In order to collect this huge amount of revenue from the people, Solomon divided Israel into twelve administrative districts, all comparatively equal in population and resources. He assigned one officer to head each district and all of them were responsible to a superior who made sure that nothing was lacking.

THE NATION PAYS AN EXORBITANT PRICE FOR A WORTHLESS GOAL

The real cost of Solomon's projects, though, was the increasingly negative attitude of the common Israelite. His forced labor disrupted family life and created resentment. His twelve new tax districts ignored old tribal boundaries, and for all practical purposes the tribal distinctions were abandoned except for temple duties and genealogies. This increased the worst suspicions of those not favorable to a powerful central government centered in the tribe of Judah. His court of splendor would have been an offense to the common man who struggled to adequately supply for his own household after his taxes had been exacted.

THE WRONG EMPHASIS DIVIDES A NATION

After forty years of reign, Solomon had brought Israel to a position of world prominence and had given his country a prolonged period of peace and prosperity. But the common people were only waiting for his death to initiate their revolt against his harsh measures. Immediately after his death, Jeroboam, one of Solomon's former administrators, led the revolt of the northern ten tribes against Solomon's son Rehoboam. The empire Solomon had spent so much time and energy in developing crumbled soon after his death because he had become preoccupied with projects rather than people.

SOLOMON CHARACTER SKETCH

WHY WAS SOLOMON SO WISE?

When Solomon inherited his father David's throne, he was still a young man. He was aware of the many pressures and difficult decisions which his father had faced. He remembered how one foolish decision by David had cost the nation seventy thousand lives (II Samuel 24:15). But that decision had been made after years of experience in leadership. He had hardly any experience and felt completely inadequate to lead such a great number of people (I Kings 3:7; cf. Exodus 3:11). His prayer to God was not for longevity, wealth or power but rather for a wise and discerning heart. His principal concern was for the people over which he was to rule, and because of this noble attitude the Lord promised him wealth and honor as well as the wisdom which he requested (I Kings 3:9-13; II Chronicles 1:10,12). His organizational ability was merely a by-product of the wisdom and discernment the Lord gave him.

WAS THE LORD PLEASED WITH SOLOMON'S TEMPLE?

Although the great temple differed from the design given by God to Moses for the original tabernacle, it is clear that Solomon's temple was approved by the Lord. The differences in the two can be explained by the fact that the tabernacle was constructed as a movable structure whereas the temple was to remain permanently in Jerusalem. Furthermore, the Lord Himself had given David the new plans, and David passed these plans on to Solomon (I Chronicles 28:11-19). The fact that the cloud, the visible symbol of the presence of God, filled the temple was a sign that God had entered it and chosen it as the scene of His gracious presence in Israel. This is exactly what had happened when Moses completed the tabernacle (Exodus 40:34,35; I Kings 8:10,11).

HOW COULD ONE SO WISE TURN HIS HEART FROM FOLLOWING THE LORD?

When Solomon was young he was so devoted to the Lord that he probably felt it would be impossible to be deceived into the worship of false gods. He may have considered himself immune from the danger of marrying foreign women who worshiped idols (cf. Exodus 34:12-16). When he realized that taxes alone would not support his many projects, he sought to raise revenue by expanding his foreign trade. Intermarriage between royal families was a common practice in the Near East often dictated by diplomatic and political expediency. Solomon took wives from the Moabites, Ammonites, Edomites, Sidonians and Hittites. He acquired a harem of seven hundred wives and princesses, plus three hundred concubines. Because he failed to maintain order in his home, his foreign wives practiced their idolatry and set up various shrines in and around Jerusalem. Solomon accomplished his goal to increase foreign trade but overestimated his strength to resist the evil ways of his wives (cf. I Kings 11:1-8). The diligence with which he maintained orderliness was evident in his strict control and leadership over those who built the temple. Because of misuse, this ability eluded him later in life, changing from a positive force to a negative one which would mar his final years with disillusionment and despair.

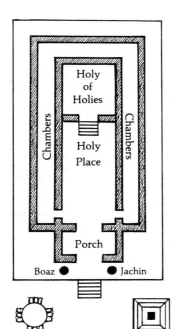

"And it came to pass, *when the priests were come out of the holy place, that the cloud filled the house of the Lord, so that the priests could not stand to minister because of the cloud; for the glory of the Lord had filled the house of the Lord.*"

SOLOMON

Orderliness

IS MAINTAINING CLEANLINESS AND GOOD GROOMING

LIVING LESSONS ON ORDERLINESS . . .

FROM THE PAGES OF SCRIPTURE

Society's outcast, she hesitatingly came as an uninvited guest. But because she demonstrated faith through an ordinary act of cleanliness, she received a priceless gift and the promise that this act of worship would be spoken of wherever the Gospel was preached.

ILLUSTRATED IN THE WORLD OF NATURE

THE BEAVER *Castor canadensis*

The energetic beaver works from dusk to dawn busily cutting trees for building material and food. The largest rodent of North America, the beaver is not too busy to maintain a comprehensive program of personal grooming and cleanliness.

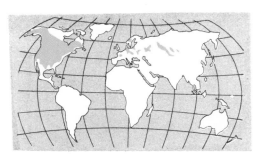

The range and habitat of the beaver

ORDERLINESS

HOW DOES THE BEAVER ILLUSTRATE ORDERLINESS IN OUTWARD CLEANLINESS?

The beaver's ability to build huge earthen dams, elaborate canals and an underwater home has earned it acclaim for its skillful engineering. But the beaver has another quality which is just as distinguishing if less familiar. The quality is that of orderliness.

The beaver takes great care and spends much time to maintain good grooming and cleanliness. Two techniques which it uses are unusual for different reasons. Both procedures require special tools—one is "built in" and the other is acquired.

The first procedure is the beaver's unconventional way of taking a bath to rid itself of irritating fleas and parasites. It ambles about, looking for a particular mound of earth. Once it finds the mound, it flops on top of it and begins to shuffle in a sprawled position. Soon ants are crawling all over its thick fur.

But rather than being irritated by these creatures, the beaver seems to enjoy their attention. To a naive bystander the procedure would be totally incomprehensible, but the beaver's actions make perfect sense to him. The ants are having a holiday as they scurry through the fur of the beaver, ferreting out and eating annoying parasites. Both parties benefit.

The second technique which the beaver employs involves its own grooming or "louse catching" claws. These claws, located on the two inner toes, are like combs. The combs are specialized—one is used for coarse combing, the other for fine. Running these claws through its fur, the beaver rakes out harmful parasites and untangles snarls which would slow its streamlined speed in the water.

These claws also aid the beaver in water-proofing its coat as it redistributes natural oils by repeated combing. At the base of the tail are two glands which provide the animal with additional oils. When a beaver leaves the water, it spends much time wiping, combing and water proofing its fur.

Because it maintains such a vigorous program of cleanliness and good grooming, the beaver is remarkably free from the parasites which plague less fastidious animals.

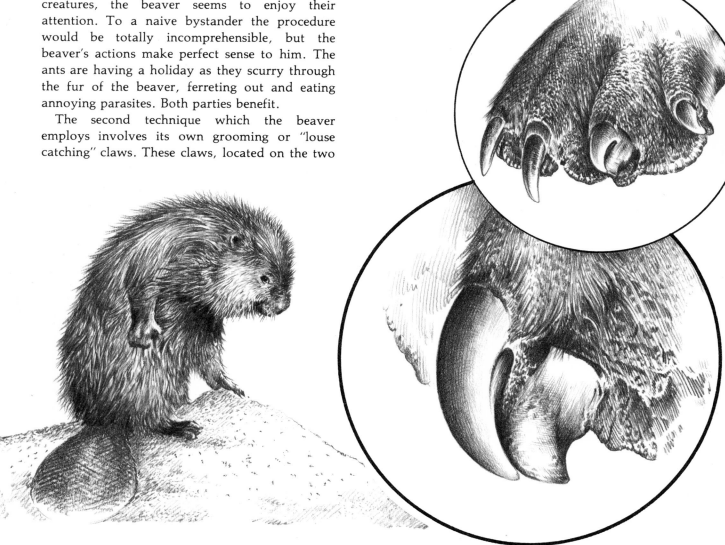

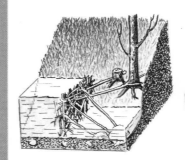

DAM CONSTRUCTION

The beaver forms a rough substructure *by pushing heavy sticks into the bottom of the stream and anchoring others to the shore. Then it interweaves branches and applies huge quantities of mud. Patching small holes with reeds, twigs and other material, the beaver makes its construction watertight.*

CHARACTERISTICS AND PHYSICAL FEATURES OF THE BEAVER

Just as the beaver is specially equipped for its unorthodox methods of maintaining grooming and cleanliness, so it is also unique in the manner in which it goes about its everyday business of eating and providing shelter. Because of its remarkable engineering abilities, the beaver is able to alter its environment and lifestyle.

HOW IS THE BEAVER ABLE TO CHANGE THE TERRAIN OF THE LAND?

Through strategic placement of logs and interwoven sticks packed with mud and stones, the beaver builds a structure which can withstand great amounts of pressure. The dam is securely anchored to the shore and river bottom. With remarkable engineering ability the beaver blocks up a stream or river and in so doing, floods the surrounding land.

HOW DO DAMS BENEFIT THE BEAVER?

The lifestyle of this animal is such that it depends on water for nourishment and protection. By flooding the land new sources of food are made accessible. The beaver is vulnerable to the attack of predators but is neither equipped nor inclined to fight. A docile and trusting animal, its only refuge is the deep pool of water created by the dam where it dives to elude pursuit.

DOES THE BEAVER REALLY HAVE AN ALARM SYSTEM?

Yes. Beavers warn each other of danger by bringing their tails up over their backs and then slamming them down on the water with great force. Any beaver hearing the sound of this crack—which may travel for half a mile on a quiet night—quickly dives beneath the surface and remains there as long as it possibly can.

The beaver's tail *has several functions. On land it supports the beaver's body while felling trees. In the water it acts as a rudder and a warning device.*

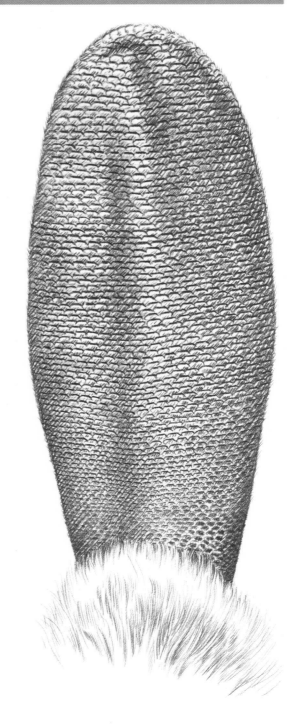

245

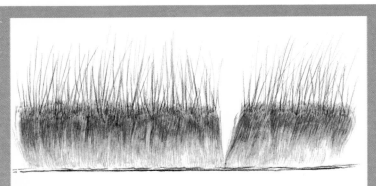

CROSS SECTION OF BEAVER'S FUR

The beaver's fur coat *provides the animal warmth and protection. Long guard hairs form a protective covering and shorter insulating fur retains body heat. Oil from oil glands is distributed enabling the fur to shed water quickly.*

HOW LONG CAN A BEAVER STAY UNDERWATER?

The beaver is equipped with large lungs and an oversized liver. As it dives, its heartbeat slows and requires less oxygen. Blood vessels which supply the extremities constrict so the oxygen supply to the brain area is not affected. By drawing on the reserve in tissues and lungs, it relaxes its muscles and slows its heartbeat, sinking to the bottom of the pond. After hearing an alarm, the beaver can remain underwater for as long as seventeen minutes without surfacing for air.

WHAT HAPPENS WHEN THE POND FREEZES?

Once ice covers the surface, the beaver lowers the water level of the pond by deliberately making holes in the dam which allow the water to flow out. This creates a gap between the water and the ice providing sufficient air and space for the beaver to breathe and swim on the water even though the surface is solidly frozen.

WHERE DOES THE BEAVER LIVE?

Usually out in the center of the pond, protected by water on all sides, the beaver builds a lodge by constructing a pile of sticks, mud and vegetation. It chisels out a tunnel and chamber above the water level.

HOW ELABORATE ARE THE BEAVER'S LIVING QUARTERS?

The design of the beaver lodge is simple and utilitarian. Each chamber has two sections, basically a dining room-bedroom division. The first floor, approximately four inches above water level, is used as a feeding area. Here the beaver eats, letting the bare twigs float away in the current. It also stands here to allow the water to drain from its coat before climbing to the second shelf, several inches higher, for sleep.

Valves over the beaver's ears and nostrils *close automatically when the animal submerges. Eyes are covered by a transparent membrane.*

Earthen Dam

WHAT HAPPENS IF THE WATER LEVEL RISES?

If a sudden storm or melting snow causes the water level to rise dangerously, the orderly beaver gnaws soil from the ceiling of its chamber and replaces it along the lower level of the den, building up the floor. If the ceiling construction suffers and becomes too thin, additional twigs and soil are gathered and replaced on top.

HOW DO BEAVERS MANAGE TO MAKE A DRY BED UNDER WATER?

The soft grasses which would seem the most likely choice for beaver bedding cannot be used in an underwater den. Because the grass would become wet when being brought to the lodge, it would mold and rot inside. Instead, small sticks must be selected and then split into long fibers. Each bed of broom-like composition is positioned separately against the wall.

DOES THE BEAVER GO WITHOUT FOOD IN THE WINTER?

An average beaver requires twenty-two to thirty ounces of bark each day. Beavers fell between two hundred and three hundred trees a year. In late autumn the beaver begins storing its food for the winter. It busily retrieves branches and anchors them by ramming them into the bottom of the pond. This maze of sticks and twigs becomes a storehouse of food. When the ice freezes over, the beaver swims to its cache, chews off a hunk and returns to its lodge to eat the bark with a revolving, corn-on-the-cob technique.

ABOVE *As the water rises, the beaver cuts away the ceiling of its chamber to raise the floor level. When the roof structure begins to weaken from this procedure, additional material is added.*

BELOW *The beaver's comfortable quarters are ventilated by an air shaft in the ceiling. Only a food shortage would force a family to abandon their lodge.*

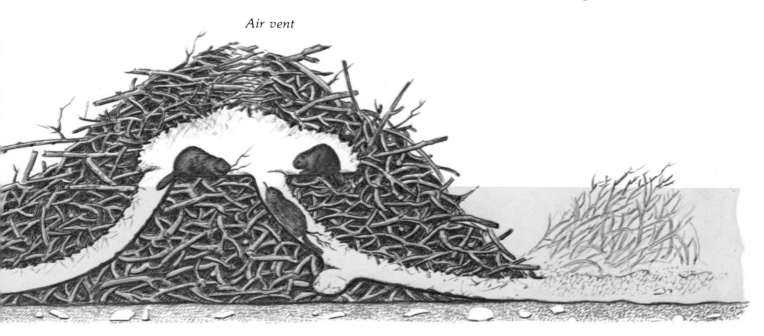

Air vent

Lodge

Food source for winter

247

ABOVE *Two flaps of skin behind its front teeth prevent wood chips from entering the beaver's mouth.*
BELOW *Three to five-inch wood chips are made when the beaver chisels through a tree by gripping the trunk with its upper teeth and tearing out the wood with its lower incisors.*

WHY WILL THE BEAVER DIE IF IT DOESN'T SHARPEN ITS TEETH?

The beaver, a member of the order Rodentia, has teeth which grow continually. If for some reason it is unable to keep them worn down, the chisel-like teeth will continue to grow through the roof of the beaver's mouth into the brain cavity, killing the animal.

DOES A BEAVER EAT THE WHOLE TREE?

Although the beaver will cut down any tree, it will not necessarily eat any tree. It keeps its menu fairly limited to birch and aspen. After felling a tree, the energetic woodsman strips and eats only the bark, perhaps using the naked branch for building material. It does not eat the wood fiber.

WHO CLEANS HOUSE IN THE BEAVER FAMILY?

The male sees to it that the lodge is neat and orderly. He also tends to any repairs on the dam. Only if necessary are the other family members recruited to share these responsibilities.

HOW DOES SCRIPTURE ILLUSTRATE ORDERLINESS IN INWARD CLEANLINESS?

Her ears were trained by practice to listen to the conversation of the street. Because she knew the pulse of the city she learned of important events such as the dinner that was about to be held.

She had pieced together the powerful teachings of One who was to attend. His words had exposed her secret life and brought deep conviction. The money that had been the object of her shameful life was now a convicting witness of her need to repent.

She took the money, representing her only means of security, and exchanged it for the most fragrant perfume she could buy. What she wanted to do would no doubt give His enemies further cause for ridicule. Religious leaders accused Him of being a friend of sinners, but those in the street quoted Him as saying that He had come to seek and to save those who were lost. These words reassured her as she slipped into the house, an uninvited visitor, and waited for the guests to arrive.

When He came she knelt down, kissed His feet and wept. Her tears splashed over His dusty feet and she wiped them with her long hair. As He gave her a reassuring and understanding nod, the host studied Him and concluded within himself, "He must not be a true prophet, or He would know how sinful this woman really is."

The same depth of understanding that reassured the woman challenged the host. "A certain man loaned two people money. Five thousand dollars was loaned to one and five hundred dollars to the other. Neither one could repay their creditor, so he graciously forgave them both and let them keep the money. Who do you think loved him the most?" The host replied, "I suppose the one who owed him the most."

By now the attention of all was upon the woman and the object lesson which her act of love became. The words brought stinging rebuke to the host and his guests.

"See this woman kneeling here. When I entered your home you didn't offer me any water to wash the dust from my feet, but she has washed them with her tears and wiped them with her hair. You refused me the customary kiss of greeting, but she has kissed my feet again and again from the time I first came in. You neglected the usual courtesy of anointing my head with oil, but she has covered my feet with rare perfume. Her sins, which are many, are forgiven for she loved much. But to whom little is forgiven, the same shows only a little love." Then He said to her, "Your sins are forgiven."

She transformed a routine act of cleanliness which others minimized into a beautiful expression of love and gratitude—an act which would be remembered for generations to come.

From Luke 7:36-50

HER ACT OF CLEANLINESS GAINED FAVOR AND FORGIVENESS FROM THE LORD

During the Lord's three-year ministry on earth, one of His most obstinate antagonists was a group of men belonging to the religious sect called the Pharisees. Many of these men gloried in their own righteousness and did good works only to be seen by men rather than being motivated by true concern. Because of their tendency toward hypocrisy, Jesus called them "whitened sepulchers" and "blind leaders of the blind" (Matthew 23:27; 15:14). Since they strictly observed external laws, they felt that they were actually fulfilling the full requirements of God's Law. As a result they considered themselves superior to those who did not observe their traditions, and they felt little need for forgiveness of their sins.

A KISS, A FOOT WASHING AND A FRAGRANCE

It was to the house of one of these Pharisees named Simon that Jesus was invited. When a person was invited to another's home there were certain duties of hospitality that every good host observed appropriate to that culture. To ignore these duties would be considered an insult. When a guest arrived at the home of his host, he naturally expected to be kissed as he entered. Each placed his right hand on his friend's left shoulder, and the host kissed his friend's right cheek. Then, reversing the action, he kissed the left cheek. It is the Western equivalent of a hearty handshake between two good friends.

Next, the guest took off his shoes or sandals before proceeding into the room. Since feet became grimy with dirt and perspiration on the hot, dusty roads a servant assisted the guest in washing his feet by pouring water upon them over a basin, rubbing them with his hands, and finally wiping them dry with a soft towel. Another custom was to anoint the head of an honored guest with oil. Inexpensive olive oil was usually used, but often it was mixed with fragrant spices. This fragrance would provide a pleasant contrast to ordinary odors of the streets which were traveled by various animals. The guest was given a drink of fresh water as a symbol of friendship and finally escorted to his place at the table.

DINNER—A COMMUNITY AFFAIR

In the time of Jesus, the Roman custom of reclining on couches had been adopted in some Jewish homes. Three couches were located on three sides of the table with the fourth side free so that a servant had access for serving. The guests reclined with the upper body resting on one arm, head raised, and the lower part of the body stretched in a reclining position. On such occasions, hospitality required that the door be barred to no one. It was customary to have the eating area open to the outside for better ventilation. For people to come in from the streets and stand around quietly observing the occasion and enjoying the conversation was quite common.

INSULTED BY THE HOST

When the Lord entered and Simon refused the customary kiss of greeting, he was saying in effect that his guest was his social inferior. When he failed to have his servant wash the Lord's feet, he insulted his guest. When he offered no oil to anoint the Lord's head, he indicated that his guest was not worthy of any special honor.

A CONTRAST BETWEEN HUMILITY AND PRIDE

Immediately after this disgraceful neglect of common hospitality on the part of Simon the Pharisee, "a woman . . . who was a sinner . . . stood at his feet behind him weeping, and began to wash his feet with tears, and did wipe them with the hair of her head, and kissed his feet, and anointed them with the ointment." (Luke 7:37,38) It would have been difficult to design a greater contrast between the actions of Simon the self-righteous Pharisee and the repentant woman.

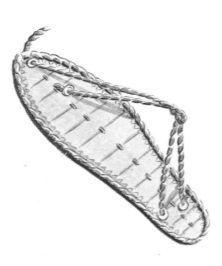

A friendly kiss *on both sides of the face is a form of greeting still used in many parts of the world.*

The sandal *worn in the warm climate of Israel left the exposed feet covered with a dusty film. Every guest looked forward to having his feet washed after entering his host's home.*

WHY DID THE WOMAN WANT TO KISS AND ANOINT THE LORD'S FEET?

This was a sign of deep affection and reverence. To kiss a person's feet was not unusual among the Jews. It was also customary among the Greeks and Romans. For a person to kiss the feet of royalty was interpreted as a token of subjection and obedience. The woman had more spiritual discernment than Simon by recognizing that Jesus was more than the son of a carpenter from Nazareth. The ointment in her alabaster container may well have represented the better part of her savings. To pour this costly perfume on the Lord's feet indicated that she had come to the conclusion that this Man was worthy of all honor.

WHY WAS SIMON SO INDIGNANT?

When Simon noticed the woman at Jesus' feet he said to himself, "This man, if he were a prophet, would have known who and what manner of woman this is that toucheth him; for she is a sinner." (Luke 7:39) The expression Simon used is often used for a woman known for her gross immorality. Such a woman was considered ceremonially unclean according to the traditions of the Pharisees, and to come in contact with her would cause defilement and create the inconvenience of purification rites. In fact, a strict Pharisee would not come within six feet of another woman in public for fear of becoming defiled. For this woman of known ill-repute to actually touch the feet of a guest eating at his table filled Simon with contempt. If Jesus were just a man, Simon's logic would have been correct, but because he was the Son of God He was able to cleanse the sinner and remain undefiled.

WHY DID THE LORD FORGIVE THE WOMAN AND NOT SIMON?

Every gesture of the woman indicated complete humility and a sense of unworthiness in the presence of a person who was worthy of her total devotion. She knew that she was a sinner and she recognized her need for deliverance from bondage. She came to Him not with boasts of good works but with her faith that Jesus' word of forgiveness was no less than God's. The Lord forgave her by His grace, through her faith, and sent her away in peace. Simon, on the other hand, did not see himself as a bankrupt sinner for he looked on the woman with contempt. He didn't even believe the Lord was a prophet much less the Son of God. Since he felt no need for forgiveness, he felt no need for a Forgiver and so he remained in his sin.

"And, behold, a **woman in the city,** who *was a sinner, when she knew that Jesus sat at meat in the Pharisee's house, brought an alabaster box of ointment."*

THE PENITENT WOMAN

Orderliness

IS REMOVING ITEMS THAT COULD HINDER ACHIEVEMENT

LIVING LESSONS ON ORDERLINESS . . .

FROM THE PAGES OF SCRIPTURE

A newly-appointed king set out to put his house in order and in so doing gained great favor with God. There were various objects in his kingdom which had to be removed because they were detrimental to the nation and hindered his people from developing spiritually.

ILLUSTRATED IN THE WORLD OF NATURE

BLACK-HEADED GULL *Larus ridibundus*

Slightly smaller in size than its relatives, the black-headed gull attains a length of fourteen to fifteen inches. Throughout its lifespan of twenty-five years, it inhabits coastlines and harbors. The black-headed gull is one of six dark-headed species found on the North American continent.

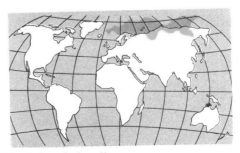

The range and habitat of the black-headed gull

ORDERLINESS

HOW DOES THE BLACK-HEADED GULL ILLUSTRATE ORDERLINESS IN REMOVING DESTRUCTIVE HINDRANCES?

The black-headed gull is a sociable bird and makes its nest in colonies. At one strategic point the parent gull removes something from its nest. The few seconds it takes to perform that simple act could mean the difference between life and death for its young.

The gull colony is composed primarily of birds of its own kind, but occasionally other species of non-preying gulls or even terns are granted the privilege of membership. Nests in a single colony may number up to several thousand. The gulls search remote seacoasts for a concealed area in which to raise their brood.

In early March the paired gulls prepare their crude nest. The birds scratch a slight depression in the ground and gather nearby vegetation and grass to line the rough nest. They fly freely to and from the colony each day. When the time draws near for the female to lay her eggs they spend less time away from the nest.

To prepare for incubation the female removes feathers from her breast. This allows her body heat to penetrate easily and warm the eggs. These featherless areas are called incubation patches. Because of its small size, the black-headed gull prepares just three such areas. As a result, only three of the brownish, black-spotted eggs are

likely to hatch even though more than three may be laid. If an egg accidentally slips outside the depression, the female carefully rolls it back into the nest.

In three to four weeks the young chicks break out of their shells. Shortly after they hatch, the parent gull does something unique. It carefully picks up the empty, broken pieces of egg shell and discards them a safe distance from the nest. By removing the shells in this manner, it reduces the threat of predatory birds which would be attracted to the nest by the white of the broken eggs.

Because of the continuous threat of destruction, parent gulls are constantly on the lookout until their young are able to defend themselves. Six to eight weeks will pass before the chicks are able to fly well enough to escape most enemies.

The eggshell served a dual protective purpose before the eggs were hatched. Its color camouflaged the egg against its surroundings, and the shell itself protected the developing embryo. But once they were shattered, the shells became a threat. Because these items that could hinder achievement were removed by the parent gull, the chicks enjoyed a greater measure of safety and a greater chance for survival.

Female stands over nesting site. *Only three of these eggs will hatch.*

CHARACTERISTICS AND PHYSICAL FEATURES OF THE BLACK-HEADED GULL

The mortality rate of black-headed gulls is staggering despite their precaution of removing white eggshells that signal the location of their chicks to predators. As many as ninety-five percent of the chicks fail to reach maturity. The gull clutch is usually two to three eggs, and both parents assume responsibility for the care and feeding of their young.

WHERE DO GULLS LIVE?

Different species of gulls live all over the world. They may be found in every state of this country sometime during the year. Living together in colonies, black-headed gulls space their nests approximately one yard apart. The birds either scrape a small depression out of the ground or construct a shallow nest of soft grasses. They favor protected or inaccessible locations on islands, peninsulas or cliffsides.

The close proximity of the nests allows the gulls to respond in a mob-like fashion when attacked by an enemy. For example, if an enemy from the air such as a raven or eagle approached, its flight toward a gull nest would infringe on the territorial boundaries of dozens of birds. The gulls take to the air in defense and it becomes practically impossible for the enemy to single out one nest for attack.

BLACK-HEADED GULL COLONY

Nests in the black-headed gull's colony *are spaced approximately three feet apart. Because they are in such close proximity, the gulls are able to ward off preying birds and animals.*

BLACK-HEADED GULL'S PLUMAGE

Immature summer

Adult winter

Adult summer

Throughout the black-headed gull's life, *its plumage changes in color as it molts in early spring and late fall. Only during summer months does the bird display the hood from which its name is derived.*

WHY ARE THE DEFENSES OF THE CHICK REALLY NO DEFENSE AT ALL?

Until they are able to fly, gull chicks are totally vulnerable to the attack of predators. If they sense danger, they simply freeze which is no defense in deterring a mammal from detecting it with its keen sense of vision and then devouring it. A chick which leaves the protection of its nest to seek refuge from wind or rain is likely to become lost and die unless the parents quickly rescue it.

WHAT ENEMIES DOES THE BLACK-HEADED GULL FACE?

Hawks, eagles, crows, ravens—all kinds of preying birds constitute a deadly threat to the survival of the eggs, the chicks and even adult black-headed gulls. Predators approaching from the ground are also attracted by large colonies of nesting gulls and may destroy dozens of birds in a single night.

WHY IS WATER A DANGER TO YOUNG GULLS?

One natural hazard which may prove fatal for the gull colony is a sudden rainstorm. If the earth fails to absorb the liquid, rain water may inundate the nesting area, and the chicks are likely to drown in shallow pools which have formed on the ground.

DOES THE BLACK-HEADED GULL KEEP THE SAME COLORED PLUMAGE THROUGHOUT ITS LIFE?

No. The bird's plumage changes when it is developing and throughout adulthood. As its name suggests, this gull is distinguished from other species by its head covering of dark feathers. Young gulls have a spotted brown head, and these feathers do not become black until the bird reaches maturity. In adult life the bird undergoes a change each winter when a molt of body feathers leaves only a few patches of black on the sides of the head and in front of the eyes.

HOW DOES THE PARENT GULL PREPARE A MEAL FOR ITS CHICKS?

The young chicks are fed many times a day by their parents. Adult black-headed gulls swallow food and then allow it to lie in their stomachs for a short time where it partially digests. Instinctively attracted to the red bill of the adult, newly-hatched chicks peck at the brightly colored underside stimulating a regurgitation action. The chicks then feed on the regurgitated food.

WHAT DO BLACK-HEADED GULLS EAT?

Everything. Fish, shrimp, dead birds, rodents, garbage, clams, fruit, eggs, grain—anything makes a meal for these scavengers. Their non-discriminatory tastes make the possibility of starvation highly remote. The gull is practically designed to eat. It has a wide mouth and an expandable gullet which increases its capacity to hold food. It can eat more than one-third of its own weight. Its heavy-duty, five-foot long digestive system has been compared to an electric mixer. Anything from bones to fish hooks can be dissolved by powerful gastric juices. The gull is useful along water fronts as an aid to sanitation for even garbage is palatable to these coastal scavengers.

WHAT IS UNIQUE ABOUT THE BIRD'S FOOD-GATHERING TECHNIQUES?

Its resourcefulness. The gull uses a special method to secure aquatic life in shallow waters. Walking backward along the shoreline, it stirs up the water with its feet and with keen eyesight detects any morsels of food in the disturbed water; it quickly grasps and swallows them.

HOW COULD THE GULL MAKE A HARD-SHELLED CRAB A MEAL?

Gulls have been observed engineering a sophisticated series of steps in order to make a meal out of a hard-shelled crustacean. They grasp the crab or clam in their bill and then fly high into the air. At this height they drop the hard shell and then quickly sweep down to retrieve the exposed animal. If the shell is not broken in their first attempt, the process is repeated until successful.

The chick of the black-headed gull *is attracted to the parent's red bill and pecks it to initiate a regurgitation response. Both parents feed the young.*

As it walks backwards *stirring up the water, the black-headed gull secures its food in a unique way. When small water life is routed from the shore bottom, the gull quickly scoops it up and eats it.*

259

GULLS RESCUE A FOREST

Just as the early settlers of Utah were benefited by the California gull, so residents of Scotland were grateful for a similar intervention by the black-headed gull. In 1947 caterpillars infested the oak forests of Perthshire. The trees would have been totally destroyed had it not been for hundreds of black-headed gulls which swept in and consumed the insect by the thousands.

Not all the eating habits *of the gull are considered beneficial. If the bird has an opportunity it will prey on the eggs of other birds—even the eggs of its own species.*

The gull uses its mouth *as a cooling system to lower its body temperature after hours of exposure to direct sunlight.*

IS THE BLACK-HEADED GULL A DIVING BIRD?

Gulls usually remain inland, and although they are excellent swimmers, they never dive. Their well-oiled plumage and double layer of down enable them to spend long periods of time on the surface of the water for resting and roosting.

WHAT'S UNIQUE ABOUT THE GULL'S DRINKING HABITS?

The gull is equipped with special glands which extract and excrete salt from the blood. Because of this asset, it can drink either fresh or salt water—a singular advantage. The kidneys of most birds and marine animals are not so equipped. Above the eyes another pair of glands strain excess salt and deposit it through openings in the bill.

HOW DOES THE GULL PERSPIRE WITHOUT SWEAT GLANDS?

Although the gull does not have sweat glands, it regulates its body temperature internally. The gull lowers its temperature by panting through its mouth causing evaporative cooling from moist lining membranes of the respiratory tract. The bird breathes rapidly through open mouth to withstand exposure to intense heat from hours of direct sunlight.

HOW DOES SCRIPTURE ILLUSTRATE ORDERLINESS IN REMOVING DESTRUCTIVE HINDRANCES?

In a war-torn and wicked kingdom a twenty-four year old prince carefully worked out a plan of action for the time when he would become king. The plan was destined to be so successful that it would turn the kingdom from wickedness to righteousness and from poverty to wealth.

He was grieved over the idolatry of his father and his nation. He had seen his own brothers and sisters burned in the fire of idolatrous worship. He watched as thousands of people had replaced the worship of God with wicked pagan ceremonies. When he was crowned as king a year later, he immediately put his plan into action. On a bright April day he gathered a group of discouraged spiritual leaders together in the street. With enthusiasm he explained the task he wanted them to accomplish.

He knew that his most difficult challenge would be removing a curious object which had come to have sacred meaning to the people. A message was carefully written inviting all in his kingdom to a celebration of worship. On the appointed day, a great throng gathered. The young king inspired them to tear down every altar that had been built to a false god, but they stopped at the altar of that curious object.

Its history began seven hundred years earlier when their forefathers had provoked God by complaining about their circumstances and questioning if God were really among them. So God sent thousands of poisonous snakes into the camp. They bit the terrified people and their bodies swelled as the deadly venom did its work. The people pleaded with their leader to intercede for them. God gave instructions for a bronze snake to be made and placed on a pole outside the camp. Thousands painfully made their way to the snake in obedience to the Lord and were healed.

The people decided to keep that bronze snake as a sacred reminder of the event. Once God had used it to test His people's obedience to His Word, but now people were looking to it as a source of healing. They imagained that the snake had power within itself. As such, it distracted them from their worship of God and many made an easy transition into idol worship by the veneration of the bronze snake.

When the throng asked the king if he really wanted them to destroy that object of worship, he answered with a resounding voice, "Nehushtan!" which means—only a piece of bronze. That command was all they needed. They destroyed this image which had for years hindered spiritual achievement.

With it removed, the people became bolder and went throughout the cities of the kingdom tearing down altars and turning the hearts of the people back to God. As a result, God blessed the kingdom and King Hezekiah—so much so that he was magnified throughout the nations of the world.

From II Kings 18:1-6

261

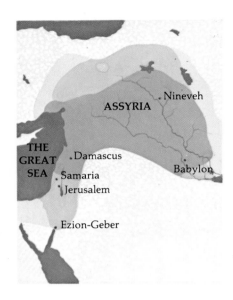

When Hezekiah inherited the throne *of Judah, the Assyrian army had already crushed the former buffer states of Syria and Israel. His successful defense of Jerusalem won him world-wide recognition.*

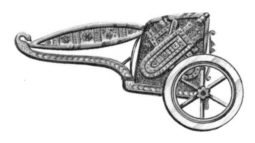

The sight of the Assyrian war chariots *caused Hezekiah's father to cower in fear.*

The "Taylor Prism" *contains an Assyrian description of their unsuccessful seige of Jerusalem. It is a hexagonal clay prism which stands fifteen inches high.*

TO SET HIS NATION IN ORDER, HEZEKIAH REMOVED OBSTACLES WHICH HINDERED SPIRITUAL ACHIEVEMENT

In order to appreciate the real significance of King Hezekiah's reform in the land of Judah, it is important to understand the state of the kingdom he had inherited from his father, Ahaz. Ahaz's rebellion against the God of his fathers and his refusal to accept counsel from Isaiah the prophet had brought economic and spiritual ruin to the nation during his sixteen-year reign.

NEIGHBORING NATIONS TAKE ADVANTAGE OF A WEAKENED KING

Early in his reign the neighboring kingdoms of Israel and Syria formed an alliance against Ahaz. They wished to replace him with someone who would join the anti-Assyrian alliance they were forming. Although Ahaz maintained his throne, the country was greatly damaged. One hundred twenty thousand men were lost in one day. The Edomites took advantage of Ahaz's weakened army by seizing a strategic naval base located on the Gulf of Aqabah. The Philistines invaded from the west and occupied border towns. Although the Mosaic Law forbad him to seek help from foreign kings, Ahaz appealed to the king of Assyria to send forces to deliver him from his enemies. The king agreed. He made Judah a satellite state of the Assyrian empire and imposed ruinous taxation on the people.

AHAZ PRACTICES IDOLATRY TO WIN FAVOR

In order to prove his willingness to submit to Assyrian rule, Ahaz imported Assyrian idols into the very Temple of God located in Jerusalem. Convinced that the false gods of Assyria were more powerful than the true God of his fathers, he became a full convert to the corrupt religious practices of Assyria. He worshipped the stars and planets rather than their Creator. He sacrificed his own children to gods that don't exist. He consulted Satanically inspired wizards and necromancers. Continuing in his twisted reasoning, he closed the Lord's Temple and made altars for himself in every corner of Jerusalem. In every city of Judah he established centers for the worship of foreign gods. Although his faithless foreign policies temporarily pacified the powerful Assyrians, the cost to the country was more than the people were able to tolerate. When Ahaz died the people refused to bury his body with past kings. Faithful Jews were praying for reform.

THE NEW KING CLEANS HOUSE

It was during this time of economic depression and religious chaos that Hezekiah, the twenty-five year old son of Ahaz, inherited the throne. To the grateful joy of the godly, Hezekiah reversed his father's policy of appeasing the Assyrian kings. He immediately reopened the Temple in Jerusalem and instructed the Levites to repair and renovate it for proper use again. The idols in Jerusalem were destroyed and thrown into the river. The Passover was celebrated for the first time in years. After the most joyful Passover celebration since Solomon had dedicated the Temple, the people went throughout all of Judah and even into the Assyrian possession of Israel destroying idols and altars. Hezekiah himself supervised the destruction of the bronze serpent which Moses had erected in the wilderness so that the people could no longer use it as an object of worship. His policy of fearing God rather than the Assyrians did not lead to the downfall of Judah as Ahaz had expected. Instead, it resulted in a new era of relative peace and prosperity. Hezekiah "did that which was right in the sight of the Lord . . . and the Lord was with him, and he prospered wherever he went forth." (II Kings 18:3-7)

YOUNG KING HEZEKIAH CHARACTER SKETCH

WHY DID HEZEKIAH HAVE TO DESTROY THE BRONZE SERPENT?

King Hezekiah destroyed the bronze serpent that Moses had made because the people regarded it as an idol and burned incense to it (II Kings 18:4). The significance of serpents in pagan rites of surrounding nations made Hezekiah's elimination of the relic especially imperative. In Canaanite, Assyrian, and Egyptian cults, altar stands with serpents modeled on them were worshipped as goddesses of reproduction or continuing life because of the snake's repeated shedding of its skin. The immoral practices of the serpent cults and the similarity of the bronze serpent prompted Hezekiah to remove the temptation for future generations.

WHY WERE HEZEKIAH'S REFORMS SO ENTHUSIASTICALLY ACCEPTED?

Although the nation of Judah was capable of great sin and rebellion against the Lord, they often seemed to recover with a godly king on the throne. Their northern brothers in Israel were never able to recover from their sin of idolatry until they were taken into captivity. When Hezekiah initiated his reforms he was immediately supported by the priests and especially the Levites (II Chronicles 29:34). When Jeroboam had eliminated the duties of the Levites in Israel, they left their assigned cities and migrated to Judah (II Chronicles 11:13,14). In Judah they resumed their responsibilities to teach the Law of God to the people, and in times of rebellion they prepared the people for reform (cf. II Chronicles 29:36). The Israelites in the northern kingdom mocked at Hezekiah's invitation to reform because they had no teachers of the Law (II Chronicles 30:10). But the godly remnant in Judah who were well-taught in the Law gave Hezekiah their full support.

HOW DID HEZEKIAH LEARN TO BE GODLY?

What Hezekiah learned about the fear of the Lord he probably learned from his Jewish mother Abijah which means "the Lord is my Father." (II Chronicles 29:1) Although it was the responsibility of the father to teach his children about the Lord (Deuteronomy 6:7), this time-consuming task was often delegated to the mother or in the case of a wealthy man to a personal tutor as well. The last chapter of Proverbs is an example of the godly instructions of a mother given to her son who became a king. As a young boy, Hezekiah must have recognized the evil of his father's idolatry and realized that his shallow compromises were made merely for political gain. He would also have been aware of the nation's strained economic condition for which his father was responsible. This awareness, combined with a desire to be a good king, were motivating factors for godly Hezekiah's reform.

The saw-scaled viper *is probably the snake which was called the fiery serpent. Its extremely potent venom is considered the most dangerous in the world. It was so feared that some Israelites worshiped its bronze image as another god.*

HEZEKIAH

Orderliness

IS PROVIDING SPECIFIC AREAS FOR DIFFERENT FUNCTIONS

LIVING LESSONS ON ORDERLINESS . . .

FROM THE PAGES OF SCRIPTURE

A wise ruler foresaw the dangers ahead and worked out an ingenious system to prepare for them. The steps he took spared his nation from that which ravaged all the nations around his own. A key in his preparation was constructing specific areas for future purposes and teaching his people the hard-learned character lessons he experienced as a boy.

ILLUSTRATED IN THE WORLD OF NATURE

THE EASTERN CHIPMUNK *Tamias striatus*

An energetic resident of hardwood forests, the eastern chipmunk makes its home in an organized network of tunnels and chambers underground. When interrupted in its search for seeds, nuts and berries the chipmunk utters several, "chips," and a "trill." It lives to the ripe age of eight years.

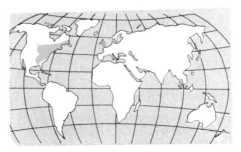

The range and habitat of the eastern chipmunk

ORDERLINESS

HOW DOES THE CHIPMUNK ILLUSTRATE ORDERLINESS IN PROVIDING AREAS FOR SPECIFIC FUNCTIONS?

The furry little ball drowsily reached down and fumbled beneath its bed, feeling the stack for something with the right shape. When it had found one that met its approval, it lazily brought it up to its mouth and began eating.

Underneath its bed was a chaotic clutter piled so high that the little animal barely had room for its bed. Its untidy appearance did not indicate slovenliness. The seeming disarray was, in fact, very orderly.

Beginning in early spring, the chipmunk had been diligent about its business. It had outgrown the protection of its mother's den and was preparing a home of its own. This would mean many days of hard work, but work wasn't a problem for the energetic animal.

It had taken care to choose a location and dig its burrow, making a tunnel two inches in diameter that would reach a depth of five feet. At the greatest depth, the base of the tunnel, the chipmunk would construct its toilet. At a higher level it would dig as many as six additional storage rooms, the contents of which would take all summer to fill. These storage bins were capable of holding as much as a bushel of food. The pantries were neatly organized and the chipmunk placed just the right kinds of foods in them. As it searched along the forest floor, it was careful not to store anything which would spoil or rot such as meats, fruits or vegetation.

A short distance from the pantry lay the master bedroom. The chipmunk took special care to choose the material for its bed and the right day on which to make it. If the day is too wet, the leaves won't dry. If there is no humidity in the air they become too brittle and break. The chipmunk scampered out to select oak leaves. It prefers oak for its thickness and fragrant smell. First, the stem is bitten off. Then, using its teeth and forelegs, it rolls up the leaves and brings them to the burrow bedroom. The slightly damp leaves make a perfect mattress.

The chipmunk took great care in providing food and comfort, but what steps did it take to ensure the safety of its burrow? In this endeavor the little chipmunk was also methodical and remarkably orderly. When the chipmunk was digging its tunnel, it deposited the excess dirt outside the hole. Once the tunnel was complete it dug another entrance, being extremely careful not to leave any tell-tale signs which would betray its location.

Finding an ideal spot among a pile of rocks for the secondary entrance, it disguised the exit and was particular to take the excavated soil a considerable distance away so as not to disclose the whereabouts of the opening. With this completed, it plugged the original entrance, carrying away any evidence of digging. An escape route was then constructed, engineered so meticulously that vegetation all the way up to the edge of the entrance was untouched.

The industrious chipmunk completed its project by late fall and was ready to enjoy a long rest which would confine it to its burrow until early spring. The chipmunk could rest, content that it had made every provision for its safety and comfort in its orderly confines.

Severt
Andrewson

CHARACTERISTICS AND PHYSICAL FEATURES OF THE EASTERN CHIPMUNK

The affectionate little chipmunk is diligent in its business of preparing for the winter. It organizes its home and stocks it in such a way that everything has its proper place. When it gets hungry in the winter, it makes a quick trip to its storehouse in the cellar and then runs back to its bedchamber—passing the winter in a leisurely manner. But this life of ease is only possible because of the boundless energy which the chipmunk exerted during the summer and fall in preparation for its retirement.

WHAT MAKES THE CHIPMUNK SUCH A LIKABLE ANIMAL?

Several things contribute to the endearing personality of the chipmunk—its neat "striped-suit" appearance, its speed and bouncing gait, its energy and peculiar habits, its astonishing ability to store away huge quantities of nuts in its cheek-pouches.

HOW DOES A CHIPMUNK RATE WITH ITS COUSINS AS A FOOD-GATHERER?

Although the chipmunk is the smallest species of the squirrel family, its olfactory sense is apparently superior to that of its relatives. When compared to the gray and fox squirrels in search for food guided by sense of smell, the chipmunk invariably beats its buddies to the pantry.

WHY IS THE CHIPMUNK'S NAME SO APPROPRIATE?

The chipmunk's name—*Tamias*—means "the steward" or "one who lays up stores." It is an appropriate description for this industrious worker. With remarkable foresight, the animal lays aside provision for times of scarcity. During the days of autumn, the striped bundle of energy labors from dawn until dark—finding and storing nuts away in its winter warehouse underground. One chipmunk is reported to have stashed away a bushel of food in three days.

Individual all-time records for chipmunk's food-carrying ability.

    13 prune stones
    16 chinquapin nuts
    31 corn kernels
    32 beechnuts
    65 sunflower seeds
    145 grains of wheat

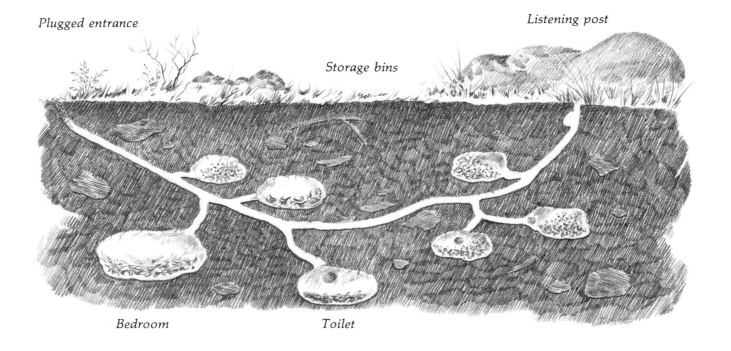

Plugged entrance

Listening post

Storage bins

Bedroom

Toilet

The chipmunk's network of tunnels and chambers *affords it protection from danger in the summer and allows it to spend a comfortable, worry-free winter. It is self-contained underground with three to six storage compartments, bedrooms, excrement chamber and nursery. After retreating to its burrow, it waits at a listening post near the entrance to detect the slightest hint of danger.*

The chipmunk is a clever little animal. *Faced with an obstacle, it quickly sizes up the situation and takes the puzzle out of the problem. In a test to determine the chipmunk's intelligence, a string was tied between two branches. Then another string was draped in tent-fasion over the taut string. A peanut was tied to one end. The nut was hoisted in the air and the other end was staked to the ground, leaving the peanut dangling. When the chipmunk was faced with this obstacle, it first tried to secure the nut by jumping up in the air after it. Failing in this attempt, it hesitated for a moment but then began tugging on the string anchored to the ground. Instead of getting closer to the chipmunk, the nut went in the opposite direction. But the little animal knew that if it pulled long and hard enough, the nut would eventually slip over the taut string and fall to the ground for it to eat.*

CAN A CHIPMUNK MAKE MUSIC?

After its winter rest, the courtship season begins for the male chipmunk. It searches for the den of a female, relying on its sense of smell. Once it finds a burrow, it calls to the female from the entrance making noises—a soft, continuous "kuk-kuk" that has a musical sound.

HOW EFFECTIVE IS THE LOVE SONG?

Chipmunk protocol requires that the female give express consent for the male to enter. Otherwise, he is literally chased from the burrow.

ARE CHIPMUNKS AFFECTIONATE?

What could be more affectionate than two chipmunks that kiss? Chipmunks occasionally greet one another with a gentle nose-touching gesture, pressing their faces against each other before scampering on about their business.

WHEN DOES THE CHIPMUNK RAISE ITS FAMILY?

Three to five young are born in the chipmunk's underground den in mid-spring. If there is a plentiful food supply, the Eastern chipmunk will raise a second brood in July.

WHEN ARE YOU MOST LIKELY TO SEE A CHIPMUNK?

In the spring, summer and early fall. During these months the chipmunk is in a frenzy of activity, busily preparing for its winter rest. A chipmunk does not actually hibernate, but it sleeps through the winter months, waking only when it is hungry. With its storage rooms full it has little need for excess amounts of fat, so it enters hibernation comfortably plump—not fat like the woodchuck.

HOW BOLD ARE THESE TINY ADVENTURERS?

Not very. A chipmunk seldom travels far from home, and it knows exactly where its entrance is at all times even though the doorway is completely concealed. When threatened, a few erratic leaps and a quick dive find the chipmunk safely back in its burrow. Once hidden, it re-emerges from its retreat to investigate the danger. Although the chipmunk is easily frightened, its inquisitive nature makes it a natural explorer. It is sociable and friendly and can be easily tamed.

Male "sings" to female in an effort to win her affections.

In no uncertain terms, the female lets her suitor know that his approach is not appreciated.

Chipmunk displays gentle, nose-touching gesture of affection and acceptance, then bounces on its way.

The chipmunk uses a ledge just below the surface at the entrance to listen for danger to pass. This pocket in the tunnel is called a listening post.

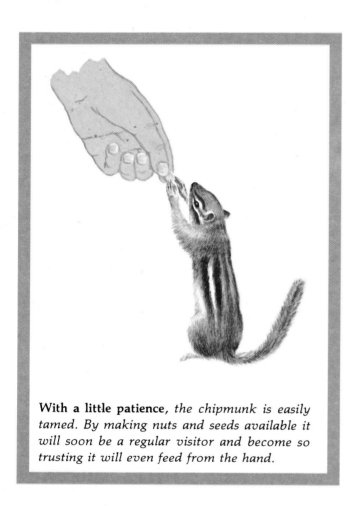

With a little patience, *the chipmunk is easily tamed. By making nuts and seeds available it will soon be a regular visitor and become so trusting it will even feed from the hand.*

In order for the chipmunk to fill its jowls *with beechnuts, it first chews off the pointed end and then fills one side of its cheek-pouch at a time.*

WHAT ANIMALS AREN'T A FRIEND OF THE CHIPMUNK?

Every predatory animal represents a threat to the tiny chipmunk. Most winged predators such as hawks, owls and falcons can sweep down from the sky and attack before the chipmunk is aware of the danger. Snakes, bobcats, foxes and weasels also hunt the chipmunk. Even small boys are a menace to this industrious inhabitant of the forest, although the chipmunk generally makes its home away from houses and barns.

WHAT IS THE CHIPMUNK'S DEFENSE AGAINST ENEMIES?

The only recourse which affords a possibility for escape is its speedy, agile run. The chipmunk leaps and bounds over grass and appears not to make any discernable path which an enemy can follow.

CAN CHIPMUNKS WARN EACH OTHER OF DANGER?

The chipmunk community is a talkative, sociable one. Using an outcrop of low branches or a small rock, several may be engaged in animated conversation. This communication network may relay more vital information than everyday chipmunk conversation, though. If a chipmunk is aware of the approach of an enemy, it races to within an easy jump of its hole and then, from that position of safety, delivers an alarm message which is quickly taken up by others.

HOW DOES SCRIPTURE ILLUSTRATE ORDERLINESS IN PROVIDING AREAS FOR SPECIFIC FUNCTIONS?

A dry desert wind blew over the land. It continued day after day until the lush green crops withered and died. For years the people of this land had enjoyed huge harvests. Now they would have to buy food from surrounding countries. But the famine covered a far wider area than anyone realized, and they didn't know it would last for many years.

When people are hungry they tend to lose their manners and their loyalties. But because of the amazing organization and leadership of a thirty-seven year-old governor, those in this kingdom developed a depth of loyalty and orderliness that was phenomenal.

Seven years earlier he had foreseen this famine and had given the ruler of the land a wise plan. Twenty percent of all the harvest was to be turned over to the ruler and stored for the time when no food would be available. When the famine began, special cities throughout the nation were supplied with an enormous reserve of grain.

Now the wisdom of his organization and orderliness was seen. Rather than giving the grain away and creating selfishness among the people, he sold it and built a respect for the value of that which they were receiving.

When the famine continued year after year, their money eventually ran out. Then they brought their cattle, horses and flocks and exchanged them for bread. But one day they said to this governor, "We will not hide our condition from my lord how that our money is spent. My lord also has our herds and cattle. There is nothing left but ourselves and our lands. Buy us and our land and we will be servants of our ruler."

The governor agreed to their plan and bought all the people and their land. Then he moved them to new cities. Instead of making them slaves, he required only as much as he did before the famine began—twenty percent of all their harvest. They rejoiced in his decision and praised him for saving their lives.

Where did he get his wisdom for such organization and building of loyalty? He learned from his own experience as a seventeen year-old boy. This governor was sold into slavery but he discovered that freedom comes by willingly serving those who are in authority over you. He, too, was moved to a new city with no possessions, but he realized that this freed him to care for and increase the possessions of those he was serving. In circumstances which would have conquered others, he learned priceless lessons of loyalty. With the foresight God gave, Joseph was able to design a plan of organization that saved the nation from famine and instilled the same attitudes of loyalty and orderliness in the lives of the people.

From Genesis 41:46-57 and Genesis 47:13-26

JOSEPH'S PREPARATION FOR FAMINE SAVED BOTH THE NATION HE SERVED AND HIS OWN PEOPLE FROM STARVATION

Camel caravans on their way to Egypt bearing fragrant balms, rare spices and occasionally slaves were a familiar sight to Joseph and his brothers.

The Ishmaelite traders carried their own balances to measure out twenty units of silver for the purchase of Joseph.

A contemporary portrayal of an Egyptian high official from the time of Joseph.

Joseph is one of the most refreshing characters in all of Scripture. Unlike those of his often-erring father Jacob, the errors of Joseph are so insignificant as to remain unrecorded. He is one of the few persons who was able to maintain spiritual stability in the peak of success as well as in the midst of trouble.

HARDSHIPS PREPARE A YOUNG BOY FOR HIS FUTURE WORK

The first mention of Joseph after his birth is when he submissively bowed down before his uncle Esau, an act he would learn to repeat as a slave in Egypt. Shortly afterward he lost the comfort and companionship of his mother during the birth of his only full brother. This was another hard preparation for the day when he would be displaced from everyone he knew and loved. Although he had ten older half-brothers, Joseph was the oldest son of his father's favorite wife and was favored above the rest. When Jacob honored Joseph with a long-sleeved robe when he was only seventeen years old, his older brothers may have discerned their father's intention to honor him with the family birthright and a double portion of the inheritance. Because of their contempt of their father's favoritism and possibly because they wanted Joseph's share of the inheritance, they sold him to slave traders on their way to Egypt.

FALSELY ACCUSED AND SENT TO PRISON

When the Ishmaelite traders reached the capital city of Egypt the young and healthy-looking Joseph was noticed by Potiphar, captain of the king's guard, who purchased him as a slave for his estate. Recognizing that this young Hebrew was not just an ordinary slave but that he excelled in everything he did, Potiphar promoted him to oversee his entire household. But the Lord had greater plans for Joseph than to spend the rest of his life in Potiphar's home. He removed him from that position in a very peculiar manner. Joseph was not willing to cooperate in Potiphar's wife's rebellion against her husband, and as a result he was falsely accused before his master and imprisoned.

THE INTERPRETATION THAT RELEASED A PRISONER

After spending the next few years in Potiphar's uncomfortable prison, Joseph was removed in order to interpret one of the Pharaoh's dreams. This ability had been discovered by the Pharaoh's butler when he was in prison with Joseph. The dream was from the Lord, and Joseph correctly interpreted it as the announcement of seven prosperous years followed by seven years of famine which were to begin immediately. So impressed was the Pharaoh with Joseph's wisdom that he raised him to be governor of all Egypt in order to supervise the economy for the next fourteen years.

BRILLIANT ADMINISTRATION SAVES THE NATION

Although Egypt and the surrounding nations benefited from Joseph's brilliant administrative efforts before, during and after the seven difficult years of famine, the real reason for his success was a promise God had made with Joseph's great-grandfather Abraham. God promised Abraham that he would be the father of a very large nation and that that nation would be the cause for all the other nations of the earth to be blessed (Genesis 22:15-18). It was because of Joseph that Jacob and his sons were preserved through the seven years of famine. In the fertile land of Goshen where Joseph placed them they prospered and grew into what later became known as the nation of Israel.

JOSEPH CHARACTER SKETCH

WHERE DID JOSEPH GAIN HIS EXPERIENCE FOR RULING THE NATION OF EGYPT?

It was no accident that Joseph was purchased as a slave by the prominent Potiphar, captain of the Pharaoh's personal body guard. To attain such a position, Potiphar must have been extremely competent and highly trusted. There is little doubt that he was well-paid and a member of the social elite. His home was probably a large and magnificent estate teeming with servants and activity. Joseph may have begun working in the smelly slaughter house or the more pleasant bakery. He may have tended the gardens, or he may have had to keep the stables. Whatever he did, he did it well and showed an enthusiasm and loyalty that was lacking in his peers. He soon was organizing the entire complex household, gaining firsthand experience in everything from small business economics to the more delicate area of labor relations. He learned how the country functioned and how the Egyptian people thought. This experience proved invaluable when he later ruled the land.

WHAT PREVENTED JOSEPH FROM DEVELOPING ROOTS OF BITTERNESS?

When Joseph was almost killed and then sold into slavery to a strange and foreign land by his half-brothers, he could easily have developed an unforgiving spirit toward them. Later he prospered as the head of Potiphar's household but was falsely accused by Potiphar's wife. When Joseph was unjustly imprisoned and forgotten for over two years, he could easily have become bitter toward God Himself. Years later when his terrified brothers discovered his identity Joseph revealed to them the reason his spirit was not bound with resentment. "And God sent me before you to preserve you a posterity in the earth, and to save your lives by a great deliverance. So now it was not you that sent me here, but God." (Genesis 45:7,8; cf. Genesis 50:19-21) As a young boy the Lord had revealed to Joseph in a dream that He had a plan for his life and that neither his brothers nor Potiphar's wife nor the Pharaoh himself could alter that plan (Genesis 37:5-11). He knew that his life was not merely a succession of coincidences but rather was being directed by a loving God.

WHAT WAS THE GREATEST LEGACY JOSEPH LEFT BEHIND?

Even though Joseph's tremendous organizational ability, his patience through tribulation, his faithfulness in fame and success and his forgiving spirit are all great tributes to his character, what stands above all others is his great faith. Joseph's faith in God and the promises that had been revealed to him were a continual reassurance as he endured the apparent unjust tribulation of slavery and imprisonment. Joseph was aware of his father Jacob's promise that his children would go to the land of his fathers. Joseph's faith was so strong that on his deathbed he made his family promise that when they did leave to go to the Promised Land they would bring his bones with them (Hebrews 11:22; Genesis 50:24, 25). This was an unusual request because at the time it was made there was no apparent reason to suspect that the Israelites would ever want to leave Egypt. They possessed the very best land (Genesis 47:11) and enjoyed the favor of Pharaoh. His faith in God was not just revealed by this dying request but characterized his entire life. It sustained and comforted him with the assurance that God had a specific plan for his life revealed to him earlier through dreams and confirmed by his father's word.

"So Joseph died, *being an hundred and ten years old: and they embalmed him, and he was put in a coffin in Egypt.*"

JOSEPH

Initiative

PART SIX

Initiative

IS EXPANDING MY WORLD BY EXPLORING NEW AREAS OF INTEREST

LIVING LESSONS ON INITIATIVE . . .

FROM THE PAGES OF SCRIPTURE

A young girl in her mid-teens wandered into a strange city with the intention of exploring and making new friends. Taking initiative which would have been contrary to her father's wishes, she exposed herself to the dangers of a city corrupted by moral decay. Every man in the city was to die because a naive girl took the wrong kind of initiative.

ILLUSTRATED IN THE WORLD OF NATURE

THE RACCOON *Procyon lotor*

An inhabitant of swamps and forests, the ring-tailed raccoon characteristically makes its home in hollow trees. Like that of the bear, the diet of the raccoon varies with the availability of food. This highly inquisitive creature scampers about, investigating every nook and cranny in the hope of uncovering a meal or simply to satisfy its own curiosity.

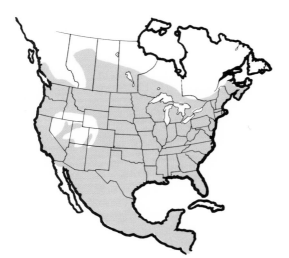

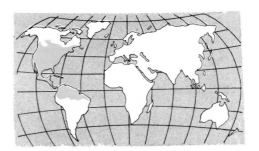

The range and habitat of the raccoon

INITIATIVE

HOW DOES THE RACCOON ILLUSTRATE THE NEED FOR CAUTION WHEN EXPLORING NEW AREAS OF INTEREST?

A leopard frog bounded into the water in an effort to elude the quick paws of the little raccoon. Its elusive tactics were no match for the bushy-tailed hunter which made a quick meal of the frog. As the masked bandit scampered on, it investigated tree hollows and interesting smooth stones in the shallows which might conceal something edible. Curious and inquisitive by nature, the raccoon is considered a highly intelligent animal because of its insatiable appetite for exploration.

Although this inquisitive tendency can lead the raccoon astray, it allows the animal to utilize food sources which might otherwise remain overlooked. Its curious nature often prompts it to investigate and carry away bright and smooth objects which are of no practical use except for play. In its enthusiasm to explore, the raccoon often neglects the need to be cautious. Then its investigative efforts may end in tragedy.

As the little raccoon continued its hunt it left the pond area and skirted the border stream of a farm. Suddenly, a glittering object caught its eye. Suspended from a low-hanging branch of a crab apple tree, the bright object fluttered in the wind, just out of reach. Without thought, the raccoon darted towards the branch. Intrigued, it danced around on its feet pawing at the object in an effort to snatch it.

An instant later a sharp crack startled the animal and burning pain shot through its leg. A farmer, capitalizing on the poultry-raider's well-known propensity to collect shiny objects, had suspended an unlikely lure from the branch and set traps beneath, hidden in the tall grass.

Frantically, the raccoon tried to free itself from the pain and the trap which it associated as one. But with each attempt, the metal jaws cut deeper into its leg. The pain intensified. In desperation to achieve freedom, the raccoon furiously bit the trap. But the unyielding metal left the raccoon with only one alternative—to sever the confined leg from the rest of its body. Turning its attention from the trap, the raccoon used its teeth to gnaw off its foot.

Freed from the grip of steel, the crippled animal hobbled away in an effort to get as far from the cruel trap as possible. Although the mishap would make a permanent impression on the young raccoon, it is doubtful that even this severe experience would deter it from the carefree and indiscriminate exploration which characterizes this inquisitive little animal.

The raccoon loves to **explore** *tree hollows and is capable of passing through openings as small as 3½ inches in diameter.*

CHARACTERISTICS AND PHYSICAL FEATURES OF THE RACCOON

After its costly encounter with the hunter's snare, the young raccoon would become extremely "trap conscious." But even this expensive lesson would not diminish its innate curiosity. Displaying initiative in its desire to explore, the raccoon expands its world by investigating any area or object that arouses its curiosity.

WHERE DOES A RACCOON LIVE?

Occasionally the raccoon makes its home in bank burrows or crevices in the rocks. But the preferred location is the hollow of a tree. These hollows are not made by the raccoon but are usually the result of holes which have been initially formed by woodpeckers or sapsuckers and then made larger by decay. The raccoon usually chooses hardwood rather than coniferous forests in which to make its home. It would be unusual to find just one raccoon in a hollow area. If room permits, as many as six may bed down together.

DOES A RACCOON EVER FALL OUT OF A TREE?

If a raccoon loses its footing because of loose bark it will fall out of its tree. The mother raccoon is aware of this danger and may remove loose bark to ensure that her young do not slip and fall. Like a cat, the animal can fall from heights without apparent harm.

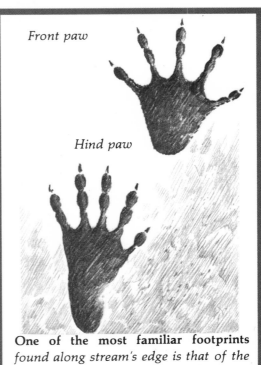

Front paw

Hind paw

One of the most familiar footprints *found along stream's edge is that of the raccoon. These prints are easily recognized. The front paw averages 3 inches in length, the hind paw 3½ inches.*

A convenient source of food *for the raccoon is the neighborhood garbage can. Only the rumbling of garbage cans as they are tipped and their contents scattered over the ground betrays the presence of this furry little bandit.*

The high intelligence *of the raccoon enables it to figure out the workings of a latch and open it, much to the dismay of farmers.*

WHERE COULD YOU FIND A RACCOON?

Basically a nocturnal animal, the raccoon spends the evening hours searching for food. On occasion one may see a raccoon during the day, but normally it spends this time resting in its den. On bright, sunny days it will stretch out in the topmost branches of a tree to soak up as much sun as possible, delighting in its unorthodox, tree-top sun bath. During its nighttime roaming the raccoon is never far from water. In one evening it may travel up to five miles—stopping at any point of interest, spending as much as an hour in one area, then bedding down in any convenient shelter just before daybreak.

WHAT'S A "COLD SLEEP?"

When the weather grows uncomfortably cold and food becomes scarce, the raccoon enters a "cold sleep." It is not a true hibernator like the woodchuck, for when the temperature rises it arouses itself and becomes active again. The drop in temperature seems to be the sole determinant for the raccoon's inactivity. In warmer regions the raccoon remains active throughout the year, never forced to enter this "cold sleep."

HOW DOES THE RACCOON HANDLE SNOW?

The short legs of the raccoon make it clumsy and slow in deep snow and place it at an extreme disadvantage both for hunting and travelling. For this reason, the raccoon chooses to remain in its den when deep snow covers the ground. Wind is another enemy. Tests indicate that the raccoon's sense of hearing is the most acute among animals. It depends heavily upon its ability to hear and smell to avoid danger. Strong winds reduce its ability to use these senses, and the raccoon usually retreats to the safety of the den.

IS THE RACCOON ALWAYS ALERT?

Even when the raccoon appears to be completely absorbed in a task, it is always listening for any sound which would indicate danger. Its acute hearing enables it to accurately detect noises even at great distances. When it hears a noise, it will raise its head to listen, becoming more mindful of danger until it finally runs to escape.

WHY WOULDN'T YOU WANT THIS MISCHIEVOUS ANIMAL IN YOUR HOUSE?

This mischievous little bandit can create quite a commotion once it gains entry to a home—opening latches to doors, unscrewing jar covers, removing corks from bottles, even turning doorknobs to open doors. Not the least intimidated by its foreign surroundings, the uninvited guest opens, unlatches and tastes everything in sight. The raccoon is able to accomplish these relatively complex tasks by the use of its forepaws equipped with dexterous fingers which it uses in the same manner as a human hand.

HAVE YOU EVER WONDERED WHO TURNS OVER YOUR GARBAGE CANS AT NIGHT?

The neighbor across the street—no . . . the cat next door—no . . . chances are it is a furry, masked rascal who has been turning over your trash and everyone else's on the block. Usually no garbage container, no matter how sophisticated its latch mechanism, is safe from these bandits. With ease it opens the lid, crawls in and checks out the contents, looking for anything which appeals to its appetite and not taking much care about leaving a mess behind.

IS THE RACCOON OMNIVOROUS?

Yes. Like a human, the raccoon eats both meats and vegetables, cooked or uncooked. It delights in feasting on an assorted menu which includes frogs, crayfish, fish, clams, poultry, corn, chestnuts, honey and sugar. It devours the last two items with special delight. The food supply of the raccoon is inconsistent. Feast or famine would be an appropriate description—the raccoon gorges itself during the summer and autumn seasons when food is plentiful but faces the threat of starvation every winter and spring.

WHAT TACTIC DOES THE RACCOON USE TO CATCH CRAYFISH?

Running its fingers under water, the raccoon gropes between the crevices of rocks and allows the defensive crayfish to clamp its pincers on its fingers. With one sweep the raccoon then pulls it out of its hiding place underwater and into its mouth, quickly devouring it. In similar fashion the raccoon gathers clams by forcing its paw between the shell halves, allowing the clam to close on its hand. Pulling the clam out of water, the raccoon chews along the muscle hinge and eventually forces the clam to break its grip. Another favorite food which takes refuge under loose sand and mud is the frog. Again the raccoon uses its agile fingers to feel along the bottom for its prey.

DOES THE RACCOON REALLY WASH ITS FOOD?

In German this animal is called "wash bear" because of a controversial habit which is performed before eating. The controversy centers around the purpose of the raccoon's customary washing procedure. Whether the raccoon dips its food in water to clean it from mud or to supplement the lack of salivary glands in its mouth is uncertain, but the latter explanation is most likely. A dog having sufficient saliva is able to swallow its food without any difficulty, but a raccoon must soften its food before it is able to swallow. When it eats food with a high moisture content it does not bother to rinse it. Because it loves to feel objects, the raccoon wets its paws and in so doing increases their sensitivity to touch.

The raccoon employs a unique fishing technique to capture crayfish.

Using its sharp teeth the raccoon gnaws away at the strong muscles which hold the clam shell shut.

Raccoon moistens food before eating. This procedure is employed to make dry food easier to swallow.

WHAT IS TAPETUM LUCIDUM?

The raccoon is equipped with special reflective cells which are situated at the rear of its eyes. This apparatus allows the animal to see in partial darkness. Light enters the eye and is absorbed. The light which is not absorbed is reflected by these "mirror" cells and it again passes through the retina, giving this light another chance to be absorbed. Through this mirroring device, *tapetum lucidum*, the raccoon is able to utilize what limited light the night affords.

HOW COULD THIS FEATURE BE DETRIMENTAL?

A popular pastime in the southern states is the use of hounds for "coon hunting." The hounds are released to find a raccoon. Once the trail is picked up a wild chase begins. All the while the hounds tell their masters the location of the coon through the pitch of their howls. Once the animal is treed the hunter can quickly locate the raccoon by merely shining a flashlight into the branches and picking up the reflective glow of the eyes.

IS THE RACCOON A MATCH FOR A DOG?

In a conflict between a raccoon and a dog, the raccoon takes initiative only to avoid a confrontation. If forced to fight, it will head for the water where it has a decided advantage. If a dog is foolish enough to follow it, the raccoon, an excellent swimmer, lures it into deep water where it climbs on the dog's back, forces its head beneath the surface and eventually drowns its attacker.

ABOVE *The special reflective eyes of the raccoon enable it to see in low light; however, they also betray the animal's presence at night when exposed by the glare of a flashlight or car headlights.*
BELOW *There is very little contest between a dog and a raccoon fighting in the water. The raccoon clearly has the upper hand.*

HOW DOES SCRIPTURE ILLUSTRATE INITIATIVE IN EXPLORING NEW AREAS OF INTEREST?

This one statement sets the stage for a tragic drama which took place only because of unguided curiosity. "She went out to see the daughters of the land."

To understand the deep lesson God wants us to learn from this story we might well relive the thoughts that may have gone through her mind as she walked toward that city. She may have considered asking her father for his counsel before making this journey. But perhaps a flood of memories prompted her to discount his opinion and his concern for her. She vividly remembered the terror of being placed by her own father in front of his favorite wife's family when they met his brother and four hundred vicious men who were coming to kill them. He certainly hadn't exercised much concern for her protection then, so why would he care if she faced danger now? She also recalled the many arguments between her mother and her father's other wife. She knew that her father preferred his other wife to her own mother. Even if something did happen to her, he probably wouldn't care. She reminded herself that only a few days earlier her father had gone into the city and bought some land from its leader. Since he traded with them it must be all right for her to meet their daughters.

But none of these reasons justified the practice of exploring new areas of interest without the protection of wise counsel. Curiosity without counsel is like a rampaging river. What was meant for our good may become the very means for our destruction. Exploring our world may also expose ourselves to danger.

When the young girl entered the city she was unaware of the sensation her attractive appearance would create. The leaders sat at the gate among whom was the prince of the country. He was more honorable than all the men of his father's household, but as he looked at her he was filled with lust and evil curiosity. He approached her and persuaded her to follow him. Before she could comprehend the impure motives of his heart it was too late, and in the tragic moments that followed he defiled her.

What began as an innocent visit turned into a devastating event. Because of what that prince had done all the men of the city were killed by two of the girl's brothers. This destroyed the reputation of her father and his family. Her father failed to provide for her protection just as she failed to ask him for it. The attraction of the city lured her into a nightmare—the tragic consequences of which became a constant reminder of her uncontrolled initiative.

From Genesis 34

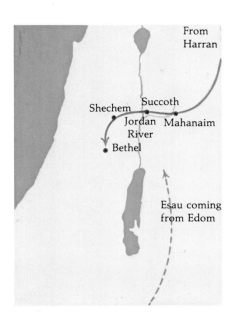

If Jacob had continued to Bethel *without delay, he would have protected his family from the godless influence of Shechem.*

In Shechem, Dinah would have been able to buy *fashionable bracelets imported from Egypt and Mesopotamia. Many of them contained images of pagan gods and were worn as a protection against evil.*

DINAH'S THOUGHTLESS INITIATIVE BROUGHT DANGER AND DISGRACE TO HER FAMILY

When Jacob fled from his angry brother to the home of his uncle Laban, he made camp near a city called Luz. That night the Lord visited Jacob and assured him of His protection, promising to bring him back to the land he was leaving. When Jacob arose he named the place Bethel (the house of God) and made a vow saying, "If God will be with me, and will keep me in the way that I go, and will give me bread to eat, and raiment to put on, so that I come again to my father's house in peace; then shall the Lord be my God: and this stone, which I have set for a pillar, shall be God's house: and of all that thou shalt give me I will surely give the tenth unto thee." (Genesis 28:20-22)

REMINDED OF A DEBT

For twenty years the Lord had protected Jacob from harm. He had blessed him with eleven healthy sons and a beautiful little daughter by the name of Dinah who no doubt was the pride and joy of her older brothers. The Lord also blessed him with great material wealth in the form of goats, sheep, camels, cattle, and donkeys. Finally the Lord reminded Jacob of his vow to return to Bethel and offer Him a tenth of his possessions. God told him to begin his journey home.

SIDETRACKED FROM HIS MISSION

When Jacob arrived at the border of the land of Canaan, he did not enter and go to Bethel to keep his promise as the Lord commanded. Instead, he built a house for himself and shelters for his livestock on the east side of the Jordan River at Succoth. When he finally crossed the river and entered the land of his birth safely as the Lord had promised, he still delayed his journey to Bethel. Instead, he purchased some land on the outskirts of the prosperous city of Shechem, whose most powerful prince bore the same name.

PROCRASTINATION BRINGS DISGRACE TO THE FAMILY

It was when Jacob was camped near Shechem that his teen-age daughter Dinah decided to seek some Hivite girlfriends living there. As a result of her journey into the city she attracted the lustful eye of the prince of Shechem who was accustomed to getting what he wanted regardless of the means. When Dinah's brothers learned of Shechem's disgraceful action they were outraged. The prince tried to appease their anger by offering them any bridal payment they desired and had his father Hamor propose a mutually advantageous trade agreement. Jacob's sons were so angry that they stooped to deceit and a perverted use of the meaningful rite of circumcision to avenge their sister. They agreed to accept Hamor and the prince's offer on the condition that all the males of the city submit to the temporarily debilitating operation. On the third day after the operation, before the men had recovered, Dinah's older brothers Simeon and Levi came into the city and mercilessly killed every male. Then they revealed their secondary motive of greed by stripping the city of all its wealth.

FEAR OF REPRISAL BRINGS OBEDIENCE TO THE LORD

When they brought back the women and children as slaves their father realized the seriousness of their crime. Jacob feared reprisal from the surrounding inhabitants after they heard of their hostile action. During this time of fear the Lord again reminded Jacob of the long-delayed payment of his vow. "And God said unto Jacob, Arise, go up to Bethel, and dwell there: and make an altar unto God, who appeared unto thee when thou fleddest from the face of Esau, thy brother." (Genesis 35:1) Jacob obeyed. He collected and buried all of the foreign idols his family had accumulated. Then he brought his family to Bethel where he paid his vow. Jacob had learned many hard lessons, and his family had suffered because of his lack of prompt obedience to the Lord. But he was once again where the Lord wanted him—in the land of his fathers.

DINAH CHARACTER SKETCH

WHY DID DINAH WANT TO VISIT THE DAUGHTERS OF THE LAND?

Dinah wanted to make new friends. She was the youngest of Jacob's seven children by his first wife Leah (cf. Genesis 30:19-21). Her six older brothers were busy in the fields all day and occupied with their own young families at night. Similarly her five half-brothers would not have provided the fellowship a young girl desires. Although there were servant girls her age, they were busy at work from early morning until late at night with their many chores. On the other hand, the city of Shechem was a relatively large and prosperous city with many girls her age. They could show her the latest styles in clothes and jewelry and talk to her about all the exciting events constantly going on in the busy city. But she was naively entering a populace whose moral standards had been perverted through the immoral rites of pagan worship. She was exposing herself to dangers for which she was neither fully aware nor properly prepared.

HOW DID JACOB FAIL HIS DAUGHTER?

Jacob should have instilled in his daughter a healthy fear of associating with the enemies of God. Unfortunately, Jacob did not provide the example himself. He welcomed their business and even allowed his own wives to possess idols and to wear pagan jewelry (cf. Genesis 31:19; 35:4). It is not surprising that Dinah was not afraid of being influenced by the Hivite daughters.

Jacob was also at fault for exposing Dinah to the temptation of visiting Shechem. He camped right in front of the city and initiated the first transaction of business (Genesis 33:18,19). He should have learned from the mistake of his older relative Lot who unwisely exposed his daughters to the wicked influence of Sodom (Genesis 13:12,13; 19:14,30-38). Jacob should have passed by Shechem on his way to Bethel without stopping.

WHY DID THE LORD ALLOW DINAH TO BE DISGRACED?

The Lord was trying to develop a nation which would one day glorify His name throughout the world. They were not to be like all of the other nations but were to worship only the true and living God. When Jacob settled in Shechem he was thwarting the Lord's plan. His family was already worshipping foreign gods. To associate and intermarry with the pagan Hivites would have increased the problem. The Lord used Dinah to warn the family of their sin and protect their daughters from the same danger in the future. Because of the abominable sins of the Hivites, the Lord would one day have the nation He was developing destroy them and their idols (Exodus 23:23,24). Dinah's tragedy would remind them of the reason for their distasteful mission.

"And Dinah, the daughter of Leah, *whom she bore unto Jacob, went out to see the daughters of the land.*"

DINAH

Initiative

IS TAKING THE LEAD IN ORDER TO RELIEVE PRESSURE FROM THOSE AROUND ME

LIVING LESSONS ON INITIATIVE . . .

FROM THE PAGES OF SCRIPTURE

In an effort to save her husband from being murdered, a concerned wife initiated the bold plan which relieved him from the immediate threat. Although her action was motivated by good intention, it was destined to bring ultimate tragedy and grief which would last for the rest of her life.

ILLUSTRATED IN THE WORLD OF NATURE

THE WHISTLING SWAN *Olor columbianus*

The whistling swan's call is actually a loud, quivering *coo*. This swan has a wingspread of eighty-three inches and may weigh up to sixteen pounds. It is a migratory bird, breeding in the northern parts of Alaska and Canada and wintering along the coast from the Chesapeake Bay to North Carolina. The majestic swan is considered the most graceful of all birds both on the water and in the air.

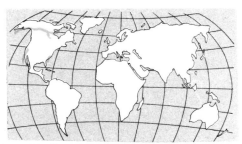

The range and habitat of the whistling swan

INITIATIVE

HOW DOES THE SWAN ILLUSTRATE INITIATIVE IN TAKING THE LEAD TO RELIEVE PRESSURE?

The cold months of winter had passed. Northern lakes were beginning to thaw as the snow melted and the ice broke apart.

Flocks of birds gathered in preparation to begin flight to their northern breeding grounds. The whistling swans were also caught up in seasonal excitement. They called back and forth to one another and busily preened their feathers. They had been eating heavily to store layers of fat for their long migration flight to the northern polar regions.

This flight would be more hurried than its fall migration. The whistling swan wants to begin building its nest as early as possible. Its nesting season is short, and if the swans are to have a successful brood, they must lay, hatch and rear their young before the water freezes and winter snow once again begins to fall.

Swans do not usually associate with other birds but fly only with their own species. Their migratory flocks may be as large as five hundred in number. At the proper time the flock slowly lifts into the air with strong, steady beats of their outstretched wings. The large body of the whistling swan lifts steadily into the air as it gradually picks up speed.

This swan is aided in flight by two advantages. First, it can fly so high that it literally becomes invisible from the ground, attaining altitudes of six thousand feet. With this advantage the swan can fly above mountains and turbulent storms. A second and greater advantage is the swan's ability to fly as a flock in V-formation. Its speed would be drastically reduced were it not for the flock's ability to fly in this manner. The whistling swan is capable of attaining speeds of up to one hundred miles per hour.

It has been calculated that twenty-five birds flying in V-formation are able to travel seventy percent farther than one swan flying by itself. This tremendous increase in distance is possible because the lead swan "breaks the trail" for the others which follow. Consequently, air resistance is lessened as each swan benefits from the upwash of the widening wake of the one preceding it. Less total lift power is required.

The lead swan has the most difficult task. When it becomes tired, it drops back and a new leader takes over, giving it an opportunity to rest. For some swans the great northerly return flight may be as long as three thousand miles. Because of the initiative of one swan in taking the lead, the swans are able to relieve the pressure from others in the flock and greatly increase the speed at which they travel.

The whistling swan is **smaller** *than the trumpeter and weighs two to twelve pounds less than its cousin. A distinguishing feature is the yellow patch found on the upper mandible of the whistling swan.*

TRUMPETER SWAN   WHISTLING SWAN

CHARACTERISTICS AND PHYSICAL FEATURES OF THE WHISTLING SWAN

The swan's ability to fly farther and faster is only possible because of the cooperative effort which allows a leader to take the initiative, breaking a trail to minimize air resistance for the rest of the flock. Even more amazing is the ability of this bird—one of the largest of waterfowl—to fly at all.

HOW DOES THE SWAN'S BODY FRAME EQUIP IT FOR FLIGHT?

The swan's rib cage and back bones are fused together, causing them to become rigid. Only the neck and tail are movable. Lightness is an essential factor in order for any bird to be able to fly. It is for this reason that both the bone structure and the quills of the feathers themselves are hollow. Larger bones of the swan are equipped with internal supports for greater strength in the air. The shaft of the feather is extremely strong yet has the necessary flexibility to lend the bird agility for aerial maneuvers.

DID YOU KNOW THAT A FEATHER IS MADE UP OF HUNDREDS OF LITTLE FEATHERS?

Hundreds of miniature, feather-like structures called barbs are attached to the shaft of each feather. These can be separated or knitted together again. The intricate structure becomes more apparent when viewed under a microscope. Each barb is made up of a number of protrusions called barbicels. These minute hooks hold the barbs in place.

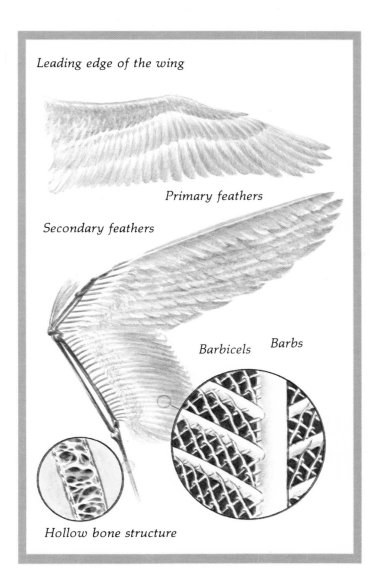

Leading edge of the wing

Primary feathers

Secondary feathers

Barbicels   Barbs

Hollow bone structure

PRINCIPLES OF FLIGHT

The curved structure of the wing's secondary feathers, those closest to its body, forces the air to go further and faster over the top of the wing than it does underneath. Thus, the pressure underneath is greater than the pressure on top of the wing. This force of air that is created which pushes the bird up into the air is called lift. Drag is the resistance of air to the bird's forward movement.

The feathers at the end of the wing which are at right angles to the bird's body are called primary feathers and act as a propeller to push the swan forward when it makes a downward stroke. The feathers are arranged in such a way that they are pressed together causing a resistance to the air. On the upward stroke the feathers open so that air can quickly and easily pass through. The tail is employed to aid the bird in steering and braking.

Like other waterfowl *the whistling swan is equipped with oil glands at the base of its tail. The swan distributes this oil and waterproofs its plumage by stroking with its bill, beginning at the base of its tail and continuing throughout its body.*

HOW MANY FEATHERS DOES A WHISTLING SWAN HAVE?

Twenty-five thousand, two hundred sixteen were counted on one bird. Eighty percent of these feathers were located on the long, slender neck. In addition to enabling the bird to fly, they provide a padding which protects the sensitive skin of the bird and acts as an insulator in aiding the bird to maintain its body temperature in extremes of cold and heat.

IS THE WHISTLING SWAN NOISY IN FLIGHT?

Once the whistling swan is airborne, it is relatively silent in flight. This is true of all white-plumaged swans with the exception of the mute.

HOW ARE THE FEET OF THREE-FOLD BENEFIT TO THE SWAN?

Besides the obvious purpose of enabling the swan to walk on land, the black webbed feet serve two other unique functions. First, the swan uses them as paddles to propel itself across the surface of the water as it vigorously beats its wings in preparation to become airborne.

Secondly, the swan walks on its webbed feet and toenails, stirring up the bottom of shallow inlets and marshes in an effort to dig up roots, wild celery or other plant life such as rhizomes and tubers. Then it turns around and swims back to where it first started, eating the tender, uprooted plants and siphoning the dislodged insects and crustaceans from the water with its bill.

DOES THE SWAN'S BILL HAVE TEETH?

The bill of the swan is not equipped with conventional teeth, but it does have a serrated bony structure. This structure resembles a fringe along the edge of the upper and lower mandibles. The serrations are called *lamellae.* When the mandibles are closed, the serrations fit together and enable the bird to sift out food particles taken into the mouth from the water.

WHY DOES THE SWAN'S PLUMAGE TURN COLOR?

The method of stirring the bottom and then using its long neck to dig up the findings often discolors its neck and underparts. The feathers turn a grey, rusty brown if the water has abundant vegetation or contains an excessive amount of iron.

WHY IS IT EASIER FOR A SWAN TO TAKE OFF FROM WATER THAN FROM LAND?

The whistling swan, like a plane, needs a long, unobstructed runway for take off. Despite its large and heavy structure the swan is able to rise up into the air with the aid of its powerful wings as long as it has clear open places to accomplish this feat. When choosing a nest location it selects only those bodies of water which have irregular shorelines for protection and those which are at least nine acres in size. If this nest site proves successful the swan will return year after year to the same spot. If the nest is destroyed when they return, the swans will either repair it or build another one nearby.

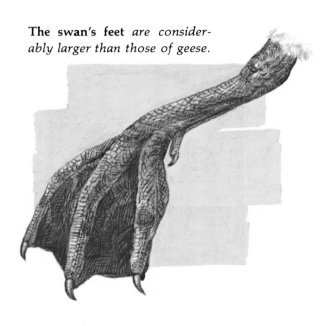

The swan's feet *are considerably larger than those of geese.*

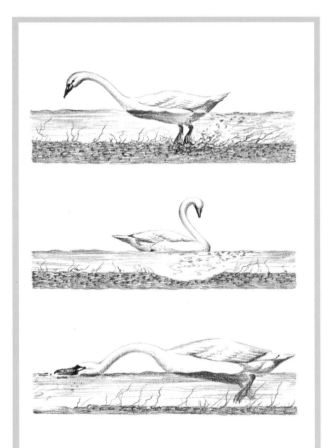

Using its feet *the swan employs a unique method to secure food in shallow water.*

ADULT SWAN IN MOLT

In late summer after the young have been raised, parent birds undergo a complete molt. In order to gain new plumage the bird loses its feathers, including those from its wing and tail. It loses the wing feathers in pairs, one from each side. Without these it is flightless and must resort to the water for safety. This molting process takes place at least once a year and may occur again in early spring.

Immature swan *unable to make long migrational flight south will be left behind to its own fate.*

Large powerful wings *serve as formidable weapons in driving off most enemies.*

HOW CAN THE WING BE AN EFFECTIVE MEANS OF DEFENSE?

A bony knuckle is located on the swan's wing. This knuckle is actually the bone joint but serves as an excellent weapon. The powerful muscles of the large wings enable the whistling swan to deliver a devastating blow. As a result, it is plagued by few natural enemies.

HOW LONG DOES IT TAKE A SWAN TO MATURE?

It takes five or six years for a swan to completely mature. By the end of its third or fourth year the bird is capable of laying eggs. Even at maturity it is only sixty-five percent successful in hatching its four to six cream-colored eggs.

WHAT IS A CYGNET?

A young swan is called a cygnet. The adult male is known as a cob.

WHY IS TIME THE CYGNET'S GREATEST ENEMY?

If a female lays her eggs too late in spring, if her young are not able to completely develop or if their preparation for the long migrational flight is shortened because of an early fall, the unprepared birds will face starvation or exhaustion and will probably die. Lack of time for the young cygnets to develop takes a heavy toll of the swan population.

HOW DOES SCRIPTURE ILLUSTRATE INITIATIVE IN TAKING THE LEAD TO RELIEVE PRESSURE?

A band of men had faithfully protected the vast herds of her husband's sheep and goats. Not one animal was missing. When they heard he was shearing his sheep, the men sent a delegation of ten to suggest that he give them a reward for the work they had done to benefit him. But he scoffed at them and their leader and claimed no obligation to repay them in any way.

This greatly angered the leader, and he planned to kill this man and all the men of his household. When his beautiful and wise wife heard that her husband was going to be killed, she recalled the many times that both she and his servants had tried to reason with him about other matters without success.

So she took five sheep, large quantities of bread, corn, raisins and figs and hurried out to meet the offended leader and his band of men. She wisely reasoned that if he killed her husband it would forever remain a grief and a burden of heart to him, especially after he became king. Her generosity and tactful words were so effective that he changed his mind and blessed her for preventing him from shedding blood needlessly to avenge himself.

Because of her action she saved the life of her husband and averted the destruction of their household. But her initiative involved taking matters into her own hands. The next morning she told her husband what she had done. He had an immediate heart attack and died ten days later. By acting on his behalf rather than simply telling him of his danger, she had temporarily protected his life only to precipitate his death.

She spared the leader of the band from the grief of having needlessly killed a man. But that memory and grief might have been the very thing which would have prevented him from later killing another woman's husband in order to cover up his sin with her. By sparing him from a failure which might have been excused, she robbed him of the necessary caution that could have prevented a great weakening of his family and kingdom.

After her husband died, Abigail became this leader's wife. He removed her from a comfortable home to the hardship of a fugitive's life. She had only one son in her new marriage and she named him Chileab. Later in life his name was changed, and the new name is officially recorded in the genealogies. The meaning of that second name is, *"God has judged me."*

From I Samuel 25

Abigail brought David *two goat skins of wine. The tightly-sealed skins, smeared with grease to prevent leakage and evaporation, kept the wine fresh and sweet.*

In exchange for food *David and his men protected livestock from thieves and wild animals.*

Abigail's gift *of bread, wine, meat, grain, raisins and figs was gratefully received by David's hungry men.*

BY TAKING INITIATIVE ABIGAIL RELIEVED TEMPORARY PRESSURE, BUT HER INDEPENDENT ACTION CAUSED PERMANENT GRIEF

David's credibility as a leader was being taxed. He was in charge of six hundred men—all distressed, in debt, and dissatisfied with the government of King Saul. They had enjoyed a brief period of rest in the land of Moab, but David had brought them back to Judah in an attempt to win the people's support. After risking their lives in order to save their brothers in Keilah from the Philistines, they were repaid by being betrayed into the hand of their enemy. A temporary truce was made between Saul and David, and the nervous men looked forward to a time of rest and refreshment.

A NOMADIC PROTECTION RING

Because of their need to move rapidly when being pursued, the men rarely carried much food. Weapons and water were burden enough. By offering protection against the seminomadic enemies of Judah, David felt justified in receiving modest provision from those he protected with which to feed his men. He did not have to ask most of the grateful farmers to pay for his services, but the situation with a man named Nabal was quite different.

A SUICIDAL INSULT

For many days David and his men had helped protect Nabal's flock of three thousand sheep and herd of one thousand goats. Since Nabal was a descendant of the godly Caleb, David may have expected this member of his own tribe of Judah to sympathize with his situation. When Nabal refused to initiate any offer of help, David sent ten men to politely ask Nabal for an invitation to the traditional sheep shearing feast. Just as farmers celebrated at harvest, so sheep men invited all of the neighbors to share in their festivities. For Nabal to refuse David's request and insult his men was inconceivably inappropriate under these circumstances. It was no less than a declaration of war.

WIFE RISKS LIFE TO REASON WITH AVENGER

When Nabal's intelligent and attractive wife Abigail heard of her husband's foolish decision, she was convinced that reason alone would not change his mind and decided to plead with David instead. Fearing for her life, she packed enough food to provide a feast for David's men and hurriedly left without telling her husband. After reaching David, she shrewdly brought him into a friendly state of mind by three well-planned arguments.

THREE PLEAS THAT AVERTED MURDER

First, she excused her husband's act of hostility on the basis that he was a fool and did not fear God. She asked David to hold her responsible for her husband's folly and then give her an opportunity to make amends. Second, she claimed that their encounter was planned by God to prevent David from committing murder, reminding him that God is the avenger of the wicked (cf. Deuteronomy 32:35). Third, she suggested to David that he would never be able to forget his bloody act of revenge, and it would be a constant source of grief throughout his life. David was impressed not only with Abigail's reasoning but also with her beauty. When Nabal died of a stroke ten days later he was convinced that Abigail should become his third wife. Little is known of Abigail after her marriage to David other than the fact that she had one son Chileab who lived and died in obscurity.

ABIGAIL CHARACTER SKETCH

WAS ABIGAIL RIGHT TO ACT INDEPENDENTLY OF HER HUSBAND?

The Biblical writer provides one significant clue in the sentence, "But she told not her husband, Nabal." (I Samuel 25:19) The same writer used the exact same sentence structure concerning Jonathan and his father Saul, "But he told not his father." (I Samuel 14:1) The two situations are remarkably similar. Both Abigail and Jonathan had good and sincere intentions. They both knew that their respective authorities were not acting wisely. They both felt that reasoning would do no good and that their request would be denied. They both felt more competent than their respective authorities and thus acted independently of their wishes. They both condemned the actions of their authorities in public (cf. I Samuel 14:29; 25:25). The Lord allowed them both to succeed in their plans. The Lord Himself pointed out Jonathan's sin (I Samuel 14:42), but no lots were thrown for Abigail. We must conclude that, although her motives were sincere, her methods were wrong and displeasing to the Lord who hates rebellion against authority even though that authority be an unwise father or a foolish husband.

WHAT SHOULD ABIGAIL HAVE DONE?

Abigail should have followed the principle established in the Law and further explained by the Lord (Deuteronomy 19:15; Matthew 18:15-17). Even though she was sure her husband would not listen, she should have confronted him with all of the facts as she knew them. If he refused to listen, she could have asked the shepherds to confirm the facts. If he still didn't listen, she could have cried out to the Lord for justice and mercy. By listening to the bad report of her husband from the young shepherd (I Samuel 25:14-17) and then initiating her own course of action, she was limiting the possibilities of God to deal with the situation in a more creative way. It is true that Abigail was successful in her scheme, but there may have been a better method.

WHAT WERE THE CONSEQUENCES OF ABIGAIL'S ACTIONS?

Rather than being killed by David's sword, Nabal died after he suffered a stroke when hearing of his wife's betrayal. It was a second stroke ten days later which was actually fatal. Abigail became David's wife, but there is no evidence that she enjoyed the blessing of the Lord or her new husband. She lived as an exile with David and his other wife in Philistia for a few years (I Samuel 27:3). She was taken captive by the Amalekites for a short period of time (I Samuel 30:5). She moved to Hebron with David (II Samuel 2:3) where she bore him his second son named Chileab (II Samuel 3:3). At Hebron she was one of six wives, and later in Jerusalem she was just one wife among many (II Samuel 5:13). Abigail's only son is not mentioned later even though he should have become the crown prince after the murder of Amnon. It is possible that she had second thoughts about her life when she changed her son's name from Chileab (restraint of the father) to Daniel (God is my Judge) (I Chronicles 3:1).

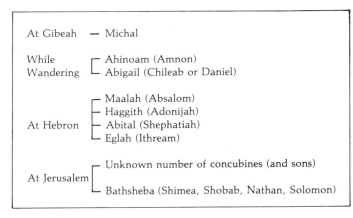

At Gibeah	— Michal
While Wandering	⌐ Ahinoam (Amnon) ⌐ Abigail (Chileab or Daniel)
At Hebron	⌐ Maalah (Absalom) ⌐ Haggith (Adonijah) ⌐ Abital (Shephatiah) ⌐ Eglah (Ithream)
At Jerusalem	⌐ Unknown number of concubines (and sons) ⌐ Bathsheba (Shimea, Shobab, Nathan, Solomon)

DAVID'S WIVES AND SONS

ABIGAIL

Initiative

IS ACTING WITH AN ASSURANCE OF THE OUTCOME

LIVING LESSONS ON INITIATIVE . . .

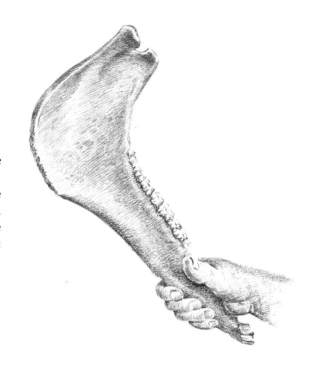

FROM THE PAGES OF SCRIPTURE

God empowered a man to free His people from the oppression of their enemies. Filled with the Spirit of God, he could act with an assurance of the outcome because he knew the power behind the special gift which was given him. But understanding his power and purpose in life were not enough. He never realized the potential that could have and should have been his.

ILLUSTRATED IN THE WORLD OF NATURE

THE YELLOW-SHAFTED FLICKER *Colaptes auratus*

Named after its call, "flicker, flicker," this woodpecker inhabits farmlands and lightly wooded areas. The thirteen-inch yellow-shafted flicker is often confused with its western cousin, the red-shafted woodpecker. Unlike most other members of its family, this flicker spends much time on the ground securing food.

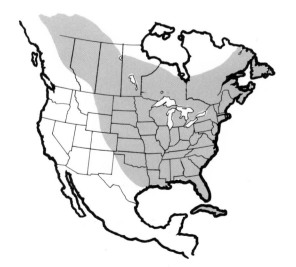

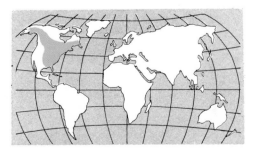

The range and habitat of the yellow-shafted flicker

INITIATIVE

HOW DOES THE FLICKER ILLUSTRATE INITIATIVE IN ACTING WITH AN ASSURANCE OF THE OUTCOME?

Rat-a-tat-tat, rat-a-tat-tat, rat-a-tat-tat is the sound one normally associates with the woodpecker as it hammers away on tree surfaces in search of bugs and other insects. But the yellow-shafted flicker is unique from its cousins in that it does not rely solely on this method to secure its food. This flicker is the most colorful of the North American woodpeckers with its various shades of yellow, brown, red and accents of black. Despite its vivid coloration, the shy bird is not easy to spot because of its tendency to conceal itself behind limbs, branches and foliage.

The yellow-shafted flicker is our only species of woodpecker that feeds on the ground. Since forty-five percent of its diet consists of ants, the flicker inhabits the open, sandy areas which are heavily populated by ant colonies. Always on the the lookout for mounds of dirt which might house these industrious little creatures, the flicker examines any likely spot for the prospect of a meal. After locating a promising mound, it initiates a procedure which is highly effective.

The flicker approaches the mound and vigorously raps on the doorway of the ant colony. This "doorway" is a tunnel which leads underground and then branches into many chambers. The energetic ants, protective of their larvae and home, unitedly respond to the threat of an intrusion. They viciously attack insects and

worms, inflicting such fatal blows with their powerful jaws that they usually succeed in warding off or killing formidable enemies which are many times larger than they.

Familiar with their response, the flicker deliberately disrupts the colony in an attempt to draw them out of their confines. It is aided in this by a special apparatus—a long tongue coated with a special sticky fluid. The tongue, impervious to the bite of the ant, resembles a spear with its barbed shaft and sharp tapered point.

As the bird vigorously pecks with its bill, it excavates the sides of the tunnel wall and forms a funnel-like cone. Then it inserts its long tongue into the ant hole. Mistaking the tongue for an intruding worm, the ants attack it in full force. As they assault this foreign object, the ants are entangled by its sticky coating. Quickly the flicker withdraws its tongue to devour the succulent insects and rapidly reinserts the blade into the tunnel. Escape is impossible for the ants that try to flee with their larvae.

So effective is this means of procurement that the flicker can annihilate an entire ant colony or inflict such damage to its population that tremendous effort is required for the ants to recover. Because the flicker initiates an action which it knows will be successful, it is able to secure great quantities of food that would otherwise be overlooked.

Severt
Andrewson

CHARACTERISTICS AND PHYSICAL FEATURES OF THE FLICKER

The yellow-shafted flicker not only uses the conventional means of gathering food which its cousins employ but is the only member of its family to secure a large proportion of its diet from ground dwelling insects. By taking initiative to use the unique features with which it is equipped, the flicker does not face as difficult a struggle for survival as other members of the Aves class do.

HOW MANY ANTS CAN THE FLICKER KILL AT ONE TIME?

Using its long tongue to scoop up insects, the flicker can consume huge quantities of ants in a short period of time. When the stomach contents of a number of flickers were examined, a single one was found to contain up to five thousand ants.

HOW LONG IS THE FLICKER'S TONGUE?

This woodpecker can extend its long, sleek tongue up to three inches beyond its beak. Proportionate to its body length, this would be the equivalent of a six foot man sticking out his tongue to a length of over a foot and a half.

THREE-INCH TONGUE

A probing, sticky tongue *and chisel-like beak enable the flicker to capture and consume thousands of ants.*

5,000 ants

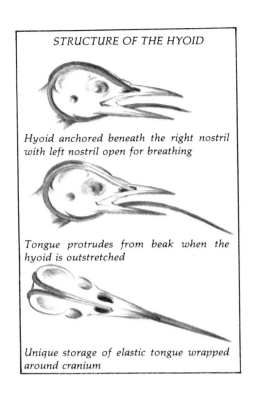

STRUCTURE OF THE HYOID

Hyoid anchored beneath the right nostril with left nostril open for breathing

Tongue protrudes from beak when the hyoid is outstretched

Unique storage of elastic tongue wrapped around cranium

YELLOW-SHAFTED FLICKER

Male

Female

Similar in appearance, *the male is distinguished from the female by a black "moustache" which extends downward from the base of the bill.*

The berry of the poison ivy plant *is included in the autumn diet of the yellow-shafted flicker.*

HOW DOES THE FLICKER FIT SUCH A LONG TONGUE IN ITS SMALL MOUTH?

The long elastic structure known as a hyoid is anchored in the right nostril and wrapped around the back of the head and jaw. When the bird extends its tongue from its mouth, it slides the hyoid along this route. The left nostril remains open for the bird to breathe through.

IS ITS BILL THE SAME AS THAT OF OTHER WOODPECKERS?

The flicker's bill is slightly curved and tapers to a sharp point. The bills of other species of woodpeckers are blunt, straight and more chisel-like in structure.

WHAT ARE THE FUNCTIONS OF THE FLICKER'S BILL?

Besides using its bill to gather food and chisel out tree hollows for nests, the bill plays an important role in courtship and communication. Males warn other males of territorial boundaries. A male flicker broadcasts its availability to prospective mates by rapping on a tree trunk. Once a female is chosen, the pair continue to communicate in this manner.

WHY DOESN'T THE WOODPECKER EVER GET A HEADACHE?

Slamming its head against a tree as many as one hundred times a minute and accomplishing this task hundreds of times a day, one would think that the woodpecker's head would become extremely sore. But this is not the case for, unlike other birds, the hard pointed beak of the woodpecker is connected to the skull by a sponge-like, rubbery tissue which has tremendous capacity to absorb shock.

DOES THE FLICKER EAT ANYTHING OTHER THAN ANTS?

Yes. Besides ants they eat a wide variety of insects such as crickets, beetles, grasshoppers and caterpillars. They search for these in the ground, under wood and also behind leaves and branches. Flickers even catch these flying insects on the wing. Nearly one-third of its food source is composed of vegetables and fruits. The grains of wheat and oats, various nuts and a range of berries supplement the flicker's diet. The bird eats raspberries, blackberries, elderberries and even the berries of the poison ivy plant, distributing the seeds and effectively propagating this unpopular plant to the dismay of those allergic to its powdery irritant.

HOW IS A WOODPECKER ABLE TO WALK UP THE SIDE OF A TREE?

The flicker's feet are zygodactyl which means that two of its four toes point forward and two point backward. The legs are short; the strong feet equipped with sharp curved claws enabling it to securely grasp the bark of a tree. It is also equipped with strong, pointed quills which extend beyond the tail feathers to prop and steady the bird. These quills resist the abrasive scraping which would shred and destroy an ordinary feather. These essential tail feathers replace themselves in a marvelous way. Not until a replacement set has fully developed will the bird molt its present ones. So well equipped is the flicker to walk in an upright position that it is rarely seen perched on a limb in a transverse position.

HOW IS THE FLICKER ABLE TO LOCATE INSECTS?

Aided by an acute sense of hearing, the flicker raps on wood in an effort to disturb any insects which might be hiding inside. This rapping betrays hollow spots which would indicate a hewn out area where insects have been at work. Once it locates a likely spot, it vigorously begins to chisel away, exposing a network of tunnels and exploring the burrows with its tongue in an effort to find any hidden insects.

HOW CAN YOU DISTINGUISH A FLICKER FROM OTHER BIRDS?

In addition to the fact that it is one of the few species of birds which climb up and down a tree, this woodpecker is also distinctive in flight. When it flies, short bursts of energy appear to sweep the bird up into the air in an irregular, wave-like pattern. Rather than the fixed-wing soaring of a hawk the flicker uses rapid, steady pumps to gain height and then glides for a short distance before repeating the action.

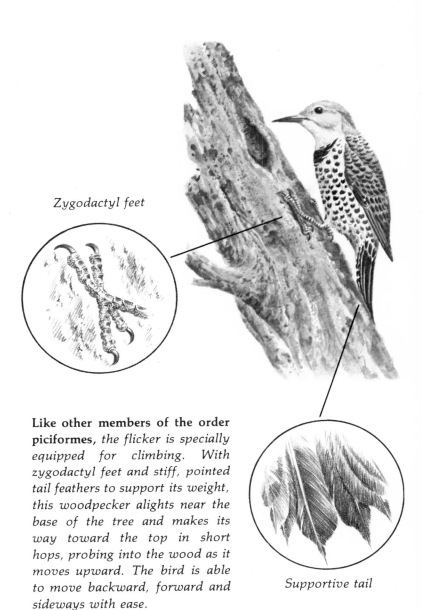

Zygodactyl feet

Supportive tail

Like other members of the order piciformes, *the flicker is specially equipped for climbing. With zygodactyl feet and stiff, pointed tail feathers to support its weight, this woodpecker alights near the base of the tree and makes its way toward the top in short hops, probing into the wood as it moves upward. The bird is able to move backward, forward and sideways with ease.*

FLIGHT PATTERN OF THE FLICKER

The flicker's erratic flight *makes it easily identifiable in the air. With rapid wingbeats the bird builds momentum, fixes its wings and then glides a short distance, creating a sputtering "out-of-gas" effect.*

Both male and female share the responsibility *for nest construction, incubation and feeding. The parents hide food under bark to teach the young to hunt for it.*

Female flicker *takes initiative to remove her eggs from danger.*

HOW DOES A MALE IDENTIFY A FEMALE FLICKER?

During courtship the male sends a communiqué to all prospective partners which can be heard for half a mile. A flicker without black patches on its head is welcomed and the two participate in a joyful, bobbing routine. A distinguishing characteristic of the male flicker is the black moustache found on either cheek. When a black patch was painted on a female's head the male attacked and drove her away from its territory, confused by this decisive marking.

DOES A FLICKER EXCAVATE ITS OWN NEST SITE?

Not if it can expand an available hollow. If it is unable to find such a cavity the paired flickers choose a decayed, deciduous tree and drill and clean their own area. The female is very particular about the nest site and usually has the final word of approval. Careful not to expose the location of the nest, the flickers remove large chips and deposit them a considerable distance from the tree.

HOW MANY EGGS WILL A FLICKER LAY?

Instances have been recorded of a single bird laying and hatching up to nineteen eggs, but the average clutch is usually six to eight white eggs. Although it is a prolific bird, this woodpecker has enemies such as crows, weasels and squirrels which would feast on its eggs. If eggs are destroyed the female lays more to replace them. It is believed that the absence of eggs against her brood patch stimulates the secretion of hormones which signal the ovaries.

WHY WOULD A FLICKER CHANGE NEST LOCATIONS ONCE ITS EGGS WERE LAID?

Because the female chooses rotten trees in which to build her nest, strong windstorms may cause the tree to split and break, exposing the clutch. If the female feels it is too dangerous to stay she will take the initiative to vacate and prepare another nesting site, transferring the eggs one at a time by carrying them in her beak.

THE UNWELCOME STARLING

In the early 1900's the starling, which is smaller than the flicker, was introduced to this country and has since become a threat to the survival of the flicker. The starling population has increased rapidly throughout the continent and these birds compete with the flicker for the same food sources. Even more devastating is the competition for nesting sites. A starling will drive off a nesting flicker, lay a covering of grass or vegetation across the eggs and raise its own brood on top of them.

HOW DOES SCRIPTURE ILLUSTRATE INITIATIVE IN ACTING WITH AN ASSURANCE OF THE OUTCOME?

In the land of God's enemies the corn harvest was ruined. Their rich fields of grain had become a charred expanse of rubble because of one man. They would teach him a lesson. They gathered a large army and marched into his country.

The people of the land trembled and asked their enemy why they were there. When the enemy explained that they had come to bind the man who troubled their nation, the fearful countrymen agreed to cooperate to appease these angry men.

They organized three thousand men and made their way to the top of a rocky hill. Then they called out to this one man, "Don't you know that these people rule over us? What is this that you have done? We have come to bind you and deliver you into their hand."

With his permission they took strong new ropes and tied his hands. He let them wrap the rope around his arms until he was so tightly bound that he couldn't move. Then they led him back to the vengeful army that had set up camp in their land. As soon as the army saw him, a great shout went up. Some shouted because their mission was now achieved. Others shouted in derision. Was this man who looked so ordinary worth all this trouble? But they didn't realize that the force behind his strength was from God.

Now with the Spirit of God upon him, the arms that were tightly bound snapped the ropes as if they had been burnt flax. He reached to the ground, grabbed the jaw bone of a donkey and began swinging it at the soldiers who rushed upon him. His defense was so furious that before they realized what was happening heaps of dead men lay on the ground. This one man with the power of God in him had killed one thousand enemy soldiers.

It is ironical that Satan would similarly defeat this man of God by introducing an element into his life, the force of which would destroy his spiritual potential. Disregarding the commands of God's Word and the wishes of his parents he fell in love with a godless woman. Her attractiveness motivated him to find reasons why it would be all right to compromise in what he knew was wrong. He reasoned that she was just a girl whom he could easily control. But the land of compromise is the territory of Satan, and behind those in his kingdom there is a force far greater than outsiders realize.

Just as that army did not comprehend the power of God in his life, so he did not comprehend the power of Satan through her life. As if to emphasize his spiritual blindness, Samson's eyes were gouged out and he died in the land of God's enemies.

From Judges 15:1-17 and
Judges 16:4-31

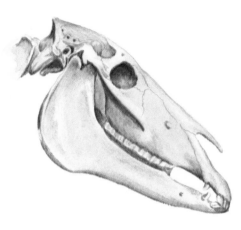

The Nazirite *knew that his whole body belonged to God, including his hair. So until his vow was fulfilled a razor never touched his skin.*

Samson used the jawbone *of a freshly-killed donkey to kill one thousand Philistines.*

Samson obtained revenge *for the loss of his two eyes during a celebration in honor of Dagon, a non-existent god of the Philistines.*

SAMSON DID NOT REALIZE THE FORCE BEHIND SATAN'S DECEPTION

The life of Samson, one of the last judges of Israel, is an illustration of the truth of Solomon's sober warning, "Better is it that thou shouldest not vow, than that thou shouldest vow and not pay. . .Wherefore should God be angry at thy voice, and destroy the work of thine hands?" (Ecclesiastes 5:5,6)

A NAZIRITE FROM BIRTH

Samson was unusual in that he was consecrated to God as a Nazirite from his birth. The Nazirite vow was normally voluntary. It involved three restrictions: contact with any dead body, the eating or drinking of any grapevine product and cutting the hair. Long hair was the outward, public sign that the person had taken the vow. Samson's story is a tragic account of misguided initiative and his threefold breaking of his Nazirite vow.

RAISED UP TO DELIVER GOD'S PEOPLE

God placed Samson under such severe restrictions because He needed a deliverer for His people who were oppressed by the Philistines. To accomplish lasting results this deliverer would have to remain free from the contaminating effect of the low moral standards to which the nation had sunk. In order to judge the nation and be a spiritual leader, he would have to set the example. The restrictions of the Nazirite vow would be a constant reminder of his mission and his dedication to God. But Samson was only interested in the surface problem of his people—their oppression by the Philistines. He was not concerned about the reason for the oppression which was the nation's disobedient worship of Philistine and foreign gods.

DISTRACTED FROM HIS GOALS

Samson's first contact with the enemy was a visit to the Philistine city of Timnah just a few miles from his home in Israel. He fell in love with a Philistine woman and wanted to marry her. On one trip to see her he killed a lion with his bare hands. On his next trip he noticed honey in the dead carcass. By scraping it out with his hands he violated the first restriction of his Nazirite vow to touch a dead body.

His fourth trip to Timnah was to participate in his seven-day marriage ceremony against the better judgment of his parents. Such feasts in Philistia would have been the occasion for much drinking, and we can only assume that the sensuous bridegroom did not disappoint his guests. This drinking would have been a violation of the second restriction of his Nazirite vow.

The wedding ceremony was never completed because of the bride's betrayal of Samson's marriage riddle. In a rage, he left to kill thirty Philistines to make payment for his lost wager. When he returned later to consummate his marriage, his best man, who was supposed to protect his interests, had married his bride. Although the Philistines burned the adulterer, Samson used this occasion to destroy his enemies' cornfields in fury. On another occasion he killed a thousand Philistines with the fresh jawbone of an ass, a questionable weapon for a Nazirite who was not to touch a dead body.

SPIRIT LEAVES WITH DISOBEDIENCE

The violation of the third restriction of his vow caused Samson's ultimate defeat. The five lords of Philistia offered Delilah the enormous sum of fifty-five hundred pieces of silver if she could find the key to Samson's strength. When Samson revealed to Delilah the real reason for his supernatural strength, it represented complete abandonment of his God-given purpose in life. As a consequence of this attitude, the Lord could no longer use him and immediately removed His power from him. Samson was easily captured, his eyes were gouged out and he was put to work grinding corn in the Philistine prison. The once-powerful deliverer of the nation of Israel now performed the humiliating task of a servant woman. Samson was a ridiculed captive of his enemies because of his apathetic disinterest toward his God-given purpose in life.

SAMSON CHARACTER SKETCH

DID SAMSON REALIZE THE SOURCE OF HIS STRENGTH?

It is significant that Samson is listed in the New Testament's list of heroes of the faith (Hebrews 11:32). It tells us that Samson did recognize that his power came from God. His error was not a lack of faith in God's power but rather his thinking that God's power would never leave him regardless of his conduct. When pressed by Delilah, Samson was able to tell that his strength was directly related to the fact that he was a Nazirite unto God from before his birth. He knew that without God he would be as weak as any other man (Judges 16:17). What is frightening is the fact that he was not aware of the Lord's departure from him when he began his final futile struggle against the Philistines after Delilah had betrayed him (Judges 16:20).

WHY DID THE LORD HELP SAMSON AVENGE HIS OWN PERSONAL WRONGS?

Two factors were involved in the Lord's answer to Samson's request for strength with which to avenge his enemies (Judges 16:28). First, the Philistines were using Samson to mock the God of Israel and justify their worship of their fish-god named Dagon. If such unbridled blasphemy were left unpunished it would have resulted in even greater religious confusion. Second, we learn that Samson's hair had again grown long (Judges 16:22). According to the Mosaic Law, when a Nazirite vow was broken, the person was to cut the hair, offer a sacrifice and start the vow over again (Numbers 6:9-12). Since Samson was in prison and unable to offer a sacrifice, his newly-grown hair was symbolic of the renewal of his Nazirite vow. The Lord filled him with strength just as before and allowed Samson to avenge their common enemies.

DID GOD PROMPT SAMSON TO DO WRONG?

Delilah was one of three women in Samson's life. The first was a Canaanite woman from Timnah whom Samson wanted to marry. The Israelites were not to marry these people on the basis that it would lead them to idolatry (Deuteronomy 7:1-4). Samson was breaking this law and not honoring his parents' good counsel in the matter (Judges 14:3). We then read the strange words, "It was of the Lord, that he sought an occasion against the Philistines." (Judges 14:4) This does not mean that Samson's disobedient actions were prompted by God. Samson's actions were prompted by his own evil lust (cf. James 1:13, 14). It is a sobering aspect of God's nature that he will give us the desires of our heart, but send leanness to our soul (cf. Psalm 106:13-15). At the same time God will use even the evil actions of men to accomplish his larger purposes (cf. Genesis 50:20).

"But the Philistines took him, *and put out his eyes, and brought him down to Gaza, and bound him with fetters of bronze; and he did grind in the prison house."*

SAMSON

313

Initiative

IS RESPONDING QUICKLY AND WISELY TO SITUATIONS OF DANGER

LIVING LESSONS ON INITIATIVE . . .

FROM THE PAGES OF SCRIPTURE

Pride prompted a king to reveal the riches and strength of his nation. His inability to respond quickly and wisely to the situation brought a severe rebuke from God's prophet. The leader's unwise divulgence jeopardized the kingdom and caused him to lose favor with God.

ILLUSTRATED IN THE WORLD OF NATURE

THE SPOTTED SANDPIPER *Actitis macularia*

A solitary bird, the long-legged sandpiper can be seen as it runs along the shoreline with its peculiar teetering motion, pausing periodically in a search for insects and crustaceans. Eighteen inches in size, the sandpiper is probably the most familiar of all shorebirds inhabiting ponds, lakes and streams throughout North America.

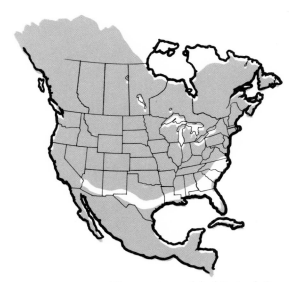

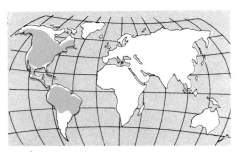

The range and habitat of the spotted sandpiper

INITIATIVE

HOW DOES THE SANDPIPER ILLUSTRATE THE NEED FOR INITIATIVE IN RESPONDING TO DANGER?

Eagerly flying northward during the protective hours of darkness, the spotted sandpiper was one of the first species to make its way to the transitional zone in early spring.

Inconspicuously arriving on the shoreline of a northern lake, the sandpiper danced along water's edge, bobbing and teetering with its head lowered and positioned forward in a search for food. Anxious to begin nesting, the bobbing little bird frequently called a loud, "hoy, hoy, weet, weet, weet" which advertised its availability and whereabouts to any prospective partner.

Three days passed before its call was acknowledged by a member of its own species. Jumping on a log the eager courter thrust its head high in the air, raised its wings and spread its tail feathers, emitting loud cries. In an amusing way it pranced in front of its partner and attempted to gain approval by repeatedly making short hops on the surface of the log.

Once the suitor gained acceptance the brief courtship culminated and the business of constructing a crude nest was undertaken. Selecting a spot on a high sandy knoll close to the water, a shallow depression was scratched in the loose surface to cradle four eggs. Once they hatched both parents took turns in the duties of incubation.

Food was plentiful. It was a mild spring with very little rain. All the elements were favorable, and a successful hatch was imminent. Everything would have been perfect had it not been for a mink which slipped toward the shoreline of the lake one late May afternoon. Spotting this dreaded enemy, the sandpiper huddled close to the eggs and froze in position.

Systematically the mink explored the shoreline in an effort to detect a movement or telltale scent which would betray the presence of prey. Unsuccessful in its search, the hungry and disappointed predator skirted the shoreline and headed towards the knoll where the sandpiper's nest was situated. The parent bird lay motionless as if frozen to the nest.

Although the intruder was dangerously close, it remained unaware of the bird and its nest. But the frightened sandpiper could remain still no longer. It suddenly startled the mink with a commotion of fluttering wings and plaintive cries as it fluttered, took to wing and flew away. The mink stopped in its tracks, saw the bird and with keen eyes discovered the nest because of the revealing flight of the parent. It quickly moved in and destroyed the eggs, crushing the embryonic life of the soon-to-be hatched sandpipers.

If the parent had responded wisely to this dangerous situation, the nest would have survived the threat of the mink's attack. Even that day the elements of nature were in the favor of the sandpiper. The nest was situated downwind from the prowling predator. Had the bird only known to remain motionless, this stealthy hunter would have continued on its way, oblivious to the presence of the nest.

The sandpiper's eggs *are just large enough for two to lie on either side of its breast. In order for them to fit, the bird carefully positions each one with its narrow end facing inward.*

CHARACTERISTICS AND PHYSICAL FEATURES OF THE SANDPIPER

Not only did the sandpiper fail to respond wisely but it failed to respond quickly to the threat of the mink. While the animal was still a considerable distance away, the sandpiper had an opportunity to leave the nest without exposing its location. The ill-considered flush, characteristic of this species, signaled the whereabouts of the eggs to the mink. Inappropriate initiative needlessly destroyed the lives of its young.

DOES THE CRUDE NEST OF THE SANDPIPER HAMPER ITS CHANCES OF SUCCESS?

Actually, the eggs are very secure because the parent bird doesn't rely on a concealed nest of vegetation as the grebes do. It depends instead on the blotched, pale eggs themselves which blend extremely well with their surroundings and form a natural protective camouflage.

HOW STRONG IS THE EGG OF THE SANDPIPER?

The egg is not strong at all. In fact, the shell walls are very thin. Light-footed, delicate birds such as the sandpiper lay delicate eggs. The structure of the egg itself is remarkable. Its porous shell allows evaporation from within and replaces the moisture with oxygen. The yolk of the egg nourishes the chick while the white liquid, called albumen, insulates the developing embryo from sudden changes in temperature.

*SEASONAL RANGES
OF THE SPOTTED SANDPIPER*

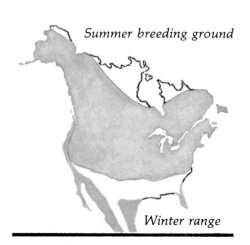

Summer breeding ground

Winter range

Within hours after the chicks hatch *they quickly adapt to their environment, no matter what the surrounding terrain may be. The breeding range of the spotted sandpiper is widely diversified. The bird is found in areas ranging in altitude from sea level to 14,000 feet.*

Upon the command of its mother, *the chick assumes a frozen position. Once danger passes the parent sandpiper signals the fledglings to return to the safety of its side. With outstretched wings it gathers them together in a gesture of reassurance and comfort.*

IS CATCHING FOOD EASY FOR THE SANDPIPER?

The sandpiper's innate agility combined with its long legs and pointed bill enable this little eight-inch bird to easily and effectively catch its food. The bird positions itself in such a manner as to make its body indistinguishable from the background soil and foliage. Pointing its bill straight at the victim, the shorebird stretches straight out and parallels its body along the level of the ground. The unsuspecting prey is unable to distinguish the bird's head because it is camouflaged against the body feathers. Assuming this position, the sandpiper slowly stalks forward and approaches within inches of the insect. Then the bird plucks it from its perch with amazing speed. The spotted sandpiper bobs up and down the water's edge in search for insects which inhabit the shallow waters, muddy pools and odoriferous rotting vegetation of the shoreline.

DOES THE SANDPIPER EVER CHANGE COLOR?

One of the most attractive and delicate of shorebirds, the little sandpiper maintains its greyish olive coloring and white underparts throughout most of the year. During courtship the plumage undergoes a color change. Between March and April a pre-nuptial molt occurs. This is a partial molt as the sandpiper loses only its body feathers; the wing and tail feathers remain unchanged. When the new plumage grows out, the white underparts of the breast become dotted with black spots. In August the sandpiper experiences a complete post-nuptial molt and at this time loses its distinctive black spots. The spotted sandpiper derives its name from the appearance of this nuptial plumage. This is the only sandpiper with a spotted breast.

BY WHAT OTHER NAMES IS THE SANDPIPER KNOWN?

This sandpiper is known by many other names such as teeter, teetertail, see-saw, sand-peep, sand snipe, river snipe, sand lark, tilt up, teeterer, teeter peep, peet weet or tip up from its nervous habit of tilting its body as it walks. The spotted sandpiper is one of the most successful species of shorebirds and is widely distributed throughout the continent.

HOW MATURE ARE SANDPIPER CHICKS AT BIRTH?

At birth the chicks are able to see, walk and even feed themselves. Their mimicry of the adult sandpiper even extends to an identical version of its characteristic teetering walk. The sandpiper's incubation period is longer than that of other eggs its size because the chicks are far more developed than most birds immediately after hatching.

HOW DOES A YOUNG CHICK PROTECT ITSELF?

When danger threatens the lives of young chicks, the protective mother cries a loud, "peet, peet, peet!" Immediately the young flatten themselves close to the ground and freeze. Their yellowish, buff-colored down with a sprinkling of brown shades enables them to blend so effectively with their background that it is extremely difficult for them to be detected even on a flat surface. When danger passes and the mother feels that it is safe to come out of hiding, she signals the brood. Once again their response is immediate as they quickly run to her side and seek protection under her wings.

HOW LONG DOES THE FAMILY UNIT REMAIN INTACT?

Two days after hatching the young begin to explore and within weeks they have separated from their parents. If conditions grow difficult for immature chicks, the adult sandpipers once again assist in caring for their brood. But usually within a month the fledglings are entirely on their own.

HOW SOON DO SANDPIPERS LEARN TO FLY?

Even before young sandpipers lose their downy coats, their wings have developed. In a matter of only ten to twelve days the young chicks are capable of flying short distances.

HOW VARIED IS THE SANDPIPER'S DIET?

Insects comprise the largest percentage of the sandpiper's diet. These include flies, grasshoppers, crickets, caterpillars and various aquatic insects. Along the water's edge and between pebbles and rocks the sandpiper searches for small crustacea. It also dines on worms, grubs, small minnows and the fry of various fish such as trout.

The sandpiper's feet *have a webbed membrane attached between the outer and middle toes. With the aid of these webbed feet the bird is adept in the water as well as on land.*

To escape the attack of one of its major enemies—*the pigeon hawk—the sandpiper may resort to diving or even walking along the lake bottom.*

The precocious chicks *are able to swim well while still in their down feathers. The fledglings develop rapidly and are capable of flying within a few weeks.*

321

A FISHERMAN'S CATCH

Returning to camp after a week's stay on a remote island in the northern wilderness, two fishermen made their way to an inlet to moor their canoe. As they approached the bank, a fluttering noise in a bush caught the attention of one of the men. After reaching shore, they headed toward the bush for a closer look.

There a frightened sandpiper struggled, hopelessly twisted and suspended by a tangled network of nylon line which had been thoughtlessly left on shore by a previous party. The bird dangled in the air. Its frenzied efforts to escape only twisted the net more tightly to the point that the bird was strangling itself against the cord. Stooping down, one of them gently cradled the helpless sandpiper in his hand and reached for a pocket knife.

He carefully cut away the interwoven cord. After the bird was released and the nylon unwrapped from its body, the man cupped the fragile sandpiper in his hand and quietly stroked its breast feathers. The bird became motionless. Sensing that it had quieted and regained its composure, he gently set it on the ground. Both men stepped back to watch.

The bird ran a few feet. Then it suddenly stopped. It turned around to face the fishermen and began its characteristic teetering. Astonished at the bird's apparent gesture of gratitude, they watched for a few moments and then walked away.

A few hours later they returned to the canoe after dinner and stopped at the beach to look for their former ward. To their amazement, the rescued bird and four fluffy chicks, no larger than half dollars, paraded along the shoreline in front of them. The female made no effort to conceal or protect herself or her young. During their entire stay on the island there had been no evidence to reveal that a family of shorebirds shared their limited quarters. After this unusual display, the men could only surmise that the uncharacteristic behavior was indeed a demonstration of gratitude on the part of the sandpiper.

Initiative can be demonstrated in many different ways. The ability to respond quickly and wisely is not limited to situations of danger but can also find expression in gratefulness. In this incident the spotted sandpiper took the initiative to show gratitude, momentarily removing barriers of secrecy and fear.

HOW DOES SCRIPTURE ILLUSTRATE INITIATIVE IN RESPONDING TO DANGER?

A curious delegation made its way down the road to the capital city. Each man was arrayed in royal apparel. Behind them were beasts of burden loaded with supplies and a gift for the king.

Their visit was designed to remove any suspicion that they were on a spying mission. When they reached the palace they bowed low before the king and explained the purpose of their visit. They told the king that the ruler they served had heard that he was sick but that he had recovered. The ruler wanted to express good wishes by sending him a gift. In that moment the king might have become suspicious. Could it be that this group came to see whether or not his kingdom would be a potential ally in the future?

He sensed the need to take the initiative and prove to his visitors that his kingdom was strong. But he did a very unwise thing. He gave them a tour of his entire palace and showed them all the priceless treasures of gold, silver and precious stones. They were overwhelmed with wonder and awe. He thought to himself, "If they are impressed with this, wait until I show them my other treasures." He led them to his secret storehouses in various parts of his domain. They eagerly listened, looked and later made notes of all they had seen.

As they left the city an uneasy feeling crept over the king. Just then the prophet arrived and asked, "What did these men say to you, and where are they from?" The king tried to reassure the prophet and also himself. "They are from a far country, even from Babylon."

"What did they see in your house?" The king replied, "All the treasures that are in my house they have seen. There is nothing I have not shown them."

With a grieved expression the prophet informed him, "The day will come when all that is in your house shall be carried into Babylon. Nothing shall be left."

What must have saddened the prophet even more was that the king had failed to show those visitors the true strength of the kingdom. He could have shown them a huge pile of rocks by the river Jordan. These were placed there as a memorial by the twelve tribes when God parted the sea and led them into the land to conquer their enemies. He could have shown them rubble from walls which had fallen flat on the ground. These were the walls of Jericho which fell outward at the command of God. He could have shown them a sun dial that God had turned back ten degrees. This was the sign that God gave him that he would become well and live fifteen more years.

In previous years this king, Hezekiah, had sought the Lord with all his heart, and God had mightily rewarded him with riches and honor. When the ambassadors came from Babylon the king failed to draw their attention to a living God who was leading His people. Had he taken the initiative to show them the evidence of God's power rather than the accumulation of his wealth, the visitors might have left with a very different impression of the strength of the nation.

From Isaiah 39

Hezekiah's name was memorialized *in this fourth-century B.C. coin inscribed with "Hezekiah" and "Judea."*

Hezekiah could have explained to his visitors *the reason for the astronomical phenomenon recently observed by Babylonian astrologers on their sundials (cf. II Kings 20:8-11).*

Hezekiah could have shown his Babylonian visitors *the stone erected by Joshua at Shechem. This was a witness of the Israelites' renewal of their covenant with the Lord—a covenant unsympathetic to their dependence on foreign military aid.*

HEZEKIAH'S INABILITY TO RESIST QUICKLY THE TEMPTATION OF PRIDE CREATED UNNECESSARY PRESSURE FOR HIS NATION

When young Hezekiah became the fifteenth king to reign in Judah, the northern nation of Assyria had become the most powerful military machine in the world. The very name of the Assyrian king was enough to send chills down the backs of the various small monarchs. The Assyrian policy of brutally torturing their unsubmissive captives intimidated most rulers, including Hezekiah's predecessor. When Hezekiah initiated his bold religious reforms and smashed all the Assyrian idols and altars, his action did not go unnoticed and was interpreted as rebellion.

WISE PREPARATIONS REPEL AN ATTACK

Hezekiah knew that Assyrian reprisal was inevitable, and he made extensive preparation in anticipation of an invasion. He built new fortifications around Jerusalem, stimulated the production of weapons and reorganized the army. In preparation for a seige of Jerusalem, he ambitiously constructed a one thousand, seven hundred seventy-seven foot tunnel through solid rock to ensure an adequate water supply. He then blocked off other sources of water in the area surrounding Jerusalem to inconvenience the invading Assyrians. When they finally invaded Judah they inflicted great damage but Jerusalem was not taken. Because the nation of Babylon was in rebellion, the Assyrians had to leave Judah and Jerusalem to quell the revolt.

VICTORY IS APPLAUDED WITH GIFTS FROM NEIGHBORING NATIONS

Hezekiah's successful defense against the hated Assyrians brought congratulations from the surrounding cities and nations which would have fallen had not Jerusalem held strong. In gratitude they flooded him with expensive gifts to help him recover his losses. It was at this time, at the very height of his popularity among the people and other nations that Hezekiah became ill. Isaiah the prophet told him he was going to die. The blow was more than Hezekiah could bear. He was only about forty years old and saw for the first time in years the opportunity to reunite the divided kingdoms of Judah and Israel. His rapport with other nations provided him the economic potential of creating an empire to compare to that of Solomon's. And now he was supposed to die. He pleaded with the Lord for an extension of life in order to accomplish his dreams, and the Lord graciously granted him an additional fifteen years.

REBUKED FOR A REVEALING TOUR OF THE NATION

It was immediately after his recovery that Merodach-baladen, the recently exiled king of Babylon, sent messengers to visit Hezekiah. He had heard of Hezekiah's successful resistance against their common Assyrian enemy and probably desired Hezekiah's support in an effort to regain his throne. In a moment of unrestrained pride Hezekiah yielded to the temptation to reveal to his prestigious visitors his vast wealth, powerful defenses and recent gifts. After being sternly rebuked for his prideful folly by the prophet Isaiah, Hezekiah repented of his ungrateful lapse of faith and led the nation into a period of prosperity the people of God had not enjoyed for many years. After the promised fifteen years, Hezekiah died and was honored by the people who loved him.

FINAL TRIBUTE TO THE GODLY KING

Although Hezekiah's kingdom never compared to the glory of Solomon's, and though he died at the relatively early age of about fifty-five, Scripture honors him with the following epithet: "He trusted in the Lord God of Israel; so that after him was none like him among all the kings of Judah, nor any that were before him. For he clave to the Lord, and departed not from following him, and kept his commandment, which the Lord commanded Moses." (II Kings 18:4,5)

OLDER KING HEZEKIAH CHARACTER SKETCH

WHY DID HEZEKIAH GIVE HIS VISITORS SUCH AN EXTENSIVE TOUR?

When Hezekiah received a fifteen-year extension of his life from the Lord, he resumed ambitious plans to restore the empire. Because of his successful stand against Assyria he received many valuable gifts from the surrounding nations and his fame grew (II Chronicles 32:23). As a result, he had accumulated vast amounts of food, animals, silver, gold and precious stones (II Chronicles 32:27,28). When the Babylonian delegation visited his kingdom, he recognized the potential of a mutually beneficial economic and military alliance. He may have recalled Solomon's strategy with the Queen of Sheba and the tour he gave her in an effort to seal a trade agreement (I Kings 10:1-13). He was trying to impress his visitors with the fact that he was a king profitable to do business with. Hezekiah was motivated by pride.

WHY WAS THE LORD DISAPPOINTED WITH HEZEKIAH?

We learn in II Chronicles 32:31 that the visitors from Babylon provided the Lord with a test to discern Hezekiah's heart. Isaiah had warned the nation of Judah not to negotiate a treaty with Egypt (Isaiah 30:1-7; 31:1-3). To do so would suggest to the world that the Lord was not able to protect His own people. For Hezekiah to make a treaty with Babylon would indicate the same thing. At this time Hezekiah had become proud of his great wealth, and his heart was lifted up (II Chronicles 32:25). He refused to resist the temptation to multiply unto himself silver and gold (cf. Deuteronomy 17:17). His great zeal for the Lord had turned into personal ambition, and the Lord had to send Isaiah to rebuke him.

WHAT WERE THE CONSEQUENCES OF HEZEKIAH'S INDISCRETION?

Isaiah the prophet told Hezekiah that because of his actions he would share in the responsibility for the future Babylonian captivity. Though he would be spared, his descendants would become captives in the palace of Babylon (II Kings 20:16-18). It was an amazing prophecy since Babylon was then under the control of the Assyrians. We can only imagine that the visitors returned with word of the tremendous wealth of Judah. A century later when Nebuchadnezzar was increasing the treasuries of Babylon, he no doubt knew of the prizes he would find in Jerusalem. He not only sacked the city of most of its valuables but also turned the princes over to the master of his household (Daniel 1:1-4). About twenty years later he returned to completely destroy Jerusalem at which time the land was stripped of all the remaining treasures of which Hezekiah had been so proud (II Kings 25:8-17).

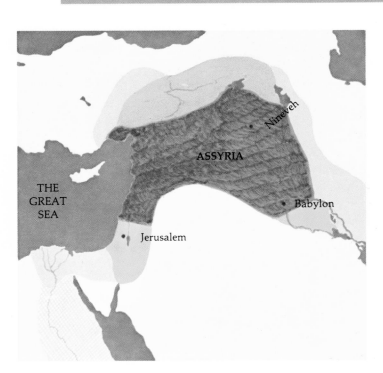

"**Then came Isaiah, the prophet,** *unto King Hezekiah, and said unto him, What said these men? And from whence came they unto thee? And Hezekiah said, They are come from a far country, even from Babylon.*"

HEZEKIAH

Decisiveness

PART SEVEN

Decisiveness

IS REFUSING TO RECONSIDER A DECISION WHICH I KNOW IS RIGHT

LIVING LESSONS ON DECISIVENESS . . .

FROM THE PAGES OF SCRIPTURE

A soothsayer was asked to curse the children of Israel, but God intervened and forbade him from making such a curse. Greed caused him to maneuver around God's command and the ultimate results were the destruction and moral decay of God's chosen people.

ILLUSTRATED IN THE WORLD OF NATURE

THE SHORT-TAILED SHREW *Blarina brevicauda*

The short-tailed shrew is one of two hundred and sixty-five species found throughout the world, thirty of which inhabit North America. This animal lives in forests, marshes and open fields which provide thick, damp ground cover. Unsociable by nature, the shrew is active both night and day.

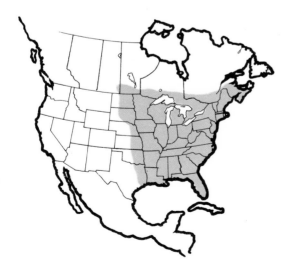

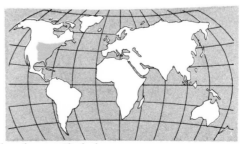

The range and habitat of the short-tailed shrew

DECISIVENESS

HOW DOES THE SHREW ILLUSTRATE DECISIVENESS IN REFUSING TO RECONSIDER A DECISION?

In an effort to secure a study specimen of the shrew, a naturalist learned how voracious this little animal's appetite really is.

One evening before retiring, he set a trap where a short-tailed shrew had been seen earlier that day. Peanut butter, a food which is highly appetizing to this insectivore, was placed on the trap as bait.

The next morning the area was inspected and he discovered that the trap was successfully sprung. Elation faded to dismay when closer observation revealed the half-eaten carcass of a shrew.

Determined to obtain a whole specimen, the naturalist reset the trap only to achieve the same result for two consecutive nights. Each time the trap was set in the evening and then inspected the following day. In each instance the unlucky victim had been almost completely devoured. Only its head remained intact.

On the third evening the naturalist set the trap earlier and checked it before retiring. As the observer drew near, a shrew raced from the sprung trap but not before it had ravaged another specimen.

Each night the bloodthirsty raider had come and ravenously devoured a hapless member of its own species which had been caught. Indiscriminate in its eating habits, the shrew was not above the practice of cannabalism. Not until the fourth morning was the naturalist's mission successful. At last, all that remained was the bait and the marauder became the final victim of the trap.

The hyperactive nature of this mammal requires excessive energy for living which is derived from eating huge quantities of food. It is not at all particular about what it eats. The only criterion in its food selection is whether or not it is able to subdue its prey. Living on a diet of meat and nuts, the shrew will attack anything smaller than a weasel. Mice which are two to three times larger than itself are unhesitatingly attacked and eaten.

Because its food requirements are enormous the short-tailed shrew eats whatever is available. When it finds a piece of carrion, no matter how rank, it considers it a delicacy and ravenously devours it. From the day it is born the shrew engages decisively in a race to maintain life.

CHARACTERISTICS AND PHYSICAL FEATURES OF THE SHORT-TAILED SHREW

The behavior of the short-tailed shrew has been compared to the ferocity of a lion. Ounce for ounce it is considered one of the most vicious animals in the world. Bent on fulfilling its massive food requirements the short-tailed shrew decisively refuses to be swayed from its task.

HOW SMALL IS THE SHORT-TAILED SHREW?

The short-tailed shrew is only three inches long, its tail representing one-third of its body length. Shrews belong to the order Insectivora and are the smallest mammals in the world. The very smallest is the pygmy shrew.

HOW DOES THE SHREW ARRANGE ITS SCHEDULE TO FULFILL ITS FOOD REQUIREMENTS?

Always in constant frenzied motion in search of food, the shrew is active both night and day. By incorporating a daily rhythm cycle the shrew alternates between spurts of intense activity followed by short rest periods. For many years a debated issue among naturalists was whether the shrew was a nocturnal or diurnal animal. Study of the species unfolded a third category. The shrew operates on a three-hour rhythm, scouring its habitat for available food then resting. Each activity period lasts for approximately three hours.

HOW MUCH FOOD CAN A SHREW EAT?

In a twenty-four hour period, the shrew will eat twice its body weight. Proportionately, an average man would have to consume four hundred pounds in order to match this voracious appetite.

Consuming huge amounts of food, *the shrew devours approximately twice its weight in a twenty-four hour period. If it goes without food for more than seven hours, it will starve.*

The shrew, one of the smallest mammals, *weighs no more than a dime and measures only three inches in length.*

With its nose thrust in the air, *the shrew sniffs for an aroma that would indicate food. Its highly developed olfactory sense is a major asset in its never-ending search for prey.*

Always on the lookout for an easy meal *the shrew is quick to seize the relatively slow salamander.*

WHY DOES SUCH A LITTLE ANIMAL REQUIRE SO MUCH FOOD?

The shrew is very nervous, short-tempered and energetic. Its heart can beat an incredible twelve hundred times per minute, and its respiration is also rapid. Because the shrew is such a small animal it loses its body heat rapidly. Much of its food intake is comprised of insects which have a high water content and are of less nutritional value than other foods. So the food requirements of the little animal are enormous.

WHAT EXACTLY DOES A SHREW EAT?

The short-tailed shrew is a member of the order insectivora which in Latin means, "insect eating." Dining on a variety of insects the shrew eats beetles, ants, flies, and caterpillars, to name just a few. Its diet also includes worms, salamanders, mice and small birds and it is not above eating carrion. An unusual aspect of this mammal's diet is its love for nuts, especially beechnuts and acorns. It also eats grasses, roots and other vegetable matter.

WHY DOES THE SHREW ALWAYS HAVE ITS NOSE UP IN THE AIR?

The highly active nose of the shrew is always in motion as it pokes for worms, mice and bugs. The shrew uses it constantly to test the air for food or possible danger. *Vibrissae*, or the tip of the nose, is very flexible and is used in a tactile capacity.

CAN A SHREW ENDURE LOUD NOISES?

The shrew's minute ears, disguised in its fur, lend the animal an acute sense of hearing. So sensitive, in fact, is its hearing that sudden loud noises have frightened the shrew to death.

HOW USEFUL ARE EYES THE SIZE OF A PINHEAD?

It is believed that they are not useful at all. The short-tailed shrew's eyes are very small, and studies indicate that the animal's vision is quite limited. The two senses on which it relies heavily are its sense of smell and its sense of hearing.

DO SHREWS HUNT IN PAIRS?

Because the shrew is volatile and unsociable it prefers solitude. Its suspicious and intolerant nature would make it highly unlikely for two shrews to hunt cooperatively.

DOES THE SHORT-TAILED SHREW HIBERNATE?

The little shrew cannot afford to hibernate. It is active all winter. Because it is such a small animal, the shrew's body chemistry is less efficient than that of larger species and as a result cannot as effectively store energy resources.

WHAT IS THE RANGE OF A SINGLE SHREW?

Always in a great hurry, the shrew burrows a network of tunnels in a maze-like fashion over the small ten yards of terrain which it inhabits. It spends most of its life in dark tunnels and matted vegetation. In the summertime when the shrew makes its subways, there is never any evidence of digging. It uses its nose to burrow and its back legs to push itself through. It disposes of loose dirt by pressing it against the side of the chamber, making a smooth passageway as it goes along. Even in the cold of winter the shrew actively digs tunnels through the snow. Relying on these passages for safety, the shrew always knows where the nearest escape hatch is located if danger threatens.

WHY IS THE SHREW'S BITE DIFFERENT FROM THAT OF OTHER ANIMALS?

When the short-tailed shrew sinks its tiny jaws in battle, its lower incisor teeth puncture the flesh of its intended prey. Then salivary glands in the shrew's mouth secrete a highly effective poisonous fluid which flows into the wound. The venom is deadly to most victims for it slows both heartbeat and breathing almost to a standstill.

HOW DOES THE LITTLE ASSASSIN KILL ANIMALS LARGER THAN ITSELF?

Its acute sense of smell enables the shrew to detect prey a considerable distance away. With lightning speed, the shrew attacks the animal by leaping from the rear and viciously slashing at the neck with its venomous teeth. The victim is soon paralyzed and the shrew begins eating—bones, hair, skin—nothing is left behind.

HOW POWERFUL IS THE SHREW'S POISON?

The glands of a short-tailed shrew have enough venom to kill as many as two hundred mice. When the shrew's poison enters intravenously it takes from three to nineteen minutes for it to kill the victim, depending on the weight of the animal and the amount of poison injected. The effect of the venom on a mouse is to cause protruding of the eyes, increased urination and partial paralysis. Just before death the doomed animal goes into convulsions. In the unlikely event that a human were to be bitten, the poison would not prove fatal but it would be extremely painful.

Active all winter, *the shrew burrows a maze of trails close to the surface of the snow with its nose and feet.*

JAW STRUCTURE OF THE SHORT-TAILED SHREW

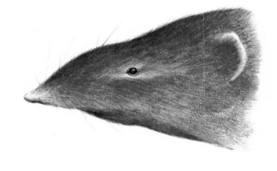

When still an embryo, *the shrew sheds its temporary teeth so that at birth the teeth with which it is equipped are already permanent.*

Wounds inflicted by the lower incisor teeth *allow the secreted venom of the shrew to creep into the wounds of the victim, paralyzing the animal.*

Extremely small, the young shrews *weigh only a fraction of an ounce at birth. Their growth is rapid. Within one month they leave the protection of their mother.*

As a means of protection, *the shrew family forms a caravan by latching onto the one in front of it. So securely do they cling to each other that if the end shrew is held in the air by its tail, the entire group will be suspended as well.*

WHAT IS THE LIFE EXPECTANCY OF A SHREW?

If the shrew is able to escape its many predators, it may live to the ripe old age of fifteen months.

CAN THESE FEISTY LITTLE ANIMALS BURY THE AXE LONG ENOUGH TO RAISE A FAMILY?

The shrew is normally a temperamental and unsociable animal and associates with other members of its species only during the mating season. At this time shrews tolerate and, in some cases, may even become very devoted to each other. During its brief lifespan the male breeds two to three times. The female may give birth to two litters during the months between spring and fall.

When the time approaches for the young to be born, the female chases the father away in order to protect the infants. The young are born in a grass nest which may be located in the ground, in a log or in a hollow stump. The nest is a ball of loosely woven material the interior of which is two to three inches in width.

WHAT DOES A SHREW WEIGH AT BIRTH?

At birth a shrew weighs just 1/200 of an ounce. The four to ten young remain close together for about a month as they mature. When the young are weaned, the family unit breaks apart. At this time they separate and regard each other as complete strangers.

WHAT UNIQUE METHOD OF TRANSPORTATION DOES THE SHREW FAMILY EMPLOY?

When the young leave the protection of their nest they assume a unique, train-like formation for travel. To synchronize their movement, they form a chain as the first infant clings to the mother by clamping its teeth on her hind parts. Each successively latches on to the one before it in the same manner, forming a straight line. If the mother speeds up or slows down, they do exactly the same. If she senses danger and freezes in place, the young shrews immediately assume the same position. If the chain happens to break loose from her and the eyes of the young are open, the mother will continue on her way without returning for the young. The one heading the group becomes the new leader.

HOW DOES SCRIPTURE ILLUSTRATE DECISIVENESS IN REFUSING TO RECONSIDER A DECISION?

The official delegation approached the house of the soothsayer. With urgency they reported a serious request from their king. "A great and powerful nation has come into our country. They will overrun the land unless we conquer them and drive them away. I will give you a great reward if you come and curse them."

He replied, "Stay here tonight, and I will give you my answer in the morning." That night God spoke to him and instructed him not to go with the men because the people whom the king wanted to destroy were blessed by God.

The next morning he said to his visitors, "Go back to your country, for the Lord refuses to let me go with you." His answer was final. The elders left. But later another delegation returned to his home. This one was larger and made up of the important princes of the kingdom. They offered him a greater reward for cursing the nation of Israel.

At that moment he was at the crossroads of his life. Had he learned the quality of decisiveness, he would have escaped the destruction and infamy that is recorded of him in Scripture. But greed made him waver and then reconsider. The seer replied, "If your king should give me a house full of silver and gold, I cannot go beyond the Word of the Lord, my God, to do more or less." That was decisive, but then he added a fatal sentence, "Stay here tonight and I will see if the Lord will tell me more."

That night God spoke to him. "If the men come to call you, get up and go with them. But only speak the words which I give you to speak." He didn't realize that the Lord was testing him. The next morning he gave the good news that he could go with them.

On the way, a series of strange events began to happen. His faithful donkey ran off the road. He beat the donkey. Then it crushed his foot against a wall. Once again it was beaten. Later, after a third beating, God opened the mouth of the donkey. It asked, "Why have you beaten me these three times?" "Because you mocked me," the soothsayer shouted. "If I had a sword I would kill you."

Then God opened his eyes and he saw an angel with drawn sword standing in front of him. The same fury that he felt toward the disobedient donkey was God's response toward him for disobeying His clear directive. God was displeased that he had asked Him a second time for permission to do what was clearly forbidden. God was angry with him for going with the princes since he knew this was contrary to His original directions.

His indecisiveness which was prompted by greed ultimately brought about the moral decay of the nation of Israel. A few years later, he was killed by the very nation that the king had asked him to curse.

From Numbers 22

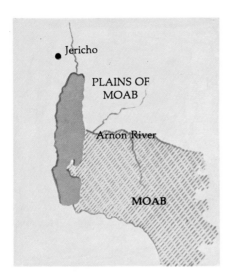

Concern over the Israelite's recent military success *prompted Moab's king Balak to contract a famous Mesopotamian soothsayer named Balaam to curse his enemy. The Israelites had temporarily settled in the Plains of Moab across the Arnon River.*

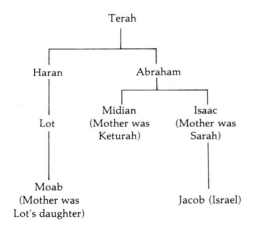

Although both Moab and Jacob *were great-grandsons of Terah, the Moabites treated the Israelites as enemies rather than relatives.*

BALAAM'S INDECISION CAUSED HIM TO RECONSIDER A DECISION HE KNEW WAS RIGHT

The awesome miracles that the Lord performed in delivering the young nation of Israel out of Egypt had terrified the kings of the surrounding city-states. For almost four decades this wandering nation of over six hundred thousand fighting men had been under constant surveillance. Various military strategies had been tried by some and observed by others. When the two powerful Amorite rulers—Sihon, king of Heshbon, and Og, king of Bashan—were utterly defeated in open combat, the Moabite king Balak resorted to more subtle designs.

ENEMIES RESORT TO MAGIC

King Balak knew of a successful soothsayer living near the Euphrates River who professed to worship the God of Israel. This soothsayer by the name of Balaam had the reputation of being able to predict the future and even influence it through his magical formulas. Since this was his vocation, Balaam charged fees for his services depending on the nature and difficulty of the request.

When Balak's initial offer for his service was rejected, he assumed it was because his divination fee was not large enough. He sent another delegation and told Balaam he could set his own fee if only he would come and curse the nation of Israel. But Balaam had received a precise and probably very rare revelation from God that he should not go to curse the Israelites. When Balaam received Balak's second offer the Lord spoke again to the soothsayer and permitted him to pursue his folly but not to speak against God's people.

CONFRONTATION WITH A DONKEY

On the long journey to the country of Moab the Lord revealed Himself to Balaam for the third time. This time the Lord reasoned with him through the mouth of his donkey. In a fit of frustration and a lapse of sanity Balaam actually argued with his dumb beast, evidencing a complete lack of spiritual discernment. After revealing the death angel to Balaam's eyes, the Lord again impressed upon him the command not to issue any curse against His people.

GREED PROMPTS A DIABOLICAL SCHEME

Three times the king of Moab asked Balaam to curse the nation he feared, but three times the Lord put words of blessing into the mouth of Balaam. The angry Balak dismissed Balaam to his home without payment, but the ingenious soothsayer had another plan to gain his fee. Although Scripture does not provide the details, it appears that after Balaam returned home he sent Balak one of the most diabolical schemes ever conceived. *If you are able to corrupt a people whom the Lord will not let you curse, a just and righteous God will have to punish them Himself.* Following Balaam's advice, Balak made friends with Israel and seduced them into worshipping the gods of Moab through marriage with the pagan Moabite and neighboring Midianite women.

THE DEATH OF TWENTY-FOUR THOUSAND—THE RESULT OF SIN

Balaam's plan worked as predicted, and the Lord disciplined His children with a plague which killed twenty-four thousand people. Had not the priest Phinehas intervened, the number would have been even greater. The Lord then protected them from further danger by commanding them not to make friends with the people who were trying to destroy them. Balaam's contemptible actions were not to remain unjudged. The enjoyment of his temporal rewards was brief, and when Israel fought against the Midianites Balaam was one of the casualties.

BALAAM CHARACTER SKETCH

WAS BALAAM A TRUE PROPHET OF GOD?

Even though Balaam was used by God to speak His words (Numbers 23:5; 24:2) and claimed to worship the Lord God of Israel (Numbers 22:18), he was not a true prophet. When King Balak sent to Mesopotamia for Balaam, he sent for a soothsayer, not a prophet. He did not want to know the future. He wanted to influence it. The fact that Balaam worshipped the God of Israel does not mean that he did not worship false gods as well. He seemed very comfortable around the altars of Baal in Moab. As a soothsayer, Balaam set fees for his services (Numbers 22:7) and used enchantments, both of which were contrary to the Mosaic Law (Numbers 24:1; cf. Deuteronomy 18:10). It is strange that the Lord would speak through a man like Balaam just as it is strange that the Lord spoke to King Saul through the woman medium at Endor (I Samuel 28:7).

WHAT SHOULD BALAAM HAVE TOLD BALAK?

Balak was more interested in protecting his own nation than in conquering Israel. If Balaam had been a prophet of God he could have told Balak that it was not God's intention for the country of Moab to be conquered by Israel. If Balaam had grasped the meaning of the words the Lord put into his mouth he could have helped Balak. Referring to Israel the Lord had said, "Blessed is he who blesseth you, and cursed is he who curseth you." (Numbers 24:9) If he had advised Balak to show common hospitality to the young nation of Israel on their journey to Canaan, the Lord would have blessed them. But to advise Balak to corrupt the nation invited God's judgment (cf. Deuteronomy 23:3,4).

HOW WAS BALAAM SWAYED IN HIS DECISIVENESS?

Balaam was told by God not to curse the children of Israel, so he refused Balak's request. A second time the king's messengers sought him, and again he answered no. But this time his reply was not as decisive. He encouraged them to stay overnight while he inquired of the Lord. Granted reluctant permission to go, Balaam journeyed to the city. Once again God forbade him to curse the Israelites as Balak requested.

He must have realized how desperate the king was. Balaam could have had anything he wanted had he been disobedient. Sent away with no payment, he may have mulled over in his mind the possibilities he had missed. The question must have arisen whether or not it was really necessary for him to miss this opportunity. Was there still a possibility for gain?

His greed resulted in a diabolical plan which he somehow justified in his own mind. He saw how he could get the reward without directly cursing the people. He contacted Balak and gave him his plan—corrupt the people from within and God will have to punish them Himself. Balaam is mentioned three times in the New Testament (II Peter 2:15; Jude 11; Revelation 2:14). His indecision and treachery have made his life a negative example to future generations.

"Balaam also, the son of Beor, *the soothsayer, did the children of Israel slay with the sword among them who were slain by them.*"

BALAAM

Decisiveness

IS MAKING PRESENT COMMITMENTS TO AVOID FUTURE FAILURES

LIVING LESSONS ON DECISIVENESS . . .

FROM THE PAGES OF SCRIPTURE

A young man committed himself to a course of action which he knew would avoid future failure. Based on the Law of God, this man fortified himself with a standard so high that even under the vengeful scrutiny of enemies who sought his life, no fault could be found in him.

ILLUSTRATED IN THE WORLD OF NATURE

THE OSPREY *Pandion haliaetus*

The magnificent osprey has a wingspan of six feet and inhabits those areas which furnish it with a sufficient stock of fish, its major food source. Admired and appreciated more than any other hawk, the osprey continues to decline in number in spite of man's efforts to save this bird.

The range and habitat of the osprey

DECISIVENESS

HOW DOES THE OSPREY ILLUSTRATE DECISIVENESS IN MAKING COMMITMENTS FOR FUTURE SUCCESS?

A piercing, shriek-like whistle betrayed the presence of the osprey. The bird was silhouetted against the blue sky as it searched for food high above the lake. Its quest was becoming increasingly difficult. The supply of fish which had abounded for years had drastically declined that spring.

The previous winter had been long and severe. Early in November, freezing weather had arrived and heavy snows covered the lake until the final April thaw.

Since the lake water was not particularly deep, the premature freezing had stilled its surface. Without the tumbling motion of the waves the fish were prohibited from receiving any further oxygen. The oxygen supply underneath the ice would still have continued to support life despite the early freeze had it not been for heavy snowfalls which blocked vital rays of sunlight. Water plants which depend on sunlight normally produce a sufficient amount of oxygen to support aquatic life. But without sunlight the plants died, and competition among fish for the limited oxygen had caused a winter kill which greatly reduced their numbers.

The osprey would be forced to work harder to find and catch the fish necessary for survival if it were to remain in this lake area. Not only was the osprey affected by this shortage, but other wildlife inhabitants were suffering as well.

Soaring up to two hundred feet in the air, the osprey scanned the water below with its acute vision. Spotting a dark object, it abruptly changed direction, circled and descended about fifty feet. Having seen just enough to determine the position of the fish, the osprey half-folded its wings, locked them into position and quickly lowered its head. It dove decisively for the fish with its sharp talons outstretched. Faster and faster the hawk's momentum increased as it plummeted toward the surface. With a burst of spray the bird's breast struck the water. Disappearing for a moment, it emerged with its talons securely clasped around the body of a rainbow trout.

On powerful wings it soared upward toward its perch where it could safely eat the catch. As it gained altitude, the hawk was suddenly over-shadowed by a huge form in the air. The threatening bird swiftly swept down from above. Startled and intimidated by the powerful wings and talons of this intruder, the osprey released its prize. Sailing down after the fish, the bold thief grasped it in mid-air and then flew towards shore to enjoy the stolen catch.

The bald eagle, another bird that lives largely on fish, had compensated for its own inadequate technique by capitalizing on the unerring decisiveness of the osprey. Deprived of its rightful catch, the osprey would resume its vigil, relying once again on its ability to make swift and accurate decisions in flight.

CHARACTERISTICS AND PHYSICAL FEATURES OF THE OSPREY

The osprey's ability to make swift and accurate decisions enables it to achieve ninety percent accuracy in capturing its submerged, slippery prey. Equipped with special talons, exceptionally keen eyesight and powerful wings, the osprey is well-suited for its "sky-diving" fishing technique.

HOW IS THE OSPREY ABLE TO HOLD ON TO A SLIPPERY FISH?

The force with which the hawk strikes the fish permits it to set long, sharp talons deep into its prey, easily penetrating the fish's protective scales. The osprey's long toes allow it to encircle the bodies of larger fish which may weigh even more than the bird itself. To ensure that the fish does not slip away, the bottom of the feet are equipped with spiny *tubercels* which create a non-skid surface.

COULD THE OSPREY EAT ITS CATCH "ON THE WING?"

The osprey is capable of eating "on the wing," but the preferred method is to have a supporting surface beneath it. The hawk is not equipped with teeth to chew its food and must rely on its talons and long hooked beak to tear apart the flesh of its catch. The bird securely holds the fish against the ground or a branch with its claws and tears strips of meat which it can easily swallow.

Included in a list of fowl which are not to be eaten, *the majestic osprey is referred to in Leviticus 11:13 and Deuteronomy 14:12.*

Similar to an owl's, *the osprey's outer toe can be moved backwards for a better grip on its prey.*

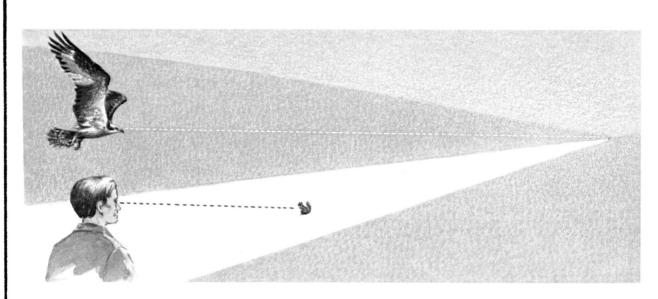

VISUAL COMPARISONS

Man's perception

Hawk's perception

ABOVE *The osprey's eyesight is eight times as acute as man's. With its telescopic-like eyes the hawk can search out objects that would be indistinguishable to the human eye. A special muscular action enables the bird to bring the object into distinct definition.*

LEFT *Comparative impression of a fox squirrel viewed from the same distance by an osprey and a man.*

OPTICAL ILLUSION

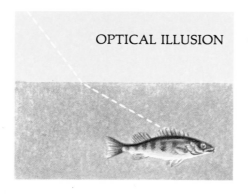

ACTUAL LOCATION OF FISH

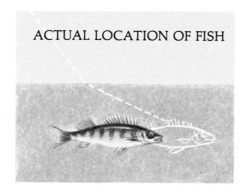

The true location of a submerged object *is difficult to determine. When aiming for its prey the osprey must adjust to overcome this optical illusion.*

DO ALL BIRDS SEE THE SAME WAY?

No. The vision of birds falls into three classifications—*flat, globose* or *tubular*. Variation among these three types lies in the distance difference between the cornea and retina and variations in the convexities or sides of the eye. *Flat* eyes are wider than they are deep. *Globose* eyes have equal distances between the cornea and retina and the side of the eyes. The cornea and retina of *tubular* eyes tend to be longer than the width, and the walls of the eye assume a distinct concave appearance. *Tubular* eyes are characteristic of birds of prey. They enable them to see longer distances, an asset which aids the bird as it soars above the ground in search of food.

IS AN OSPREY'S VISION BETTER THAN A MAN'S?

A man would need a device to increase the strength of his vision eight times in order to see as well as the osprey. The hawk is equipped with monocular vision. A muscular action adjusts the lens of the eye in a manner similar to a "zoom-in" focus feature of a telescope. In addition, the osprey's binocular vision increases its ability to judge distance by an overlapping of each eye's field of vision.

DO THE HAWK'S EYES HAVE TO BE LARGE IN ORDER TO ACHIEVE SUCH EXCELLENT VISION?

The osprey's eyes are actually equivalent in size to that of an average man. In fact, the eyes are so large that they occupy more room in the head of the hawk than the brain.

IS THE OSPREY COMPLETELY SUBMERGED WHEN IT DIVES?

The easiest catches for an osprey are those fish that bask in the sun near the surface of the water. When catching these, the hawk is able to make a shallow dive. Only its talons strike the water. This is the preferred procedure, but if necessary, the bird completely submerges itself in order to make a strike in deeper water.

WOULD AN OSPREY EVER GET WATERLOGGED?

No. The osprey's plumage is specially designed to prevent such an occurrence. Its strong feathers are constructed very close to each other and an oil gland at the base of the tail provides an effective water-repellent. Water is quickly shed, and the feathers remain dry even after its brief immersion.

DOES THE OSPREY EVER TAKE A BATH?

One would think that a bird which submerges itself so frequently would never need a bath, but such is not the case. Periodically the osprey flutters in the water to rinse its feathers and then flies away to a nearby branch to preen and oil them. The osprey has a unique method of washing its talons free of the protective slime which coats fish. Gliding close to the surface, it submerges its feet in the water and rinses them as it flies along for several hundred yards.

ARE FISH CARRIED AWAY IN ANY PARTICULAR FASHION?

The manner in which the osprey carries a fish depends upon the size of the catch. Small fish can be carried away with one foot. Larger game require both claws. The osprey carefully positions each foot—one in advance of the other—and points the nose of the fish into the wind to reduce air resistance.

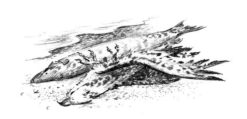

A FATAL MISJUDGMENT

Occasionally a fish hawk is found on the shore—its talons deeply embedded in the back of a large fish. The osprey's grasp is so strong that once its claws are locked in position the bird may not be able to release its grip. If for some reason it misjudges the size of a fish and attempts to seize one which far surpasses it in weight, the fish may drag it beneath the surface and drown the bird. Large pike and muskie are two species capable of such a feat.

DOES AN OSPREY HAVE ITS OWN DINNER TABLE?

The osprey becomes very attached to a convenient tree limb or other preferred location to which it returns with its catch. The hawk uses this area regularly unless it is disturbed in some way either by a hunter or another bird. It is unlikely to abandon its favorite dining spot unless threatened.

Diving on a dead branch, *the osprey breaks off sticks to build its nest.*

The beautifully colored eggs *of the osprey were once sought by collectors.*

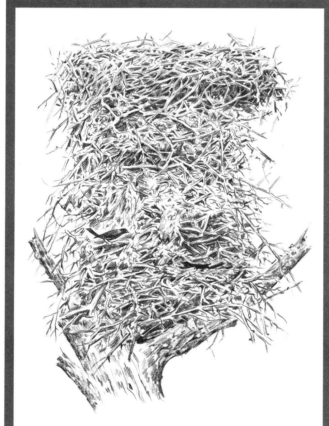

The huge nest of the osprey *houses more than just the builder's family. It is not unusual to find other small birds nesting in lower areas of the tiered construction.*

HOW BIG IS AN OSPREY'S NEST?

The osprey returns to the same nest year after year and adds new materials to its home every season. The birds may live for twenty years; consequently, the nest can attain enormous proportions. Nests have been recorded which weigh as much as half a ton, becoming so heavy that the tree in which they are constructed breaks under their weight.

HOW DOES THE OSPREY DECORATE ITS NEST?

Plummeting down on the branch of a dead tree as it would a fish, the osprey breaks branches and twigs loose to add to its nest. Particular about its construction, the parents line it with moss, evergreen branches and brush. In its care not to get the nest dirty the adult ospreys even clean their feet before entering. The hawks have a flair for decorating and place shiny objects such as shells in different sections.

DO BOTH PARENTS PARTICIPATE IN THE REARING OF THE YOUNG HAWKS?

Ospreys usually mate for life and both parents participate in building the nest, incubating the eggs and feeding the young. After the eggs hatch, the male gathers food and brings it back to the nest for the female to partially digest and feed to the young. As soon as the fledglings are old enough to handle the food, the parents simply drop it in the nest for them to feed themselves.

HOW DOES THE OSPREY RESPOND TO INTRUDERS?

The large nest of the osprey may serve as a tenant building for other birds as well. Not threatened by this hawk, both the starling and the English sparrow have been known to make their homes in the lower sections of its large, airy nest.

HOW SUCCESSFUL ARE THE OSPREYS IN RAISING THEIR YOUNG?

The ospreys experience a high loss of eggs and young during the first eight to ten weeks of life. If given an opportunity when both parents are away from the nest, predators such as gulls will raid the eggs. On occasion the parents themselves smash the eggs if forced to make a hurried exit.

HOW DOES SCRIPTURE ILLUSTRATE DECISIVENESS IN MAKING COMMITMENTS FOR FUTURE SUCCESS?

One hundred and twenty-two fearful men secretly worked out their evil plot. Any previous arguments which they may have had among themselves were set aside in an effort to protect their present power and influence. Their futures depended on success in finding some fault in the life of one man who was mighty in spirit.

They interviewed those who knew him, investigated the records of his previous activities, listened to his words both in public and in private and observed his actions. But early in life this godly man had made a vital decision which was to frustrate their efforts.

After a diligent search, the disappointed men gathered for their second meeting. "They could find no occasion nor fault: for as much as he was faithful, neither was there any error or fault found in him."

His godliness forced them to reveal their ungodliness. Since their original plan had failed, they devised a new scheme. When it backfired, they were killed by the king whose favor they were trying to preserve. Their power and honor were then given to the one whom they had tried to destroy. But what was the decision which enabled him to avoid destruction in later years?

As a boy he had been challenged by the courageous pronouncements of the prophet Jeremiah against the wickedness of the king and the nation in which he lived. His people refused to change their ways and scoffed at the punishment which the prophet predicted.

A few years later that very judgment fell on the nation as foretold. Their king was chained and led from his country with thousands of others to a heathen land. This young man was among that captured group. Everything had been taken from him—his home, his family, his possessions, his freedom.

But these circumstances revealed what was of lasting value. He observed that compromise with evil always results in punishment to the compromiser and to those around him. He visualized the compromises which he might face and made the decision that he would not defile himself or violate God's Word in any way.

In so doing he chose to be governed by a higher and stricter law than that which the one hundred twenty-two men followed. Not only were his standards higher but his motivation to keep them was stronger. He was keenly aware that God was watching and evaluating every one of his words, thoughts, actions and attitudes. His very name Daniel means, *"God is my Judge."*

From Daniel 6

AN EARLY COMMITMENT ENABLED DANIEL
TO AVOID FOUR FAILURES

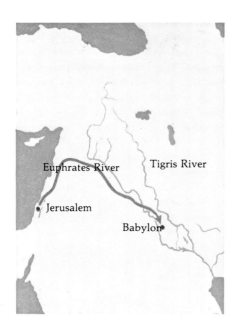

Daniel is the only man in Scripture other than the Lord who was called "beloved" in a message sent from heaven (Daniel 9:23; Matthew 3:17). His record is without blame. Just as Pilate had to proclaim to the Lord's accusers, "I find in Him no fault" (John 18:38) so Daniel's accusers "sought to find occasion against Daniel. . .but they could find no occasion nor fault. . .neither was there any error or fault found in him." (Daniel 6:4)

DISCIPLINE DURING A TIME OF PLENTY

The key to Daniel's truly successful and prosperous life can be traced to an important decision he made as a young man. "Daniel purposed in his heart that he would not defile himself." (Daniel 1:8) His career can be outlined by describing how he remained firm to that early decision on four separate occasions scattered throughout his long life.

When Daniel was found to excell in appearance, intelligence, understanding and discernment he was placed in a three-year training course to prepare for service in the king's court. Because of his privileged vocation he was offered endless varieties of meats, fish and game from the table of the king.

His first test involved deciding whether or not to eat this food which had been defiled by contact with Babylonian idols and which was unclean according to the list of prohibited animals in the Mosaic Law (cf. Leviticus 11). Daniel did not use these unusual circumstances to make provision for his appetite but creatively substituted unquestionably clean vegetables for the unclean foods.

BOLDNESS IN THE FACE OF DANGER

His second test consisted of deciding whether to reveal to Nebuchadnezzar an extremely pessimistic interpretation of one of his dreams. Daniel tactfully but boldly told the king that he would become insane for a period of seven years as a consequence of his sin and iniquity. Apart from the protection of God such a prediction would have meant certain death.

A FORECAST OF DEFEAT

His third test was similar to the second when he faced Nebuchadnezzar's grandson years later to interpret a strange inscription written on the palace wall. He predicted his defeat by the Medes and Persians and rebuked him for pride, immorality, idolatry and blasphemy.

DEATH RATHER THAN DISOBEDIENCE TO GOD

His final test occurred when he was an old man during the reign of Darius. The king had been tricked into signing a law which in effect prohibited prayer to God. Although the penalty for disobedience was a violent and certain death in a lion's den, Daniel decided he could not conform. He chose to face lions rather than displease his God. Again the Lord miraculously honored Daniel's decision by sparing him from the jaws of death. Because of the commitment which Daniel made as a youth and his faithfulness to that decision, he was a blessing to the world and to his exiled people for over seventy years.

When the young Daniel approached Babylon he would have noticed immediately the three hundred foot temple of their god, Marduk. The sight may have strengthened his decision to remain loyal to God.

Because of his high social standing, Daniel was among the first Jewish captives taken to Babylon in 605 B.C. by Nebuchadnezzar.

DANIEL CHARACTER SKETCH

WHY DID DANIEL'S ASSOCIATES WANT TO DISCREDIT HIM?

When King Darius appointed three commissioners over the one hundred and twenty governors of the various Medo-Persian possessions, his motive was to prevent loss of revenue through political corruption. Since each governor had a fixed levy to collect, it was easy for him to collect more than required and pocket the difference unless properly supervised. The only way the governors could continue their thievery was to bribe the commissioners. Daniel would not tolerate dishonesty in himself or in others. When King Darius considered setting him over the entire kingdom, the governors and other commissioners feared that their corruption would be exposed. Since they couldn't accuse him of dishonesty, their only alternative was to find something against him in regard to the law of his God (cf. Daniel 6:1-5).

COULDN'T DANIEL HAVE CONTINUED TO PRAY IN SECRET?

The fact that Daniel knew that the law against prayer had been signed but continued to kneel and pray three times a day indicates that he was well aware of the consequences of his actions. Daniel knew that the law was unjust. The king had been deceived by his counselors. But Daniel was willing to test the law by accepting the consequences and appealing to the very court of God Himself. There was another stronger motive for Daniel to maintain his daily prayers toward Jerusalem. When Solomon dedicated the temple there, he prayed that when the nation would be taken captive and the people would pray toward the Temple in Jerusalem that God would hear their prayer and have compassion on them (I Kings 8:48-50). Although unquestionably loyal to his foreign king Darius, Daniel's heart was with his people and the land of his birth.

HOW WAS DANIEL PREPARED FOR DIFFICULT TESTS?

Daniel was born into a prominent Judean family probably about the time of godly King Josiah's reformation in 621 B.C. He was raised in an atmosphere where idolatry was condemned. Obedient worship of God was encouraged both by family and government. Daniel was just a teen-ager when the beloved King Josiah was killed in a battle against the Egyptians. Three months later the nation lost its independence. He no doubt was familiar with the prophet Jeremiah's early warning about the developing Babylonian threat to the north, and he may have at this time decided what he would do if taken captive by an ungodly nation. His worst fears materialized in 605 B.C. when he was among the first group of Jewish captives taken to Babylon by Nebuchadnezzar, but he was both mentally and spiritually prepared for the tests that lay ahead.

A glazed brick panel from Nebuchadnezzar's Processional Way *at Babylon portrays the type of animal from which Daniel was miraculously delivered by God.*

DANIEL

Decisiveness

IS DEVOTING ALL MY ENERGY TO A COURSE OF ACTION WHICH I KNOW IS RIGHT

LIVING LESSONS ON DECISIVENESS . . .

FROM THE PAGES OF SCRIPTURE

A young widow's determination was rewarded because she did what she knew was right. The desires to dwell in the land of God's people, to provide for her mother-in-law and to perpetuate her husband's name were all granted because of the spirit and pure motivation with which she pursued these goals. From her unselfish determination came a blessing which would benefit all mankind.

ILLUSTRATED IN THE WORLD OF NATURE

THE BADGER *Taxidea taxus*

The badger is a member of the weasel family. Measuring thirty inches in length, this low-slung ground-dweller inhabits dry, open country. The female gives birth to a litter of two in an underground nest lined with grass. Silent by nature, the badger follows a definite pattern in its nocturnal prowls.

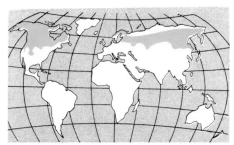

The range and habitat of the badger

DECISIVENESS

HOW DOES THE BADGER ILLUSTRATE DECISIVENESS IN DEVOTING ENERGY TO RIGHT ACTION?

The sheepherder gazed over the large expanse of pasture. It was a beautiful time of year. A promise of life was in the air as buds began to unfold their leafy contents. Fields of grass were beginning to turn green and would soon provide feed for his prize sheep. He credited his high quality of stock to his rich pasture lands. It was important to him that the grazing lands be correctly managed. Careful not to allow the sheep to overgraze any one area and destroy the root system of the grass, he rotated the flock on a systematic basis.

His purpose this day was to make sure that the fences were in good repair to contain his sheep and strong enough to discourage predators from entering. His livelihood depended on how well he was able to manage and provide for the sheep. His was a one-man operation, and he had to work long, hard hours caring for his stock. He took great pride and satisfaction in owning this five-hundred acre ranch.

Within a few weeks the young lambs arrived. These small, woolly animals were wobbly at first on their uncertain legs, but soon they playfully ran about enjoying their new world. They grew rapidly.

Early one morning as the sheepherder made his routine rounds to check the flock, he noticed something strange in the dirt by the north fence row. He knew and feared what this mound represented. The burrow had been made by an animal which would probably never attack the sheep but which still represented a major threat to their well-being. Because of an unpleasant encounter two years earlier, the sheepherder recognized the mound as the work of a badger. He knew that to protect his flocks he must quickly

eliminate it. Two years before he had had to shoot some of the sheep which had broken their legs as they stumbled in the underground shafts.

A strong digger, the badger makes long, extensive tunnels in an effort to secure food. It periodically breaks the surface creating dangerous holes which can easily cripple livestock. The sheepherder immediately moved his flock to a grazing area free from the hazardous pits. He then came back with a shovel and filled in the threatening holes.

Aware of the badger's nocturnal habits, he returned to the field early that evening. He had used the last of his ammunition during the previous hunting season and had not had an opportunity to make the long trip to town to purchase shells. Armed with only a shovel, he decided to dig the animal out and dispose of it. As he began his vigil, a slight movement several hundred yards away caught his eye. Hurriedly, he started toward the movement and picked up speed when he realized that the badger had spotted him.

But by the time he reached the badger, it had already dug itself out of sight. Furiously, he began digging in pursuit. The more he dug, the deeper the badger went—easily outdistancing the man and staying out of range of the shovel. He waited for the animal to make another appearance until it grew too dark to see. Discouraged, the man went home.

The next morning he returned to the field to see what further damage the badger had done. To his surprise there was no additional tunneling and a search each evening for the next few nights revealed that the badger had wisely sought a safer hunting ground. The badger's life was saved by its decisive nature which prompted it to swiftly dig itself free from danger and leave the area.

CHARACTERISTICS AND PHYSICAL FEATURES OF THE BADGER

Were it not for the badger's decisive movements, it would have been destroyed by the sheep herder. An effective and swift excavator, the badger is capable of digging itself out of sight in ninety seconds. Endowed with special equipment which aids in digging and defense, the burrowing badger is well-known but seldom seen.

DOES THE BADGER ALWAYS RUN FROM DANGER?

No. Like its cousins in the weasel family, the badger is a fierce fighter. With powerful jaws and long sharp teeth, it viciously wards off anything foolish enough to tangle with it. This animal has few natural enemies. The badger's response to its only real threat, man, is unpredictable. It may choose to fight by snapping at the man's legs, or it may make a quick retreat to its burrow. If no shelter is available, it quickly disappears by digging headfirst into the ground.

HOW DOES A BADGER RETREAT TO ITS BURROW?

A badger may temporarily bluff its opponent by standing its ground only to retreat quickly at the last possible moment. It enters its den in one of two ways. It either descends headfirst or backs into its refuge, ready to use its powerful teeth and claws against its pursuer.

RETREAT TACTICS

Option Number One: Forward Exit
The speediest retreat possible—headfirst.

Option Number Two: Back-In
The battle may continue as it withdraws—backwards.

The badger's two-inch claws *are kept sharp by constant digging. The animal takes care to keep them well-manicured, deliberately cleaning each set of claws by scraping one paw with the other.*

The badger's acute sense of smell *compensates for poor eyesight and informs it of the presence of an underground animal.*

IS IT POSSIBLE TO PULL A WOUNDED BADGER FROM ITS HOLE?

It is always dangerous to confront a badger, much less to brave the fury of a wounded animal which has retreated to its den. Disaster may result if a wounded badger backs into its burrow and a man is foolish enough to try to pull it out. The badger has been known to send long incisor teeth deeply through the arm and then retreat farther into the tunnel, tightly bracing itself by sinking its claws into the earth of the walls. The badger anchors itself so securely that it is virtually impossible for either to free itself. If help does not arrive, both man and badger will starve to death.

HOW DOES THE PHYSIQUE OF THE BADGER HELP IT MAKE ITS LIVING?

A muscular, low-slung body structure affords the animal great leverage and strength as it digs its way beneath the earth. Short, powerful legs effectively maneuver in close quarters, enabling it to move backwards and forwards. Strong, curved claws easily pierce packed dirt. Combine these elements in one animal and the result is a powerful earth-moving machine effective in search for meaty ground-dwellers on which it survives.

WHAT KEEPS A BADGER BUSY?

The badger routinely reviews the status of its holdings to determine whether or not they are yielding income. It frequently visits abandoned burrows which it has previously dug in the hope of finding a new and unsuspecting resident. Often rabbits and other small burrowing animals have moved in, and the badger capitalizes on their innocent intrusion.

WHAT WOULD A BADGER DIG FOR?

Basically anything. Omnivorous in taste, the badger selects from a wide variety of food including grains, roots, vegetables, fruits, insects and nuts. It easily outdigs moles, ground squirrels and chipmunks under the surface. Rabbits are another ground-dweller which account for a large proportion of its diet. Given an opportunity, the badger will even excavate and enjoy a bee's nest.

WHY IS THE PLACEMENT OF THE BADGER'S HAIR UNIQUE?

The hair of animals that live above ground is placed or "set" in such a fashion that it goes in one direction only—backwards. But the badger passes through burrows in both directions. The excavator not only moves quickly forward but moves backward rapidly, as well. Its hair is "set" in such a manner that it can lie easily in either direction. When the badger is pursued or in pursuit of prey, its uniquely placed hair does not hinder movement or slow the animal down.

WHAT IS BADGER BAITING?

The inhuman practice of badger baiting involved a contrived contest between a dog and a badger. For sport, a dog was deliberately set to taunt and provoke a caged badger. This cruelty is now illegal, but from the practice came the term *badger* meaning, "to annoy, harrass or tease in an unkind manner."

IS THE BADGER ANY MATCH FOR A DOG?

A formidable opponent, the badger is able to defeat and kill dogs up to four times its weight. For this reason, an experienced hunting dog has great respect for its fierce adversary and is not likely to provoke a fight.

WHAT MAKES THE BADGER PRACTICALLY INVULNERABLE TO ATTACK?

The badger's hair is so thick and its skin so loose that an attacker is unable to maintain its grasp or penetrate the animal. This powerful mammal is also sheathed in a protective armor of tough muscle, insulating vital organs from wounds. In addition, the badger is equipped with a protective plate and "interparietal" ridge of bone on the back of the skull which protects the head. Its long, sharp teeth and claws form vicious weapons which can inflict deadly blows on an enemy.

WHAT HOUSEHOLD ITEM IS DIRECTLY CONNECTED TO THE BADGER?

Before the invention of the electric shaver, lather was applied to the face with a shaving brush. If you really wanted a good applicator, you bought one that was made of badger bristles. During that era, badger's hair sold for as much as eighty-five dollars a pound. Today, the hair is still used for finer artist's paint brushes.

What does shaving have to do with a badger?

A coyote
unsuccessfully *tries to grasp the badger. Each attempt to bite a vital organ only results in a mouthful of loose skin.*

WHAT IS THE HEBREW BACKGROUND FOR THE SCRIPTURAL REFERENCE TO A BADGER?

The Hebrew word for the animal mentioned in Exodus 25:5; 26:14 and Ezekiel 16:10 is tachash. The word is thought to be associated with the Arabic tuchasun or tuchash meaning all sea animals. It is likely that the animal referred to is actually the sea cow, readily available at the time. Its two distinct skin textures could either be used for a fine, ornamental sandal or the coarse covering of a tent.

The badger's coat is so loosely attached to its body *that it can practically turn around in its skin. This is an asset which effectively protects the animal from assault.*

A mother badger *boldly defies a horse and carriage so that her young may cross the road.*

Farmers and ranchers do not appreciate the handiwork *of these ambitious excavators. The tunnels which the badger constructs impose a danger to the well-being of their livestock.*

IS THE EVER-BURROWING BADGER CLEAN?

The badger's personal grooming as well as its surroundings are immaculate. It is careful to clean the dirt from underneath its claws and is fastidious in combing and washing its fur. A study of freshly acquired specimens revealed little evidence of infesting parasites. The badger digs holes for its droppings and has even been known to bury its dead. Once a year, just before winter sets in, the badger family joins in a cooperative effort to clean the entire den. The ambitious animals remove accumulated debris and spread it out in fan shape in front of their exit. Not to be overlooked is its straw bedding which is changed on a regular basis.

WHAT IS UNUSUAL ABOUT THE BADGER'S LIVING QUARTERS?

The badger's home has two unusual aspects. First is its dimension. Spacious in size, the living quarters may be as long as three hundred feet. A second distinction is the depth at which this animal builds its nest. Excavating a long tunnel, the badger may build its nest six feet underground.

IS THE BADGER A GOOD NEIGHBOR?

The badger's ability to get along with other species is a unique quality. It is happy to share its spacious home with foxes or coyotes. In some cases the animals even work cooperatively in the capture of ground-dwellers. A badger may burrow down the passageway of a rodent while a coyote stands post at the back door, ready to pounce on the emerging prey.

WHAT KIND OF PARENTS DO BADGERS MAKE?

With some help from her mate, the female affectionately cares for the young which are born in May or June. In their own playground the playful cubs engage in such games as leapfrog and somersaults, frolicking under the protection of her watchful eye. By the time they are almost grown, they accompany the mother when she hunts for food. The family separates in late September.

HOW DOES SCRIPTURE ILLUSTRATE DECISIVENESS IN DEVOTING ENERGY TO RIGHT ACTION?

God gave explicit instructions to a man. "Leave your father's house and come to a land that I will show you." This man obeyed and brought his nephew with him; however, the land wasn't adequate to support both of their vast flocks and herds.

The uncle suggested to his nephew, "You choose the land which you want and I'll take the remainder." The nephew saw and chose the lush, green valley of the Jordan, certain that it would meet all his needs. But in that country lived the wicked inhabitants of Sodom and Gomorrah. Years later, God's judgment fell on those immoral cities, and the man barely escaped with his own life and those of his two daughters.

They had lost everything. Most of all they had lost God's standards of morality. As a result, both of his daughters became involved in immoral acts, and from one sinful union the nation of Moab began.

Many years later, God's judgment fell upon His own nation. Armies invaded the land, and famine and disease destroyed their harvests and their health. The famine in Israel drove a sickly family of four to the land of Moab. A young woman became a part of their family through marriage.

But then her husband died as well as her brother-in-law and father-in-law.

Now she was faced with a decision—return to her mother's house and their false gods or go back with her mother-in-law to Israel. She knew that the true God was worshipped in the land of Israel, so with all of her heart and mind and soul, she spoke those famous words to her mother-in-law. "Entreat me not to leave thee, or to return from following after thee: for whither thou goest I will go; and where thou lodgest, I will lodge: thy people shall be my people, and thy God my God. Where thou diest, will I die, and there will I be buried: the Lord do so to me, and more also, if aught but death part thee and me."

Her mother-in-law marvelled at her decisiveness because she knew that there was no more hope of her fulfilling the desires of her daughter-in-law. But this young woman looked beyond her mother-in-law's inabilities and was content to receive whatever God had for her as long as she was in the right place and serving Him.

As if to underscore how basic her decisions were to illustrate the whole Gospel message, Ruth not only met the man of God's choosing, but from their children came the line of Christ.

From Ruth 1

The distance from Bethlehem to Moab *was about fifty miles. On foot the return trip would take Naomi and Ruth four or five days.*

When Ruth returned from the fields *with the precious grain, she and Naomi still had to separate the kernels from the stalks. The kernels were then ground into a coarse flour and used for bread.*

RUTH WAS REWARDED FOR HER DEVOTION IN A DECISION SHE KNEW WAS RIGHT

When God judged His people in Israel with a severe famine because of their disobedience, Elimelech had to decide how he was going to provide for his wife Naomi and two sons. Rather than trust God to provide their needs during the crisis, he decided to leave the land he had inherited from his father.

A JOURNEY TO A STRANGE LAND

He sought refuge in the fertile but ungodly land of Moab. He could not have fared any worse had he remained in his own land. Within ten years Elimelech and his two sons died, leaving three penniless widows to fend for themselves.

The bereaved Naomi and one Moabite daughter-in-law gathered their meager belongings and began the four to five day journey back to Naomi's former home in Bethlehem of Judah. Orpah, the widow of her younger son, reluctantly remained with her family in Moab. But Ruth decided to help care for Naomi and refused to stay behind.

BENEFITED BY A LAW THAT PROVIDED FOR THE POOR

Their arrival in Bethlehem coincided with the spring grain harvest, a period which lasted from mid-April to about mid-June. A large supply of grain waited to be cut by young men. Young women then bound the grain into bundles called sheaves. According to the Mosaic Law, the poor were to be allowed to follow the binders and gather the random stalks that were left behind (Leviticus 19:9, 10). The once proud and prosperous Naomi was now among the destitute of Bethlehem. She had sold her husband's land to meet her need for shelter, and Ruth offered to go into the fields and glean for food.

In a rapid sequence of events, Naomi's bleak prospects for the future brightened. The first field in which Ruth obtained permission to glean happened to belong to Boaz, a relative of Elimelech. He had heard of Ruth's noble decision to leave her family and come to a foreign land in order to comfort and provide for Naomi. He instructed his workers to intentionally leave some stalks of grain for her to gather easily.

A NOBLE PLAN TO PERPETUATE A NAME

After the harvest, Naomi instructed Ruth to approach Boaz and formally ask him to marry her. Boaz immediately recognized Ruth's pure motives in this request and praised her for her willingness to provide Naomi with a grandson that could maintain the family name. Although Boaz was drawn to Ruth's beautiful character, he was not immediately free to accept her proposal. It was the custom of the day for the nearest relative to have the first opportunity to provide for the widow. When the younger relative declined, Boaz was free to marry the young Moabitess without criticism. He bought back the property that Naomi had sold and provided his grateful young wife with a son by the name of Obed.

REWARDED FOR HER DEVOTION

Because of Ruth's decision to exchange her pagan customs for the worship of the true God and to accompany her lonely mother-in-law to a foreign land, she had the privilege of comforting Naomi in her sorrow and became a key figure in the history of the nation of Israel. Her son Obed was the father of Jesse, and Jesse became the father of King David whose house, kingdom and throne were established forever (II Samuel 7:16).

RUTH CHARACTER SKETCH

WHY DID NAOMI ENCOURAGE RUTH TO REMAIN IN MOAB?

Naomi was concerned for Ruth's welfare. Ruth was a Moabite and faced a hostile reception in Israel. The Moabites were descendants of Lot's son, Moab. The nation had begun as the result of an incestuous relationship, and the impure rites of their fertility cults and their practice of offering human sacrifices were an abomination to the people of Israel. It had been Moabite women, under the counsel of Balaam, who caused the men of Israel to become involved in immorality and idolatry (Numbers 25:1-3). Because of this sin the Israelites were to have nothing to do with the Moabites for at least ten generations (Deuteronomy 23:3-6).

WHY DID BOAZ PRAISE RUTH FOR ASKING HIM TO MARRY HER?

Boaz was aware of the motive behind Ruth's seemingly indiscreet request. She was not seeking her own pleasure and security but was pleading with Boaz to deliver Naomi from her shame of having no male descendant. She was appealing to one of the ancient customs of Israel which provided for a childless widow to marry her dead husband's nearest willing relative. The first son of this marriage was to maintain the name of the dead husband and keep the family property intact by becoming the legal heir. Ruth's first son would become Naomi's legal grandson and inherit her husband Elimelech's name and property.

WHY DIDN'T ELIMELECH'S NEAREST RELATIVE WANT TO MARRY RUTH?

When Boaz asked the younger and nearer relative to purchase back Naomi's property he quickly agreed. But when he found out that he would also have to marry Ruth he reversed his decision (Ruth 4:3-5). His consideration to buy the land was purely economic. For a moment he shrewdly saw an opportunity to increase his property. But since Naomi had no legal heir, his first son by Ruth would become heir to the property under Elimelech's name, not his (Ruth 4:6). The gain that he would have made in property by the marriage would be lost since, according to the Mosaic Law, property reverted back to its original owner or legal heir every fiftieth year (Leviticus 25:10).

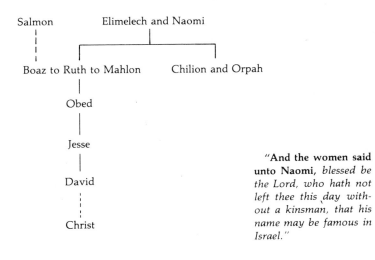

```
Salmon          Elimelech and Naomi
   |                    |
   |         ┌──────────┴──────────┐
Boaz to Ruth to Mahlon      Chilion and Orpah
          |
        Obed
          |
        Jesse
          |
        David
          |
        Christ
```

"**And the women said unto Naomi,** *blessed be the Lord, who hath not left thee this day without a kinsman, that his name may be famous in Israel.*"

RUTH

Decisiveness

IS EVALUATING COURSES OF ACTION QUICKLY AND ACCURATELY

LIVING LESSONS ON DECISIVENESS . . .

FROM THE PAGES OF SCRIPTURE

One man refused to give up when the pressure to abandon a task increased. Because he was able to evaluate a course of action and outmaneuver and stall his opponents, others were inspired to finish a monumental task. This project, completed thousands of years ago, still stands—a lasting testimony to this man's decisiveness.

ILLUSTRATED IN THE WORLD OF NATURE

THE RED FOX *Vulpes fulva*

The red fox, easily recognized by its bright amber coat and white tipped tail, is the most familiar of all North American species. It roams a home range of two to five miles and may live as long as twelve years. The red fox attains a length of forty-two inches and raises a brood of frolicsome kits each spring.

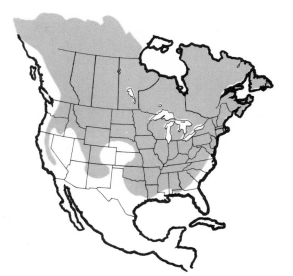

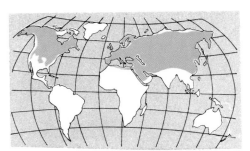

The range and habitat of the red fox

DECISIVENESS

HOW DOES THE RED FOX ILLUSTRATE DECISIVENESS IN MAKING ACCURATE EVALUATIONS?

The subject of many fireside stories is the sly red fox which has earned a reputation for its cunning and wit.

The fox is born with an innate fear of anything that is strange or foreign and exhibits a timid and cautious nature. Rigid training of the young begins early in life as the kits learn from their parents what is really dangerous and what is not to be feared.

Learning from each experience, the red fox accumulates a repertoire of valuable lessons and tricks which are essential to its future survival. If a young kit is not forced to leave the area in which it was raised, its chances of survival are greatly enhanced. For the fox learns its terrain thoroughly, knowing every nook and cranny, river and stream, grove and thicket that would enable it to confound even the most experienced pursuer. Its familiarity with its own range coupled with its sleek, slender body which is designed for speed make the fox seem almost to enjoy a good chase.

Depending on its age, intelligence and experience, a single fox is easily able to outrun and outmaneuver a pack of dogs. Keeping a safe distance between itself and the pack, the fox runs a circular course of two to three miles in length and draws from its reservoir of tricks in an effort to outwit and elude its pursuers. It even refreshes itself periodically as it rests and feeds during the chase. The average dog is much slower and is not afforded such luxury. Foxes have been known to run dogs for as long as four days. While they remain relatively fresh, the unfortunate hounds have grown gaunt in the interval, and the rigorous chase has taken its toll in the worn pads of their feet.

At every opportunity the elusive fox tries to conceal its trail by executing one of its tried and true ruses. The fox cleverly uses shallow bodies of water to its advantage. It wades through the water for as long as possible and then leaps high onto the bank at a decisive point in an effort to throw off the dogs. The water covers both the tracks and the scent, forcing the dogs to waste time as they race up and down the shore to retrace the missing trail.

The fox has even wittingly used cows to cover its trail. Running through pasturelands, it intermingles its scent with that of the cows and manure of the field. The pursuing dogs are not only confused by the clouded scent, but they create mass confusion as they try to follow a trail underfoot of the pasturing animals.

Another trick which can always be drawn upon is the old double-back technique. The crafty fox turns in its tracks and actually runs back in the direction from which it came. Retracing its steps for a considerable distance, it chooses the most strategic point at which to leave the trail. The unsuspecting dogs lumber past, noses stuck to the ground as they zip by the hidden fox. Amused at having outsmarted them, it trots away in the opposite direction as the confused dogs reach a dead end.

In the wintertime, when the surface of ponds and rivers are frozen, the crafty fox uses even this to its advantage. A bewildered vixen was running out of options trying to elude the threat of pursuing dogs. Having maneuvered them to the shore of a frozen lake, the light-footed fox gingerly stepped across the thin ice, knowing all the while that the heavier hounds which were following close behind would crash through. True to form, the dogs didn't disappoint the vixen. Glancing back over her shoulder she was assured that the chase had ended when the cold, wet dogs scrambled from the shattered ice back to the safety of the shore. Because the clever fox has learned to outwit its would-be adversaries it is thriving today.

Severt Andrewson

CHARACTERISTICS AND PHYSICAL FEATURES OF THE RED FOX

Because the fox is able to evaluate quickly different courses of action, it has gained for itself a reputation of being sly and crafty—two descriptions which have come to be synonymous with its name. In addition to its cunning and wit, it is endowed with physical features that further enhance its ability to survive.

WHY IS A FOX'S NOSE ALWAYS WET?

The noses of members of the Canidae or dog family characteristically glisten with moisture. The liquid covering actually intensifies and accentuates the aromas in the air. This is an important feature since the fox relies heavily on its sense of smell for hunting. The lubricating liquid on the damp, rough surface of the nose gives the fox a keener ability to distinguish the messages of the wind and the trail.

CAN A FOX'S NOSE DETECT YOUR FEAR?

When you are afraid, your body emits strong odors even though you may not be aware of them. The fox analyzes a person's odor with its acute sense of smell. Your scent conveys a number of messages among which are frustration, anxiety or fear. If you're frightened, the fox is sure to know it. This distinct message will affect its response toward you. If it detects fear, it will respond aggressively and hold its ground. If it senses confidence, the fox will probably retreat.

The moist, rough surface *of the red fox's nose increases its sensitivity to smell and aids it in tracking down a scent.*

The fox incorporates three hunting techniques—*each appropriate for a different kind of prey.*

DOES A FOX PREFER TO BE UPWIND OR DOWNWIND?

It depends. Upwind and downwind are terms that refer to the position of the animal in relation to the direction that the wind is blowing. If a fox is hunting, it is likely to trot upwind. With the wind blowing against its face, any scent is intercepted by its keen nose. But a rabbit in a downwind position is safe even a few feet away from a fox since the wind will blow its scent in the opposite direction.

HOW FAR AWAY CAN THE SQUEAK OF A MOUSE BE HEARD?

Although the fox depends the most on its ability to smell, hearing is also an important sense. If conditions are favorable, the faint squeak of a small mouse such as a whitefoot can be heard as far as one hundred and fifty feet away.

WHAT DISTINGUISHES THE FOX FROM OTHER MEMBERS OF ITS FAMILY?

Its eyes. The fox is the only member of the canidae family with elliptically shaped pupils. The others are round in shape. Although the eyesight of the fox is good, it is not considered as vital an asset as its senses of smell and hearing. Like most other animals, the fox is color-blind.

IS IT POSSIBLE TO TELL WHAT A FOX IS UP TO BY THE WAY IT HUNTS?

A major portion of the red fox's diet is composed of rabbits, woodchucks and ground squirrels, and mice. These animals represent three different styles of hunting, and it is possible to tell exactly what a fox is after simply by watching it hunt.

CAN YOU TELL WHAT THIS FOX IS HUNTING BY THESE THREE PICTURES?

WHAT ARE THE THREE HUNTING STYLES OF THE FOX?

RABBITS

With body held low and parallel to the ground, head outstretched and ears cocked forward, the fox stealthily stalks its prey. Using whatever cover the terrain affords, the fox creeps as near as possible to the unsuspecting rabbit. Once it gets within ten to fifteen feet, it breaks into a run and pounces with lightning speed. If the rabbit manages to escape the deadly pounce the fox will run it down.

WOODCHUCKS AND GROUND SQUIRRELS

The fox watches closely from the sidelines for the burrowing animal to go underground. Then it runs quickly to the entrance and, as best as it can, conceals itself with whatever ground cover is available. When the unsuspecting woodchuck comes out, the fox rushes in before it has a chance to turn around and retreat to the protection of its burrow.

MICE AND VOLES

Relying on its sense of hearing, the fox listens for the slightest movement in the concealing grass where mice and voles make their home. When its keen ears pinpoint the location of a sound, the fox leaps into the air and pounces on the movement, hoping for one of these two rodents.

WHICH IS FASTER, A COYOTE OR A FOX?

If you guessed a coyote, you're wrong. The red fox is faster; in fact, it is one of the fastest animals in North America. It is capable of running with strides of up to twenty feet and easily reaches speeds of twenty-six miles an hour. Although the legs of the fox are long in proportion to its body, in deep snow they are not long enough to enable it to move as swiftly as it usually does. At that time, the coyote with its longer legs is faster.

HOW DOES A FOX KEEP ITS FEET WARM IN WINTER?

The pads of the fox's feet serve a distinct function. They allow the animal to release body heat. The pads of foxes which live in cold regions are smaller in size than their cousins inhabiting warmer areas. Because they are smaller, more heat is retained in winter. The fox has a growth of stiff hair between its toe pads. This thick growth provides warmth and also forms a protective covering to guard against cuts. In addition, the hair affords the animal better footing when crossing slippery ice.

FRONT FOOT OF THE RED FOX

The red fox prefers to dig in loose soil. *It uses its claws to excavate its den, dig out prey and bury caches of food. The female, in particular, stores large quantities of food in preparation for the arrival of her kits. The heavy growth of hair on the fox's paw insulates it from cold and ice.*

Although the crow is no threat to the fox, *it is a nuisance. Crows in the area are quick to expose and broadcast the presence of a fox with loud, warning squawks. Their alarm ruins the fox's chances for a sneak attack.*

Two "reds" outfox a pack of hounds

A TAIL FOR A MUFFLER

During cold nights of winter, *the fox prevents frostbite from occurring on its nose and foot pads by drawing itself up tightly into a ball and wrapping its tail around these two exposed parts. The tail is also used in defense to deflect or cushion blows.*

IS THE FOX'S FLUFFY TAIL A BENEFIT OR A HINDRANCE?

Both. The graceful, fluffy tail with its white tip enhances the appearance of this beautiful animal and aids the fox in maintaining balance when turning corners at high speed. But it becomes a distinct disadvantage when its fur is matted with water and ice. Weighted down by the heavy tail, the speed of the animal is considerably reduced. This is one of the few circumstances which would force the fox to seek refuge in a den if pursued.

DO FOXES HUNT IN PACKS THE WAY WOLVES DO?

No. Unlike the wolf which may travel and hunt in groups, the fox hunts by itself. But it is sociable by nature and has close family loyalty.

WHO HAS THE MODEL MARRIAGE OF THE ANIMAL WORLD?

None other than the red fox. The paired foxes are dedicated to each other and demonstrate a high degree of affection and loyalty. The male fox takes an active role in the rearing of the young and the two remain with each other during the rest of the year, long after family responsibilities have been completed. They mate for life and are considered one of the highest examples of union in the animal world.

DO FOXES EVER HELP EACH OTHER?

In winter when foxes begin to pair up, loyalty and comradeship grow strong. When one partner is in trouble, it is not at all uncommon for its mate to come to its rescue. When a vixen was pursued by a pack of dogs, the owner, hearing the tiring tone of his hounds, wondered how a single fox could maintain such stamina and endurance.

The fox had been running a circular path for a distance of approximately one mile. Situated on a high knoll, the observer could see the dogs and the fox at regular intervals. A considerable distance separated the fox and the hounds, and as time went on the hounds dropped farther and farther back. But the vixen seemed to be maintaining a constant speed with ease.

As the cycle repeated itself, the bystander suddenly saw what was happening. There was not one fox involved in the chase, but two. In a cooperative effort, one mate ran the large circle in marathon fashion, completing the course by running through the hollow core of a large fallen log. "Dropping the baton", the partner replaced its mate in the chase, giving the latter an opportunity to rest. The clever exchange tactic wore down the dogs and explained the amazing endurance which had perplexed the observer.

HOW DOES SCRIPTURE ILLUSTRATE DECISIVENESS IN MAKING ACCURATE EVALUATIONS?

A leader and his companions silently slipped into the night air. They carefully made their way to the edge of the city. Concealed by darkness, they skirted the surrounding wall and made mental notes of all they saw. Shocked and grieved by the conditions, they returned to their homes convinced that their task was of great importance.

The success of their mission depended on time and strategy. The leader was aware that jealous surrounding nations and even individuals within the city would take every opportunity to oppose the effort once they learned of it. For this reason the men concealed their observations by a blanket of darkness, after waiting until the third night to begin their investigation.

In no way did this leader want to give his opposition an advantage to thwart his plan. Limited by time, his actions would have to be decisive and correct. He was aware that any delay might cause the project never to be completed.

After the spying mission they gathered the city leaders together and explained their bold plan. The leaders agreed to its necessity but staggered at the tremendous amount of work which the plan required. Under the leader's direction, they initiated the monumental task with enthusiasm and teamwork. Laboring from sunrise to sunset they were inspired by his determination to complete the impossible job.

Once the project was made known the anticipated opposition began. The leader was now faced with the task of outmaneuvering the would-be saboteurs. The king had given permission to begin the task but the leader knew that his enemies would try to slander him and convince the ruler to stop the project. In a decisive move, he motivated the people to work even harder to complete the job before these enemies could reach the king and return with a message.

So determined was the leader that he didn't even take time to change his clothes. Through his example, others gained the morale and strength which were necessary to complete the colossal task. Because of his ability to evaluate his courses of action quickly and accurately, he was able to construct a massive wall twelve feet wide and thousands of feet long in the incredibly short time of fifty-two days.

Nehemiah's decisiveness was rewarded by the permanent fortification of their city. Free from attack, the inhabitants were now able to live in peace and safety.

From Nehemiah 2:11-20 and Nehemiah 6

Before serving the king, *Nehemiah would pour a little wine into the palm of his hand and drink it. If the wine were poisoned it would be discovered before causing injury to the king.*

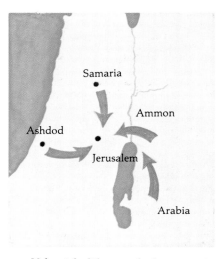

Samaria

Ammon

Ashdod

Jerusalem

Arabia

Nehemiah did not only face opposition *from the Ashdodites, Samaritans, Ammonites and Arabians. He also struggled against enemies within his own country.*

A battering ram was a heavy beam *which might be several hundred feet long. At one end a huge metal ram was used to butt against a wall or gate. Nehemiah wanted Jerusalem to be able to withstand such powerful weapons (cf. Nehemiah 4:3).*

NEHEMIAH DECISIVELY EVALUATED COURSES OF ACTION TO THWART OPPOSITION AND COMPLETE A MONUMENTAL TASK

After King Nebuchadnezzar of Babylon leveled the city of Jerusalem in 586 B.C., godly Jews had prayed daily for its restoration. The city which had housed the beautiful temple built by Solomon and had gained fame throughout the world for its wealth, power and glory was now an object of contempt by its enemies. The once strong city wall which had formerly protected them from the Philistines, Ammonites, Moabites, Midianites and Syrians now lay in ruins, leaving the few remaining inhabitants prey to marauding bandits.

A KING GRANTS PERMISSION FOR AN EXILED PEOPLE TO REBUILD THEIR HOMELAND

In 538 B.C. Cyrus, the new King of Persia, reversed Nebuchadnezzar's policy of exile and gave the Jews permission to return to their homeland to rebuild the temple that they might worship God as they had formerly done. It was an exciting day when the people began rebuilding their temple. But their governor, Zerubbabel, was not able to maintain the type of leadership needed to overcome the resistance of their unsympathetic neighbors. The people became discouraged and quit almost as soon as they had started. It was not until the prophets Haggai and Zechariah rebuked the people for their lack of determination sixteen years later that work on the temple was resumed. The temple was completed four years later, but the city remained deserted since few people desired to live in an unprotected city without walls.

A CITY WITHOUT WALLS HAS LITTLE APPEAL

Fifty-seven years after the temple was rebuilt, Ezra requested permission from King Artaxerxes to go to Jerusalem in order to teach the Mosaic Law and also to refurbish the temple. Ezra's plan was militarily advantageous to Artaxerxes. Egypt had just revolted by ousting the Persian tax collectors, and the loyalty of Israel was crucial for his plans against the rebellious Egyptians. The Jews of Babylonia were often substantial citizens and could be trusted to be loyal. By allowing Ezra to return as a respected religious leader, he may have expected him to quell the cries for revolt. Ezra's mission was successful in that he established some much-needed reform, but he found it difficult to accomplish lasting results. Most Jews refused to migrate back to Jerusalem until they had protective walls and as a result, the maintenance of the proper and orderly worship of the temple was impossible.

A CONCERNED CITIZEN QUIETLY ATTEMPTS TO RESTORE HIS CITY

In the twentieth year of King Artaxerxes' reign, Nehemiah, the king's cupbearer, heard that the situation in Jerusalem was still a disgrace. Four months later he received permission to rebuild the city and its wall. Nehemiah was officially commissioned as governor and given all necessary provisions to accomplish his task. When he arrived in Jerusalem the report of the deplorable conditions was confirmed. Not wanting to arouse opposition, he concealed the true purpose of his mission for a few days during which time he secretly inspected the walls and assessed the situation. After outlining his plan to rebuild the wall he recruited priests, Levites, merchants, goldsmiths, perfumers and farmers for the job. He assigned teams to work simultaneously on all sections of the wall, and the project proceeded at a furious pace.

DESPITE THREATS, BLACKMAIL AND FALSE ACCUSATION—AN INCREDIBLE TASK IS ACCOMPLISHED

When Sanballat, governor of Samaria, Tobiah, governor of Ammon, and Geshem, leader of the Arabs who lived to the south of Judah heard of Nehemiah's action, the three joined in an informal coalition to prevent the reconstruction of the wall. They first tried to discourage Nehemiah, then they demoralized the people. Next they gathered an army for a direct attack and then tried to blackmail Nehemiah by accusing him of treason. But these men failed in their attempts to trap Nehemiah because of his ability to outmaneuver his opponents.

Nehemiah finished his task in the incredibly short time of fifty-two days, but even then he did not consider his mission accomplished. He continued to use his influence to make Jerusalem a safe and attractive place to live. Because of his determined effort, the Lord used him to reestablish Jerusalem as the vital center for the Jews' worship of their God.

NEHEMIAH CHARACTER SKETCH

HOW DID NEHEMIAH WIN FAVOR WITH THE KING?

Although Artaxerxes allowed Ezra to beautify the Temple in Jerusalem in his seventh year (Ezra 7:8), he expressly forbade the building of the wall (Ezra 4:16,21). The city had a long and infamous record of rebellion (Ezra 4:15,19). The fact that four months passed before Nehemiah made his request to the king indicates its serious nature (cf. Nehemiah 1:1; 2:1). For Nehemiah to be made governor of Judah and be able to fortify its capital revealed the tremendous trust the king placed in his cupbearer. Because he was indirectly involved in the assassination of his father, Artaxerxes was well aware of the danger of poisoned wine. Nehemiah had the responsibility of protecting the king's life by keeping the poison out of his cup. It was a high position of trust which he faithfully and competently fulfilled. Artaxerxes was now looking to Nehemiah as he had in the past to preserve his interests in Israel by allowing him to fortify Jerusalem. If Nehemiah led Judah into a revolt against Artaxerxes by making an alliance with Egypt and Athens, the king could have possibly lost the entire area south of the Euphrates River (cf. Ezra 4:16). However, if Nehemiah remained loyal to his master, as Artaxerxes fully expected, it would do much to stabilize the entire area.

WERE NEHEMIAH'S MOTIVES PURE?

Nehemiah's concern for God's reputation above his own is apparent in his humble and reverential prayer (Nehemiah 1:4-10). He lived in the splendid winter capital of the pagan Persian Empire while Jerusalem, the residence of the Temple of God, lay in ruins. Like Jeremiah he could weep and say, "How doth the city sit solitary, that was full of people; how is she become a widow! She that was great among the nations, a princess among the provinces; how is she become tributary." (Lamentations 1:1) Nehemiah knew that the cause of the situation was the disobedience of his own people, but other nations would think that the God of Israel was less powerful than their gods. Nehemiah's concern was for the spiritual restoration of his people, and he realized the importance of rebuilding the city which was the center of the nation's spiritual activities. He was willing to leave his position of prestige and safety in order to help accomplish this task.

HOW WAS NEHEMIAH ABLE TO GET THE JOB DONE SO QUICKLY?

Nehemiah had won the favor and confidence of the king; however, he knew that when governors Sanballat, Tobiah and Geshem learned of his ambitious project these jealous leaders would go to the king to stop the reconstruction.

Nehemiah calculated that he had only a few months before the king's message could be delivered and returned from Jerusalem to Susa (cf. Ezra 7:8,9). It was imperative, therefore, that he get the job done within that period of time. He accomplished this by having each man concentrate on a small section of wall which bordered his property. By working long hours and not being distracted or discouraged by their opponents' diversionary tactics, they were able to complete it in the alloted time period. Nehemiah met each opposition of the enemy wisely and accurately, careful to choose a course that would nullify their undermining efforts.

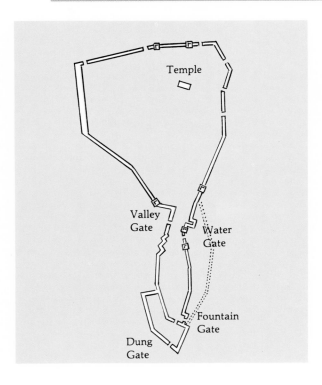

"And I went out by night by the gate of the valley, even before the dragon well, and to the dung gate, and viewed the walls of Jerusalem, which were broken down, and its gates were consumed with fire. Then I went on to the gate of the fountain, and to the king's pool... Then went I up in the night by the brook... and turned back, and entered by the gate of the valley."

NEHEMIAH

INDEX

Listing of names, places, animals and selected words.
Bold numerals indicate illustrations.

INDEX OF SCRIPTURAL REFERENCES

A. Hammarberg

A. Hammarberg